IGCSE
English
as a Second Language:
Focus on Writing

Alison Digger

HODDER
EDUCATION
AN HACHETTE UK COMPANY

Acknowledgements

The Publishers would like to thank the following for permission to reproduce copyright material:

Reproduced by permission of the University of Cambridge Local Examinations Syndicate. *IGCSE English as a Second Language*: **p.120** May 1998, Paper 2 Part 3, Exercise 3 Q29; **pp.142–3** 2006 Specimen Paper 1, Exercise 1; **pp.143–5** 2006 Specimen Paper 2, Exercise 3; **pp.146–7** 2006 Specimen Paper 1, Exercise 4; **pp.158–9** November 1996, Paper 2 Part 2, Exercise 2; **pp.164–5** May 1996, Paper 2 Part 2, Exercise 3; **p.169** November 1998, Paper 2 Part 2, Exercise 3; **p.174** June 2004, Paper 3 Part 2, Exercise 1 Q7; **p.175** June 2004, Paper 4 Part 2, Exercise 2 Q8; **p.179** June 1997, Paper 4 Part 3, Exercise 1 Qs21–6.

p.169 'Out in the wheel world' by Alf Alderson

Every effort has been made to trace all copyright holders, but if any have been inadvertently overlooked the Publishers will be pleased to make the necessary arrangements at the first opportunity.

Although every effort has been made to ensure that website addresses are correct at time of going to press, Hodder Education cannot be held responsible for the content of any website mentioned in this book. It is sometimes possible to find a relocated web page by typing in the address of the home page for a website in the URL window of your browser.

Hachette's policy is to use papers that are natural, renewable and recyclable products and made from wood grown in sustainable forests. The logging and manufacturing processes are expected to conform to the environmental regulations of the country of origin.

Orders: please contact Bookpoint Ltd, 130 Milton Park, Abingdon, Oxon OX14 4SB.
Telephone: (44) 01235 827720. Fax: (44) 01235 400454. Lines are open 9.00–5.00, Monday to Saturday, with a 24-hour message answering service. Visit our website at www.hoddereducation.co.uk.

First published in 2007 by
Hodder Education,
an Hachette UK company,
338 Euston Road
London NW1 3BH

Impression number   5
Year   2010

Cover photo © Royalty-Free/Corbis
Typeset in 11 on 13pt Galliard by Phoenix Photosetting
Printed in Italy

A catalogue record for this title is available from the British Library

ISBN 978 0 340 92806 6

CONTENTS

INTRODUCTION

IGCSE English as a Second Language is designed primarily for students preparing for the International General Certificate of Secondary Education (IGCSE) examination in English as a Second Language, but will also be extremely useful to students taking a course in English as a first language.

All parts of the exam are covered, with strong emphasis on the written component, which is the area where students usually need most help. Detailed units, geared to exam techniques, cover each aspect of the written paper, including letter writing, formal writing, school magazine articles and summaries.

The skills needed for the written component are taught through the extensive use of examples in a step-by-step, hands-on guide, designed to boost students' confidence in their ability to answer exam questions successfully. Equal attention is paid to the importance of style and content as well as accuracy, with reference to regular mistakes made by students in these areas. Many units include students' answers to previous exam questions, annotated with teachers' comments.

Much emphasis is placed on the correct use of different registers, and a unit in the reference section outlines many of the common register mistakes made by students and how to overcome them. Also included in the reference section is a selection of grammar points relevant to the requirements of the IGCSE exam.

In an attempt to ensure that there is no barrier to understanding for the student working alone, every effort has been made to use clear, carefully selected language throughout, and grammatical terms are included only where absolutely necessary.

The IGCSE English as a Second Language exam is very demanding, requiring intimate knowledge of both language and culture. To bridge the gap of cultural difference, the final section of this book, Database of topic-related vocabulary and ideas, provides students with relevant cultural information and encourages both development of ideas and ways of expressing them.

IGCSE English as a Second Language is an invaluable guide for students preparing for the First Certificate in English (FCE) and Certificate in Advanced English (CAE) exams, for any students keen to improve their level of language proficiency and writing skills, and for teachers of students at these levels.

■ Exam overview

The IGCSE exam is offered at both Core and Extended tier. Candidates who take the Core tier may obtain Grades C to G. Candidates who take the Extended tier may obtain Grades A* to E.

At both Core and Extended levels there are two compulsory papers and an oral component. Marks for the oral component do not contribute to the overall grades candidates receive for the reading, writing and listening components. Results are given on a separate certificate with grades from 1 (high) to 5 (low).

Reading and Writing Paper 1 (Core) or Paper 2 (Extended)

Weighting: 70 per cent. Reading and writing skills are equally weighted within the component.

At both levels the question paper is divided into seven exercises.

- Exercises 1 and 2 are reading exercises.
- Exercise 3 requires you to read a passage and then complete a form or some notes using the information from the passage.
- Exercise 4 requires you to read a passage, and make notes using information from the passage.
- At Core level, exercise 5 is linked to exercise 4 and requires you to write a paragraph-length summary about an aspect of the passage you read using the notes you made in exercise 4.
- At Extended level, exercise 5 requires you to read another passage and write a paragraph-length summary about an aspect of it.
- At Core level, exercises 6 and 7 each require you to write 100–150 words of continuous prose in response to a statement and/or prompts.
- At Extended level, exercises 6 and 7 each require you to write 150–200 words of continuous prose in response to a statement and/or prompts.

Listening Paper 3 (Core) or Paper 4 (Extended)

Weighting: 30 per cent.

At both levels there are three parts.

- Part 1 involves listening to six short spoken texts and giving short answers.
- Part 2 involves listening to two longer spoken texts and using the information to complete a form or chart.
- At Core level, Part 3 involves listening to two longer spoken texts and ticking True/False boxes.
- At Extended level, Part 3 involves listening to two longer spoken texts and giving short or sentence-length answers.

Oral Component 5 (Examination) or Component 6 (Coursework)

Oral exam

The oral exam lasts about 10–15 minutes. It includes:

- conversation on general topics such as the student's family, hobbies, future. This part is not assessed, and allows the student to relax and 'warm up' (2–3 minutes)
- talk by the student on a topic from an Assessment Card (2–3 minutes)
- assessed conversation between the student and the assessor, developing the topic (6–9 minutes).

The exam is assessed internally.

Oral coursework

Oral coursework is devised by individual Centres, and involves students being assessed on three oral tasks which are assessed internally.

For both of the oral components, a recorded sample of candidate performance is sent for external moderation by Cambridge International Examinations.
For ideas and development of likely topics in the oral component, see the Database of topic-related vocabulary and ideas towards the end of this book.

■ How to use this book

This book may be used as a course book in class or by students working alone. In order to benefit from the material included in the book you should work through the units in order from the beginning. It is essential that you spend time working through the exercises methodically. If using it as a course book, your teacher may ask you to do certain exercises in pairs or groups. Whenever possible, compare your answers with other students. You can learn about your strengths and weaknesses this way.
Remember that there are many different ways of producing good answers from the prompts given, and the answers provided in this book are only suggestions. Under no circumstances should you learn any of the suggested answers in order to reproduce them in an exam – this will be seen as cheating. Every answer must be original.

Various features are used throughout the book to help you:

■ **Remember** boxes remind you of very important information.
■ **Exam tips** contain useful information about what to do in the exam.
■ **Language Point** boxes highlight and explain various important language features.

Colour is used in Sections 1 and 2 to show the key features of informal writing.

■ Words or phrases in this colour are being used to create **interest**.
■ Words or phrases in this colour are being used to make the writing more **personal**.
■ Words or phrases in this colour are being used to **support** a point.

Colour is used in Sections 3 and 4 to show the key features of formal writing.

■ Words or phrases in this colour are expressing **generalisations**.
■ Words or phrases in this colour are expressing **suggestions**.
■ Words or phrases in this colour are expressing **opinions**.
■ Words or phrases in this colour are expressing **views** or **arguments**.
■ Words or phrases in this colour are being used as **time fixers**.
■ Words or phrases in this colour are being used to **introduce** points.
■ Words or phrases in this colour are being used to **join** points.
■ Words or phrases in this colour are being used to **support** a point.

★ **Note**
When you read the examples of students' work included in this book, you will notice that not every mistake has been corrected. This is because individual errors are not always relevant when teachers and examiners are looking for overall linguistic merit.

IMPROVING YOUR INFORMAL WRITING

The first unit in Section 1 explains what is meant by key words referred to in the IGCSE syllabus and gives examples of different levels of English, both written and spoken, to make you aware of the differences. The following units then concentrate on the informal written language you need in the exam, using examples to show you how to begin to write informal or 'friendly' letters.

UNIT 1 — Different kinds of English

In order to achieve the best possible grade in the exam, it is important to be aware of what the examiner expects from your answer. The IGCSE syllabus for the writing paper states that you should be able to 'employ **appropriate register**/style'. It also states that the tasks for the writing paper 'will be distinguished by requiring different purposes/formats/audiences/register'.

When referring to language, **register** can be defined as 'the use of socially appropriate language' – in other words, using the correct **level** of language to suit a particular situation.

Most languages have different registers or levels. The register you use when **speaking** to your **friends** will be very different from the register you use to **speak** to your **grandmother**. The words you choose will be different because your grandmother is probably not familiar with the modern expressions you use with friends. The sentence structure you use with friends will be more flexible, too. Even the grammar could be more relaxed. Compare these examples of spoken language:

Hey Saz! You alright? You goin' up the city Monday?
(young person speaking to a friend)

Hello Grandma. How are you? Are you going to the city on Monday?
(young person speaking to his grandmother)

If you are **writing** rather than speaking, there will again be differences – these will depend on whom you are writing to. **Writing generally uses a more formal register than speech**. Compare these examples of written and spoken language:

Please let me know when you're arriving.
(informal, written)

I should be grateful if you would inform me of your expected time of arrival.
(formal, written)

Could you fill in this form, please?
(formal, spoken)

I should be grateful if you would kindly provide the necessary information on the form attached.
(formal, written)

In the exam, you are expected to show awareness of the differences between formal and informal registers and the ability to use the correct register according to the situation in the question.

Friendly register

In the IGCSE exam you may be asked to write a letter to a friend, a penfriend or a relative. We will call all such letters 'friendly letters', because you need to use informal or 'friendly' register when you write them. So what is **friendly register**?

- Although it is called **friendly**, it is *not* as informal as the language you would use when **speaking** to a friend.
- Although **written**, it is *not* as formal as the language you would use when writing a letter applying for a job.
- In other words, **friendly register** is a **level** of language which comes between informal spoken language and formal written language.

■ Writing in friendly register

When writing in friendly register, be careful *not* to make your level of language **too informal**. Do *not* include the following three features which are often used when speaking to a friend:

1 Words, phrases or sentence structures which use **slang**:

- ✖ I like to <u>chill out</u> at the beach.
- ✔ I like to <u>relax</u> at the beach.

- ✖ <u>Hanging out</u> at the club is real <u>cool</u>.
- ✔ We enjoy going to the club.

- ✖ My Mum, well she <u>kinda like freaks out</u> when I tell her about ...
- ✔ My Mum gets upset when I tell her about ...

- ✖ My friend, she <u>went, like</u> ...
- ✔ My friend said/replied ...

2 Words shortened to look **phonetic** (in other words, to look the way they sound), such as:

- ✖ How ya doin?
- ✔ How are you?

3 Text message/SMS-style phonetics, such as 'u' for 'you', or small 'i' instead of 'I', or a number to represent a word, for example '4' instead of 'for', and so on:

- ✖ How r u?
- ✔ How are you?

On the other hand, when writing in friendly register be careful *not* to make your level of language **too formal**:

- ✖ Social interaction can be one of the benefits of sport.

This looks like a sentence from a textbook!

In fact, when writing in friendly register, you should try to simplify your language as much as possible. When you try this, you will find that **simplifying** language very often involves **expanding** it; a larger number of simple words are needed to explain or replace bigger words.

For example, imagine your friend is having difficulty understanding a certain section of a science textbook and asks you for help. When you begin to explain what the text means, you find that you automatically replace long, complicated words with shorter, easier ones; you also need to use more words, and this helps to make your language less formal. Applying this to the example above, the meaning of the phrase:

social interaction

could be expressed in friendly register by a phrase such as:

mixing and getting on with people

and the phrase:

benefits of sport

could be replaced by a phrase such as:

one of the good things about sport

So the whole phrase could be rewritten in friendly register as:

One of the good things about sport is that you get to be with people and learn how to get on with them.

Exercise 1 Rewrite the following sentences using friendly register.

1 Taking up employment in a children's holiday camp offers excellent opportunities for adventure.
2 Demand for water is doubling every two years.
3 It is essential that measures are taken to prevent motorists from exceeding speed limits.
4 Regular exercise is beneficial to health. Moreover, it may result in weight reduction.
5 Tourism represents a significant contribution to the national economy.

The Register unit on page 182 helps you to understand more about the difference between formal and informal register. It also shows you how to change from formal to informal register and gives examples. As you work through this book, you will also find some pieces of work which were written by students and have been corrected to show their register mistakes. This should help you avoid making the same mistakes.

Friendly letters: the basics

Before you write

★ **Remember**
Every piece of information contained in a question is there for a reason – for you to respond to. Imagine how different your answer would be to a maths question if you ignored half of a mathematical equation!

Before you begin to write your answer in the exam, it is extremely important to read the question several times and analyse it carefully.

Often some parts of the question are **implied** – in other words, not all the details about the situation are actually given to you. However, you must show that you are aware that information is missing by referring to it or including it in your letter.

Many students are unaware of this; others, perhaps because of exam nerves or lack of time, fail to recognise the implied part and lose many marks. Only the students who are well prepared will find the hidden implications and supply a full answer. Look at this example of a friendly letter question:

Write to a relative who missed a family celebration, telling her/him all about it.

A full answer will not only give details about what happened at the celebration, but also inform the reader *why* the relative missed the party. (We will look at more examples and how to deal with them in this and the following unit.)

As you read a question, try to follow these steps:

- Establish the facts according to the information both **given and implied** in the question. *Where* are you writing from? Home? Another town? Another country? *Why* are you writing? How do you *feel* at the time of writing?
- Establish the **audience**: *Who* are you writing to? You may be asked to write to a relative, a friend, or a penfriend. (A penfriend is usually someone who lives in another country – England is a good choice for the purpose of this exam – and whom you have probably never met, but to whom you write mainly to improve your English.)
- Establish the implications.
- Establish which **type** of friendly letter is required (see Section 2).

Format of a friendly letter

Friendly letters can be divided into the following sections:

- Greeting
- Paragraph 1: Introduction
- Paragraph 2: Transition and body
- Paragraph 3: Body
- Paragraph 4: Conclusion
- Ending and signature

There are several different types of friendly letter you may be asked to write in the exam. The body of each type has certain features, which we will look at separately in the four units of Section 2, together with the relevant conclusions. We will look at the other sections of a friendly letter in this unit.

Greeting

Be sure that you know the ways of starting a letter to different people.

- ✔ To a friend: *Dear* + first name

- ✔ To a brother/sister: *Dear* + first name
- ✘ *Dear Brother Omar*

- ✔ To your mother/father: *Dear Mum/Dear Dad*
- ✘ *Dear Mother/Dear Father*

- ✔ To your parents: *Dear Mum and Dad*
- ✘ *Dear Parents*

- ✔ To a cousin: *Dear* + first name
- ✘ *Dear Cousin Omar*

- ✔ To an aunt: *Dear Auntie* + first name

- ✔ To an uncle: *Dear Uncle* + first name

In every case, use only the standard *Dear*. Do *not* be tempted to write:

- ✘ *Dearest*
- ✘ *My Dearest*
- ✘ *My Best Friend*

★ **Remember**
Keep the name short and simple. Groups of consonants, such as *kh, gh, dj, hm*, are difficult for English readers, for example *Khadija, Mahmoud*.

Although most people now write their letters on computers, remember that the type of letter you will be writing in the exam is hand-written. Paragraphs need to be clearly shown by indenting the first line of each new paragraph so that it lines up under the comma following the name:

Dear Omar,

      It was lovely . . . .

. . . .

      I live in a large house . . . .

. . . .

      I'm really looking forward . . . .

★ **Remember**
One of the main aims of the exam is to test your aware-ness of different registers and your ability to handle them, so an introduction written in the appropriate register will be very effective.

Introduction

Most types of friendly letter should have a short introduction. As this type of introduction is only used for friendly letters, it distinguishes them from any other kind of letter. It would be quite wrong, for example, to use this type of introduction in a formal letter. More importantly, as soon as the examiner reads your introduction she will know whether you are able to show that you understand different registers.

What is the purpose of the introduction?

The introduction warms the reader up and prepares for the main part of the letter, so the reader knows what to expect and can get in the right mood. Look at this example of a letter *without* an introduction:

✖ *Dear Uncle Omar,*
　　　　　　I'm writing because I want to come and stay with you for a month.

This sounds very blunt and rude. Even if Uncle Omar agrees to your request, he may consider your language inappropriate (not suitable)!
　Here is another example:

✖ *Dear Heba,*
　　　　If you want my advice on how to lose weight, stop eating chocolate.

Again, this sounds very cold and definitely *un*friendly! Although the advice itself may be relevant, the language used to express it sounds uncaring because it is too direct.
　The introduction also establishes the relationship between the writer (you) and the audience (the person you are writing to). Look at this phrase:

I'm sorry I haven't written this week, but ...

The phrase this week tells us how friendly the writer and the reader are, because it **implies** (and we understand) that they usually write to each other every week – so they must be good friends.

What do I write in an introduction?

There are several set, or fixed, ways of writing an introduction. In each case, the grammatical structure of the sentence must not be changed. However, the other parts of the sentence can be adapted to suit the question.

1 Using an apology
2 Not using an apology
3 Personal reference

1 A favourite way to begin an informal letter is by using an apology. There are two kinds of apology introductions.

　a) Apologising when there is a genuine reason why the writer has not written

Apology	Reason

I'm sorry I haven't written for ages, but I've been busy studying and haven't had the time.

How can the sentence be adapted?

■ The construction with *for* (+ length of time) could change to *a long time* or to *so long*.

I'm sorry I haven't written for { *ages / so long / a long time* }

■ The construction with *for* could be replaced by a construction with *since* (+ specific time).

$$\text{I'm sorry I haven't written since} \begin{cases} \textit{your birthday} \\ \textit{the party} \\ \textit{we last met} \end{cases}$$

■ The actual reason for not writing can change.

$$\text{... I've been busy} \begin{cases} \textit{moving.} \\ \textit{settling into my new house.} \\ \textit{rehearsing for the school play.} \\ \textit{getting fit at the gym.} \end{cases}$$

If no reason is given or implied in the question, then 'studying' or 'revising for my exams' can be used. Suggesting that you are a serious, hardworking student will probably make a good impression on the examiner!

★ **Language Point**

❑ Notice the use of the contracted (or short) form of the verb in the introductory sentence (**I'm, haven't, I've**). Do not think that to shorten the verb is poor English. In fact, the short form is most appropriate in friendly register – so it must be used in this part of the exam, and only in this part of the exam.

★ **Remember**
The short form of the verb should only be used in friendly register writing.

b) Apologising when there is no real excuse for not writing

I've been meaning to write for ages, but I'm afraid I just haven't got round to it.

How can the sentence be adapted?

■ The construction with *for* can change, as we have just seen above.
■ Again, the excuse can change, but because there is no real reason for not having written, the phrases used are very vague:

I've been meaning to write since the party ...

$$\begin{rcases} \textit{but things kept cropping up and} \\ \textit{but what with one thing and another} \end{rcases} \begin{cases} \textit{I'm afraid I just haven't got} \\ \textit{round to it.} \\ \textit{I'm afraid I just haven't} \\ \textit{had the time.} \end{cases}$$

Look again at the two examples of 'apology' introductions:

I'm sorry I haven't written ...

I've been meaning to write ...

Both **imply** that the writer has been thinking about the reader and feels bad about not having written. They also imply that the reader has been expecting a letter and may be feeling disappointed not to have received one. In other words, this is obviously a letter between friends.

2 Other introductions to friendly letters do not involve an apology.

$$\text{It was} \begin{cases} \textit{lovely} \\ \textit{great} \end{cases} \text{to} \begin{cases} \textit{get your letter} \\ \textit{hear from you} \end{cases} \begin{cases} \textit{yesterday.} \\ \textit{last week.} \end{cases}$$

★ **Language Point**
- ❑ Notice the use of the word *get*. This is the friendly register equivalent of *receive*, which would be too formal here.
- ❑ Notice the use of the word *hear*. This is the correct word to use, even though we use our eyes, not our ears to read a letter. **To hear from** means 'to receive news from' and is used in informal situations.
- ❑ *yesterday/last week*: it is important to say *when* something happened at the end of sentences like this, otherwise the sentence does not sound complete to the English ear.

★ **Exam tip**

Always keep in mind that a composition of 100–150 words (Core) or 150–200 words (Extended) is not very long, so every word is important and must be carefully selected. Marks will not be given for simply filling the page with words; every word must be the right one and in the right place.

3 An introduction to an informal letter can also begin with something very personal, to show your friendship.

Congratulations on passing the exam!

I hope ⎱ *you're feeling better.*
⎰ *you've got over the flu.*

★ **Language Point**
- ❑ Notice the phrase **to get over** is informal register and is used instead of **to recover from**, which would not be suitable here.

Transition
How to write a transition sentence

After writing a suitable introduction, the next step is to write a transition sentence. This will be the first sentence in the second paragraph of the letter, and it is needed to link the introduction to the main body of the letter. We will now look at three different ways to begin the transition:

1 Using the words *Anyway,* or *Anyhow,*
2 Using the past tense
3 Using other methods

1 A common way to begin the transition is to use the words *Anyway,* or *Anyhow,* especially after an apology-type introduction. Remember to put a comma after these words.

✔ *Dear Sarah,*

I'm sorry I haven't written for ages but I've been busy rehearsing my part for the school play.

Anyway, I thought I would drop you a line to ...

In other words, what the writer has been doing, 'rehearsing for the school play', is not really important or interesting to Sarah and is not the main reason for writing.

Be careful about using *anyway* or *anyhow* incorrectly. Both words suggest that anything referred to in the previous sentence does not matter and is not important. In effect, they cancel out the sentence that comes before them. In some situations it can be completely wrong to use these words.

Look at these examples:

❋ *Miss Smith has given us loads of maths homework tonight. Anyway, I won't have time to do it because there's a good film on TV.*

The meaning of the example above is 'The fact that I have a lot of maths homework is not important. Watching the film is more important to me.' or even 'I don't care about my maths homework. What really matters to me is the film on TV.'

Clearly, this can sometimes give a bad impression. Here is another example:

❋ *I was sorry to hear you feel lonely and are missing your friends. Anyway, we are all fine and going to play tennis tomorrow.*

The use of *anyway*, gives the following meaning to the sentence: 'I don't care if you are lonely. What matters to me is that I have friends and things to look forward to. These are more important than my friendship with you.'

2 The second way to begin the transition is to use the past tense.

I thought you might like to know something about …

The English way of showing respect for the person you are writing to, and that you accept that your news, suggestion or advice may not seem interesting, important, wanted or welcome to the other person, is to use the past tense.

★ **Language Point**

❏ Notice that the sentence using the past tense sounds more respectful when compared to the following example of what students often write in a descriptive letter about home and family:

❋ *I am going to tell you about my family.*
❋ *I will tell you about my family.*

❏ Notice the use of the words **will** or **going to** is very strong and forceful in English and should be avoided in this situation.
❏ Notice that the word **tell** is not appropriate: a letter is written, not spoken, and the verb **tell** is generally related to speech.

Here are some more examples of transition sentences introduced by the past tense:

I thought I would drop you a line to let you know something about my family.

Again, the meaning is 'I hope you don't mind if I …'.

★ **Language Point**

❏ Notice here the phrase **drop you a line** can replace **write to you** in informal register.

I <u>thought I would</u> drop you a line to let you know I'm really happy you can come to stay with us.

★ **Language Point**
- ❏ Notice how the phrase **let you know** replaces the formal word **inform**.
- ❏ Notice the word **that**, which sometimes follows **let you know**, has been dropped from the sentence; this is another feature of friendly or informal register.

3 Other ways to begin the transition include:

Just a } (short) note / quickie   to let you know ...

★ **Language Point**
- ❏ Notice the use of the word **note** in this phrase, even though referring to a letter.

✖ *I'm just writing <u>to you</u> to let you know ...*

This is an obvious statement. Who else are you writing to except the reader?

Exercise 1   Write the greeting, introduction and transition of a letter to:
- ■ a penfriend who is coming to stay with you
- ■ a friend who is going for an interview
- ■ a relative who missed a family celebration.

Signature

When you have finished writing the letter and appropriate ending, write on a separate line, either on the left or in the middle of the page, one of the following:

Love,
Love from
With love from
Yours,

Note the use of capital letters and which phrases need a comma after them.
    When you sign at the end of a friendly letter, do not include your family name. Write your name in your normal hand-writing. It is not a formal signature.

✖ With love from
    Anna Hutchins
✔ With love from
    Anna

The different types of friendly letter you may be asked to write in the exam, together with their individual features, including appropriate conclusions and endings, will now be considered separately in the following units.

Section 2 looks in detail at four types of friendly letter – descriptive, advice, narrative and descriptive narrative. The four units show you the techniques for producing each of these letter types, by highlighting certain features and giving examples of how to use them accurately and effectively.

When answering a writing question in the exam, you should aim to write four paragraphs. You are usually asked to write between 100 and 150 words (Core) and between 150 and 200 words (Extended). This means that each paragraph should contain 25–40 words (Core) and 40–50 words (Extended). On the basis of ten words to a line (for average-size hand-writing) this means you need to write about three or four lines (Core) and four or five lines (Extended) in each paragraph.

UNIT 1 Friendly letters: descriptive

The key words 'describe' or 'write about' in the exam question indicate that a descriptive friendly letter is required. Descriptive letters need to be written in friendly (informal) register. These are letters written either to a relative or to someone the same age as you, such as a friend or a penfriend. A penfriend is someone who usually lives in another country and to whom you write, mainly to improve your knowledge of the language of that country. You have probably never met each other.

There are usually only a few things you can be asked to describe, including:

■ your home
■ your family
■ your school
■ your hobbies/free time.

We will look at each of these in this unit.

The main points to keep in mind when writing about any of these topics are:

■ create interest
■ personalise for the reader
■ support each idea
■ do not list.

Before considering exactly what these points mean, and how they help you to produce an excellent letter in terms of content and style, you should remember that the basic principles of writing a letter in the exam should be no different from writing a real letter.

When you write a real letter to a friend, you know something about the character of the person you are writing to. You have a mental picture of that person. You may even know about where they live, what they enjoy doing, how many brothers and sisters they have, and so on. Every sentence you write is with **that particular person** in mind.

In the exam, before you can begin to write anything at all, it is essential to have a **real** picture in your mind of the person you are writing to, so that you can include that person in your letter in order to make it sound real. (We will be looking at exactly *how* to achieve this later.) Without this, your letter will only consist of factual information about your family, school and so on, and will sound formal.

A typical exam question for a descriptive letter might be:

Write to a penfriend who is coming to stay with you for a month. Tell her/him about your home, your family and your school.

In reality, you probably do not have a penfriend. You cannot write a friendly letter to someone you do not know. So you should start by creating a penfriend in your mind. Build up a mental picture of this person. Make a full character, so that even you can believe your penfriend exists. As you do this, write down the answers to the following questions:

■ Where does my penfriend live? In a house or a flat? In the city or the country?
■ Is my penfriend sporty? Studious?
■ What is my penfriend's favourite food?
■ What subjects is my penfriend good or bad at?
■ What kind of music does my penfriend enjoy listening to?
■ What kind of TV programmes/DVDs does my penfriend like to watch?
■ Is my penfriend quiet and shy or out-going and fun-loving?

These details will be used to help you create interest, support your ideas and personalise.

Now that you have a clear picture of your penfriend or friend, it is time to consider the best way to describe your home, family, school and hobbies in a letter to this person.

★ **Exam tip**
Creating a believable penfriend takes time! You should practise doing this *before* you go to the exam until you can write without thinking. Use your imagination.

■ How to describe your home

Before looking in detail at ways of describing your home, it is worth being sure that you know the different kinds of houses in England.

■ A *flat* – all the rooms are on one floor. There may be other flats on the same floor. The building is called a 'block of flats'.
■ A *house* – most people in England live in houses. Usually they have living rooms downstairs and bedrooms upstairs. Most have a garden at the back of the house and some also at the front. A 'detached house' is usually expensive because it does not join onto any other house. A 'semi-detached house' (or 'semi'), as the name suggests, is joined to a neighbouring house on one side.

■ A *terraced house* – one of a row of houses joined onto each other.
■ A *bungalow* – all rooms are on one level, like a flat, but a bungalow stands alone at ground level, and usually has its own garden.

There are no villas in England. Villas usually have flat roofs and are found in hot countries where there is not much rain.

Houses in your country may have a special name or a particular design. If so, you should say what the house is called, and give a brief description of it:

I live in a (give the name of the house). *It's a house built on stilts to keep us above water in the floods.*

However, the important thing is to make sure you:

■ do not list
■ do not state the obvious.

What is wrong with this sentence written by a student?

✖ *My house consists of ten rooms – a kitchen, a living room, a dining-room, four bedrooms and three bathrooms.*

a kitchen, a living room, a dining-room, four bedrooms and three bathrooms is an example of listing.

To mention that you have a kitchen and a bathroom is stating the obvious.

★ **Language Point**
❏ Notice that there is inappropriate use of register in this sentence.
❏ *consists of* – This is formal register.
❏ The sentence begins with a noun: **My house**. Replacing the noun with **person + verb**, for example **I live ...**, will make the sentence less formal.

It would be better to write something like:

I live in a four-bedroom house.

(The number of bedrooms indicates the size of the house.)

Describing location

Describing the location of your house is one way to create interest.

Where can houses be located? Here are a few ideas to start you thinking. Be careful with the **prepositions** (words like *in, on, of, with*); these are difficult in English, and give a **bad impression if incorrect**. Make sure you **learn them perfectly**.

Describing an inner city location

(quite) near the city centre

(right)	in the centre / in the heart	of	the city / Paris

... with a	lovely / marvellous / wonderful / great / fantastic	view of	the busy/noisy market square / the famous/well-known river Nile / the bus station / a park/lake / the cathedral/mosque

★ **Remember**
It is not necessary to describe your real house. You are free to **use your imagination**. This is your chance to create the house of your dreams if you wish!

★ **Remember**
Listing is boring and suggests to the examiner that
❏ your style is weak
❏ your knowledge of vocabulary is basic
❏ you know only words, not constructions.

or

... overlooking
{
the busy/noisy market square
the famous/well-known river Nile
the bus station
a park/lake
the famous/well-known cathedral/mosque
}

For example:

I live right in the centre of Paris, with a marvellous view of the river Seine.
I live quite near the city centre, overlooking a park.
I live in the heart of Cairo, with a fantastic view of the famous mosque.

Describing a location on the outskirts (edge) of a city

not far from
on the outskirts of
in the suburbs of
} + name of city

about half an hour's
{
walk
drive
bus ride
} from + name of city

For example:

I live on the outskirts of Athens.
I live about half an hour's drive from Madrid.

Describing a location in the countryside

in the heart of the
in the middle of the
} country(side)

... with a
{
lovely
marvellous
wonderful
great
fantastic
breathtaking
}
view of
{
the snow-covered mountains
the pine forest
fruit orchards
}

or

... overlooking
{
the snow-covered mountains
the pine forest
fruit orchards
}

For example:

★ **Remember**
Make sure your prepositions
are **accurate**.

I live in the middle of the country with a wonderful view of the pine forest.
I live in the heart of the country with a fantastic view of the mountains.
I live in the heart of the countryside, overlooking fruit orchards.

Exercise 1   Use the examples above to write two different descriptions of where you live, one real
and the other imaginary.

Adding support

Describing the location of your house to your friend also involves adding support. Look at a sentence without support:

I live right in the centre of Athens.

In order to find what to include in the support phrase, ask yourself:

■ Why am I telling my friend this?
■ Why should this interest my friend?

I live right in the centre of Athens, so we can go sightseeing any time.

The support phrase will depend very much on the character and personality of your 'friend' and how well you know this person. Think back to the friend or penfriend you imagined on page 13, and consider the following points.

If your friend is looking for social life, wants to meet new friends, go to parties, go sightseeing and perhaps join in some sport activities, then a house in a rural location, far from city life, will not seem attractive to her (or him) (unless there is public transport available). This type of friend would be happy to discover you lived in a city! The same may apply if her own house is in a quiet area and she would appreciate a change of scene.

If, on the other hand, your friend is hoping to relax and unwind after a hectic school term, then being in the middle of nowhere with no local facilities may be just what she is looking for. The same will apply if your friend lives in a noisy, polluted city and is longing for some fresh air and peace and quiet.

If you know your friend enjoys shopping, for example, you could write:

I live right in the centre of Milan, so we can go shopping whenever you like!

Make sure that the support phrase links to the friend's character.

... so you'll never be at a loose end	(she gets bored easily)
... so we can go shopping whenever you like	(she enjoys shopping)
... so we can easily walk to the tennis club	(she is sporty)
... so we can sit and watch the world go by	(she is happy to stay at home)
... so you can put your feet up, relax and enjoy the view	(she comes from a stressful environment)

If you realise the location may not be what your friend was hoping for, then you should support it in a favourable way, to persuade her.

I live on the outskirts of Paris, only half an hour by train from the centre – so we can go shopping whenever you like!

If you live in the middle of a mountain range or a desert, and shops are days away, it would be better not to mention this aspect at all. Instead, try to persuade your friend that a complete change will be a totally new experience, which she would definitely not want to miss.

Exercise 2   Refer back to exercise 1 and add support to each description of where you live.

Creating interest

One of the best ways to create interest when you write is through contrast. So, when you 'invent' your imaginary friend or penfriend, try to make his life different from yours. If you choose your house to be in the countryside, why not imagine your friend is living in a big city? However, do not try to draw a contrast in every single case, or your letter will not sound natural. Look at the following example sentence, describing where you live:

I live in a three-bedroom house right in the centre of the city. It's very different from your quiet village and **there are so many things to do, you will never be bored**!

Notice the following:

- ■ *I live* – Always use **person + verb** instead of a noun (*my house*) to create friendly register.
- ■ *in a three-bedroom house* – Why should this interest your friend? The number of bedrooms in a house usually gives an indication of its size. If your friend is coming to stay, this might interest him.
- ■ *right in the centre of the city* – Why should this interest your friend? This will probably be a contrast with where he lives.
- ■ *It's very different from your quiet village.*
  - – This creates interest through contrast.
  - – This personalises the situation for your friend because it is relevant to his personal life.
  - – This also shows the reader that your relationship is a friendly one because you know your friend lives in a quiet village.
- ■ *there are so many things to do, you will never be bored!* – This supports your statement by explaining *why* your friend will enjoy coming to stay in a noisy city.

Exercise 3   Refer back to exercise 2 and try to add interest to each description of where you live.

Describing living arrangements

Describing your house also involves describing the living arrangements, especially if your friend is coming to stay. Consider the following points:

- ■ Where will he (or she) sleep?
- ■ Will he have a room of his own, or will he have to share? Some people do not like to share, others welcome the idea – they may feel more secure in a strange house, or they may just find the idea fun, especially if they are an only child, or have never shared with anyone before.
- ■ Will someone have to 'move in' with a brother or sister so that the guest can have his own room?

Use the **past tense** as a polite way of giving information. It would be quite rude to write to your friend:

✱ *We've only got three bedrooms, so you'll have to share with me.*

or

✱ *You will stay in the guest room.*

The use of *will* and *going to* can be very strong in English. It is far more considerate and polite to use the past tense. Look at these examples:

I <u>thought</u> you might like to share my room with me, so we can listen to my music together, but the guest room is all ready, if you prefer.

I <u>thought</u> you might like some privacy, so you can have my brother's room if you like, and he'll move in with me.

Note that it is polite to give your guest a choice. Remember, he may prefer not to share, or he may feel unhappy to be alone in a strange house.

Mum has got the spare room ready for you, but if you prefer, you can share my room.

Support your sentence and take the opportunity to personalise – in other words to show how well you know the person you are writing to. A list of phrases used for personalising can be found on pages 24 and 25.

I know you share a room with your younger brother, so I thought you might like the luxury of having a peaceful room all to yourself!

My room is on the other side of the house from my younger sister's, so bring those favourite CDs of yours and we can listen to them at full volume without having to worry about disturbing anyone!

Do not fall into the trap of listing when discussing the advantages of your bedroom.

✱ *In my room there's a TV, a CD player, a DVD player, a computer, a piano, a mini-library and a PlayStation.*

★ **Remember**
- ❏ Use the past tense as a polite way of giving information.
- ❏ Support your sentence and take the opportunity to personalise.
- ❏ Avoid listing.

This just sounds like showing off. Choose one of the items in your room that is interesting to your friend so that you can support and personalise it. If your friend spends a lot of time playing football and watching horror films at the cinema, he probably will not be interested in your piano or your stamp collection!

You'll be glad to know I've got the old family computer in my room, so we can spend hours playing your favourite games, if you like!

Exercise 4   Write a description about where you live and the living arrangements for a visitor. Include interest, support and personalising.

■ How to describe your family

What is wrong with the following sentence written by a student?

> ✱ *My family consists of five members – my father, my mother, my brother, my sister and myself.*

my father, my mother, my brother, my sister and myself is an example of listing.

★ Language Point
- ❑ Notice that there is also inappropriate use of register in this sentence.
- ❑ **consists of** – This is formal register.
- ❑ The sentence begins with a noun: **My family**. Replacing the noun with **person + verb** will make the sentence less formal.

A better way to write the sentence might be:

I have an older brother, Mark, and a sister called Maria, who is two years younger than me.

Notice how important it is to give brothers and sisters **names**. These are supposed to be real people whom your penfriend will soon meet and get to know.

There is not enough space in a 150–200 word composition to describe each member of the family. It would also be a form of listing, and would definitely be boring – for you and for the examiner. Instead, pick *one* person – perhaps the one with a strong personality, or the one your penfriend will see most while he stays with you.

My older brother, Mark, is mad about computers, just like you!

(*Just like you* – In other words, I know you well enough to know how interested you are in computers.)

I'm sure you'll get on well with my Dad. He loves football almost as much as you!

(*I'm sure* – In other words, I know you well enough to judge who you will like. I also know how much you love football.)

This gives your friend a clear picture of your brother or father. The support phrases inform your friend that your brother and father share the same interests as your friend (that's why you mentioned them) and this will make your friend keen to come and stay. The personalising phrase again emphasises your friendship.

My sister Maria is two years younger than me and loves to sing at the top of her voice whenever I am trying to study! Don't worry – she's going to summer camp so we won't be seeing much of her!

(*Don't worry* – In other words, I know you so well that I am aware of the things that worry you. Why tell your friend that your sister is going to summer camp? So he knows she will not be there to bother him! This suggests that your friend prefers a quiet life!)

★ Remember
- ❑ Keep asking yourself: *why am I telling my friend this?* and *why* should this interest him?
- ❑ Support each sentence and personalise it for the reader if possible.

Ideas for describing family members

Here are some ideas to help you describe members of your family. You can use the vocabulary and phrases in your sentences.

Mother/Father

- Is she a football fan/computer nut (= someone very keen on computers)/television addict?
- Is she easy to talk to/to get on with/always interested in other people's viewpoints?
- Is she a workaholic (= someone addicted to work), always at the office/business, so you don't see much of her?
- Is his bark worse than his bite? (In other words, is he strict? Does he shout a lot, but never take any real action or carry out his threats?)
- Does she fancy herself as a linguist, and is she looking forward to trying out her English (which she hasn't used since school) on your penfriend?
- Is she young at heart? (In other words, does she still have the outlook of a young person?)
- Is he easy to talk to/always ready to lend an ear?
- Is he a brilliant cook? Can he make your penfriend's favourite food?

Be careful not to make these common mistakes:

   ✱ *My father is a tall man with black hair.*

Of course your father is a man! This is stating the obvious. Only describe a physical feature if it is unusual in some way.

   ✱ *My father is nice.*

This is stating the obvious. Of course your father is nice – and if he isn't, you would not tell your penfriend, as this would definitely discourage him from coming.

   ✱ *My mother is an excellent cooker.*

(*cooker* = a kitchen appliance!)

Older brother/sister

- Is he hard-working/studious/always in his room?
- Do you never really see her – not even at weekends?
- Does he listen to music at full volume whenever he's at home?

Younger brother/sister

- Is she a nuisance/always disturbing you/always playing tricks on you?
- Is he a bookworm? (In other words, does he read books all the time?)
- Does he have any particular features? Round face/orange hair/spiky hair/thick-rimmed glasses? (Think of a cartoon character!) Does he (or she) look cheeky, innocent, a genius?

Now ask yourself: *why* am I telling my friend this and *why* have I selected this piece of information? By answering these questions, you will provide the support for your ideas.

Exercise 5 Practise on your own, trying to write as many things as possible about different people in your family in the same way and trying to use some of the phrases above – or others of your own. Remember, they do not need to be the real members of your family. You are free to *use your imagination*. Try to add a little humour if you can, to make the examiner laugh!

■ How to describe your school

When asked to write a letter to a friend describing your school, all the points mentioned previously apply.

Describing the school building

Is there anything special about your school or its buildings?

Is it very old?

I go to a very old school – it was } founded } almost   two hundred years
                                    built   nearly   ago.

Is it very new?

I go to a very modern school. In fact it was only built last year!

Is it near your house?

It's only a } fifteen-minute } walk   to school from } my house.
             half-hour   bus ride   where I live.

It only takes me ten minutes to bike to school (from home).

Or is it far away?

I have to get up at six o'clock to catch the bus to school – it takes almost an hour/it's about an hour's trip!

You'll be glad to know it's only a ten-minute walk to school from my house, so you won't have to get up early!

Do not give a guided tour of your school buildings.

> ✷ *On the left is administration and two bathrooms, on the right are three classrooms.*

Why are you telling your friend this? She will almost certainly not be interested. What can you find to interest your friend, to make her look forward to coming to school with you? You have to create interest. Think back to the mental picture you produced of your imaginary friend, and consider her (or his) interests.
   If she is keen on (= enjoys) sport:
■ write to her about the new gym – it should be finished by the time she arrives
■ tell her how popular the volleyball court is at lunch breaks. If she is part of a team at home/a brilliant player, everyone will want her to join the school team while she is staying with you

- you could mention the Olympic-sized indoor/outdoor swimming pool (heated if you live in a cold climate, cooled if you live in a hot country). She can relax/get her exercise there each day/after school/at weekends.

If he is keen on music:

- write about the music room – he can practise the guitar at lunch break
- perhaps he can join the school orchestra/choir.

If she is keen on reading:

- write about the well-stocked library. She can shut herself in there whenever she likes – while you are playing football, if she is not keen on sport.

There are other topics you can mention to make your friend interested.

Describing the teachers

Describing teachers is another way to create interest and should be approached in the same way as describing your family. Choose only one teacher to describe (do not fall into the trap of listing). In order to be interesting for your friend, the teacher you choose should either have a strong personality or have some connection with your friend's particular interests. You may describe the sports teacher, for example, if your friend is sporty.

Although it is not a good idea to be rude about teachers (remember it is teachers who mark your exam paper!), you can be light-hearted about them. Exaggeration is often a good way to produce a comic effect.

Wait till you see Mr Jones, our absent-minded physics teacher! He never remembers to comb his hair, his jacket sleeves are too short and he's always dropping things!

Be careful not to make these common mistakes:

✖ *There are teachers in my school.*

This is stating the obvious.

✖ *My teachers are nice.*

Nice is a weak adjective.

✖ *At my school I study maths, biology, physics, chemistry, history, geography, economics, business and English.*

This is an example of both listing and stating the obvious – these are subjects which almost everybody studies at school, not stamp collecting or skating!

Describing your school friends

Of course you want to include your friends in the letter, but avoid stating the obvious.

✖ *My friends are nice.*
✖ *My friends are very friendly.*

Try something indirect:

... they can't wait to meet you!
... they're really looking forward to meeting you!
... they're dying to meet you!

This reassures your friend that she will not feel lonely and will probably encourage her to come.

Exercise 6   Describe your school to a penfriend. Include interest, support and personalising.

■ How to describe your hobbies and free time

The best way of approaching this is to be **realistic**. How much free time do you really have each week? Studying probably takes up most of your week and some of your weekend, too. Your penfriend is about the same age as you, so he will probably also be busy. This is something you have in common. Why not start by saying that, like him, you do not have much free time during the week because you are studying for your exams?

Perhaps you have an hour or so free in the evening? How do you spend it? Watching television? Playing computer games? Talking to your friends on the phone?

What about weekends? Do you have a morning or an afternoon or an evening off (not studying)? Do you do the same thing every weekend?

By using *sometimes* or *if I have time* or *if he is not busy* with standard activities such as *go round to my friend's* or *listen to music together*, your letter will sound natural and therefore convincing.

How many different hobbies do you have? Do not be tempted to write down all the hobbies you can think of, and then string them together – and do not feel that you should be doing something adventurous all the time.

> ✳ *On Saturday morning I go deep sea diving. Then at ten o'clock I go mountain-climbing. At eleven I go water-skiing. After lunch I go trekking. Then I go sailing. In the evening I go …*

What is wrong with the sentence above? It is clearly an example of listing.

As with the rooms in your house, the members of your family, and the teachers at school, choose one or two hobbies to describe.

Choose a popular sport. Why do you enjoy playing squash? The answer to this question will be your support phrase: it keeps you fit/gives you a chance to meet other people of the same age.

Does your friend share the same hobby or enjoy the same sport? If so, this is an opportunity to personalise. Perhaps she does not enjoy sport of any kind. This is a chance to personalise/create interest through **contrast**. Writing this way involves your penfriend and the examiner, avoids listing and makes the whole letter sound interesting and natural. It takes practice, though!

When writing about your free time, one of the dangers is, once again, listing. Do not be tempted to write a complete timetable of your week, starting from when you get home from school.

> ✳ *On Monday, I come home from school at 2.30. At three o'clock I have a shower. Then I eat lunch. After lunch I go to sleep. At 5pm I wake up and watch TV. At 6pm I play computer games. Then I do my homework. At 8pm I …*

This is repetitive and not interesting for the examiner to read.

★ **Remember**
Support your ideas.

★ **Remember**
Create interest by including your friend and emphasising the similarities and comparisons between you.

Exercise 7 Describe how you spend your free time to your penfriend. Include interest, support and personalising.

Exercise 8 Describe your hobbies to your penfriend. Include interest, support and personalising.

■ Personalising phrases

Here is a list of phrases which help you to join your ideas together and also personalise them for the reader – in other words, these phrases will make the reader feel that he is included in your thoughts as you write and that his feelings and opinions have been taken into account. Using these phrases will result in a more personal and friendly letter. These phrases apply to all types of friendly letters.

1 You'll be glad to know …

2 I know / I'm sure } you'll { love … / get on (really) well with …

3 Wait until you { see … / meet … / taste …

4 You'll really enjoy …
5 I can't wait till you …
6 As you know, I …
7 I know you …
8 … – (just) like you!
9 … – as usual!

The following examples show you how to use these phrases.

Phrase 1

You'll be glad to know there's a fitness centre near where I live, so we can work out in the gym anytime.

You'll be glad to know = personalising; it shows you know something about what makes your friend happy, her hobbies, character, etc.

there's a fitness centre near where I live – Why tell your friend this? To create interest.

so we can work out in the gym anytime. = personalising again, because it shows you know your friend likes to work out. It is also support, because it explains why your house is in a good location for your friend.

Phrase 2

I'm sure you'll get on really well with my brother Sami! He's mad about football, just like you!

I'm sure you'll get on really well with my brother Sami! = personalising

He's mad about football, = support

just like you! = personalising

I know you'll love my mum's cooking! She can make almost anything – especially your favourite, pizza!

I know you'll love my mum's cooking! = personalising; it shows you know your friend well enough to know what food she likes.

– especially your favourite, pizza! = personalising again; you know your friend loves pizza. It is also support.

Phrase 3

Wait until you taste my mother's cooking! You'll never want to go home! Wait until you meet our physics teacher!

What can you put to support this sentence?

Phrase 4

You'll really enjoy not having to walk to school **in the mornings!**

You'll really enjoy not having to walk to school = personalising; you know your friend hates walking to school. He's lazy!

Phrase 5

I can't wait till you meet my friends! (Support this.)
I can't wait till you get here! (Support?)

Phrase 6

As you know, I'm not much good at swimming, **but** …

As you know, I'm not much good at swimming = personalising; this shows you have told your friend personal things about yourself.

… **but** (support?)

Phrase 7

I know you enjoy sightseeing, so I thought you might like to go and see the Pyramids.

I know you enjoy sightseeing = personalising

… **so I thought you might like to go and see the Pyramids.** = support

I know how much you love music, so …

I know how much you love music = personalising

… **so** (support?)

Phrase 8

My sister adores pizza – just like you!

Phrase 9

At the weekends I am quite lazy – as usual!

as usual! = personalising; your friend knows your habits.

■ Conclusion of a descriptive letter

The conclusion for a descriptive letter should be quite short; probably two or three lines, and, if possible, should return to the point which began the letter. For example, if you are writing to a friend who is coming to visit you for the first time, your introduction might have started something like this:

It was lovely to get your letter yesterday and to hear that you're coming to stay! I thought I'd drop you a line to give you some idea about life over here.

Your conclusion should reflect the points made in the introduction and also bring the reader back into the letter.

Anyway, I hope this gives you some idea about us here, and that you're getting excited about coming!

This is particularly important if you have been writing mainly about yourself, for example, your hobbies.

Anyway, now you know all about how I spend my free time. Maybe when you write you could tell me what you do in yours.

If possible, add a personal sentence:

Don't forget to let me know what time your flight arrives.
Don't forget to pack a swimsuit!
Write soon and let me know whether/when/where ...

■ Ending and signature

(I'm) looking forward to seeing you } *soon.*
on Friday.
next week.

Looking forward to hearing from you!

And finally,

With love,
Love from
With best wishes,
Yours,

+ your first name *only*, in writing that the examiner can read.

■ Further exercises to improve your descriptive letter writing

Exercise 9   Create an imaginary friend for yourself from your local area. This means she will share the same culture as you, know what facilities are available, what time school starts, which days are the weekend, what festivals your country celebrates, the type of food you eat in your country, and so on. This person can be based on a real friend, if you like.

Make notes about your friend under these headings:

- physical appearance
- characteristics
- likes and dislikes
- hobbies
- family

and make a note of how these are different from, or the same as, yours.

Now create an imaginary friend from another country – probably England, or another English-speaking country, who you know through writing and receiving letters (a penfriend). You may not know this person quite as well as the friend from your local area, and he probably lives in a totally different kind of area and different house, goes to school at different times, has a different weekend from you, eats different food, has different customs, and so on.

Exercise 10   Make a list of phrases to support the characteristics of the imaginary friend you created in exercise 9. If possible, personalise them at the same time. Look at some examples of how to add support and personalising phrases about a friend who likes reading.

★ **Exam tip**
Adding support and personalising phrases is *not* easy to do under exam conditions. Practise as much as you can *before* the exam. Try to keep improving on your support and personalising phrases.

You can read my brother's collection of novels. He won't mind – he's at university now. He's a bookworm, just like you!

You'll be glad to know the town library is not far from where I live. You can have a look round while I go to football practice, if you want. I know how much you dislike sport!

I know you love reading, so I'm sure you'll want to join the school book club.

Exercise 11   Write about a member of your family. Try to describe two or three people to start with, then select the one you feel most happy with. Try reading it out to friends and ask their opinion – or ask your English teacher. Remember that the person you finally choose should have some *relevance* to your imaginary friend, in order to be convincing. Add support and personalising phrases to the description of the chosen member of your family.

Write descriptions of your home, school and how you spend your free time in the same way.

Spend time producing these descriptions. Write them. Leave them for a few days. Then read them again, edit and improve them. You may need to repeat this procedure several times until you are satisfied. When you are sure you cannot make any further improvements, try writing one or two from memory, until you become familiar with them and feel comfortable about the whole concept of descriptive letter writing in friendly register.

■ *Exam-style questions*

Now you are ready to attempt the following exam-style questions.

Question 1　You are going to take part in an exchange visit with someone from another country. She/He will be coming to stay with you and your family in three months' time. Write a letter about 150 words long in which you:

- say something about your family
- describe your local area
- explain what activities you can do together
- suggest places to visit.

★ Note

Exchange visits are very common between students in English schools and other countries in Europe. Not all students understand the phrase, because they do not experience them in their particular country. Exchange visits are usually arranged between schools. A group of students from an English school goes to France, for example; each student stays at the home of a French student and accompanies the French student to school for a week or two (usually at the end of the school year). The following year, the French students go to England and stay with the English students. This gives both nationalities the chance to improve their foreign language. Sometimes the students will have been writing to each other, as penfriends, for a year or more; sometimes the school places them with a student they have never written to before.

Before you begin to answer question 1, consider the following points:

- Decide how well you know the exchange student, and make it clear in your answer.
- Do you need to mention your visit to the exchange student's country?
- As you are writing in English, it makes sense for the exchange student to come from an English-speaking country.
- Remember to write something about all four of the points given and be particularly careful to avoid listing.

Question 2　An English student who has never been to your country before is coming to stay with your family for three weeks and will also go to school with you. Write a letter about 200 words long telling the student about your home and school and the sort of things you do.

Question 3　Write to your penfriend about how you spend your free time after school. Describe your usual evening and weekend activities.

Question 4　A cousin you have never met before has written to say she/he is coming to stay. Write and tell her/him about your family, your home and the area you live in.

★ Exam tip

Consider the **implications** of a question. Here (question 4), although you have never met, you are writing to *your cousin* who has probably seen photographs or heard about your part of the family. Use this knowledge when you write.

I suppose you've heard about James (the youngest)!
I'm sure you've seen the photos of my birthday party!

Question 5 A friend from your old school is coming to spend a few days with you in the new area you have recently moved to. Write and tell her/him about the area, your new house and what you will be able to do together. Before you begin, think carefully about your relationship and how well your friend knows your family.

■ *Students' descriptive letters*

Read the following selection of descriptive letters written by different students in response to exam questions, and the comments related to them.

★ Note

These are original letters written by IGCSE students and may still contain minor mistakes. In the comments column, the letter **R** refers to points in the Register unit on pages 182–5, and the letter **G** refers to points in the Grammar unit on pages 186–99. The arrow (→) points to what the text in the letter should be changed to or replaced with.

Question 1 Write a letter to a penfriend who is coming to stay, telling her/him about the area you live in and your school.

Dear Sam,

How are you? It was nice to get your letter last week and even nicer **to know that you are❶** coming to Dubai for a three-week stay with us.

Anyway,❷ I thought I'd drop you a line about **my place❸** and the school I go to. **You will be living with us in our semi-detached house❹** in the country. It has 4 bedrooms **one of which❺** you might like to stay in, that I have already **prepared.❻** But of course you are welcome to stay in **any bedroom you would like,❼** perhaps share my room, where we could enjoy listening to music together or watching DVDs. I hope you don't mind **being set up in practical jokes,❽** as my younger brother is always at it. He is actually very different from my sister – she's 'the quiet type'. You will recognise my father because he's got a bushy moustache. He's quite understanding and **I think you would enjoy❾** talking to him, as well as my mother (not with a moustache!)❿ Although we live far from my school the school bus comes right up to my house and takes me to school just in time for the first lesson. The school is quite large with a nosy principal, but quite caring teachers and friends.

Anyway, I'm looking forward to seeing you soon.

Best wishes

Hisham

Comments

Lovely opening paragraph

❶ R6 → to hear you're

❷ Unnecessary

❸ R1 Replace noun with person + verb → **where I live**

❹ Too strong, not needed → **we have a 4-bedroom semi in the country**

❺ Inappropriate register → **My mum has got one of the rooms ready for you.**

❻ R3 → **got ready**

❼ Confused grammar → **any bedroom you like**

❽ Confused phrase → **being set up** or **having practical jokes played on you**

❾ Good personalising

❿ Nice humour!

General comments

● This letter has a good introduction.
● The student has succeeded in creating interest.
● There is no listing.
● There are not many grammatical or register mistakes.

However:

● Instead of writing about the area he lives in, as the question asked, Hisham has written about his house and family. This is an example of *not* answering the question, and would lose many marks in the exam.
● The body of the letter is one very long paragraph.

Question 2 Write a letter to a penfriend who is coming to stay, telling her/him about your home,
Answer A family and school.

Dear John,

      I'm sorry for not writing to you for so long, but we had exams and I had to study. **Anyway,**① I was glad to know that you're coming to stay with us **here**② and I thought you might like to know something about life over **here**.③

      To start with④ **I'll tell you**⑤ about my **home and family**.⑥ **The house is**⑦ a 5 bedroom flat on the 17th floor of a building in a **well-known area**.⑧ **Everyone of us has his**⑨ own room and I thought you might like to **stay in my room**.⑩ **Well,**⑪ if not, **there is a room**⑫ ready for you where you can be free. I would like to warn you about my twin sisters. They love playing tricks on people. They'll try to drive you crazy by exchanging their clothes every now and then. But I'm sure you're going to love them because they are kind-hearted.

      About school,⑬ **it is situated**⑭ in a remote area near a military **base**.⑮ The best thing about our school is our **sports gymnasium**.⑯ It is one of the biggest in the city and **any kind of sport can be done**⑰ there. **Also**⑱ I'd like to tell you about the most spectacular personality of our school. She is our Headmistress. She is an old lady who **dresses up**⑲ as if she's only 16 years old.

      As for my free time,⑳ I'm never **free**㉑ during the weekdays because studying takes all of my time. I hardly get an hour to watch TV or play computer games. **Well,**㉒ during **the weekend, which is, by the way, different from yours,**㉓ I go horse-riding, and **well**㉒ occasionally I go to **the cinema with my friends**.㉔

      I hope this gives you an idea about life over here and that you're excited about coming. Don't forget to tell me **when your flight will be**.㉕ I'm **looking forward to see**㉖ you soon.

Love,

Moutaz

Comments

① Used correctly. His study is not as important as John's visit.
② Where else would he stay? Not needed.
③ Repetition. Remove the first, irrelevant **here**.
④ Listing
⑤ → I thought you'd like to know
⑥ Avoid repetition of wording of title. It is formal register.
⑦ Replace noun with person + verb → I live in
⑧ Why tell him this? Support
⑨ Incorrect grammar → **We each have our**
⑩ Why? Support
⑪ A feature of spoken language which is inappropriate here: remove.
⑫ → **The spare room is**
⑬ Continuation of listing
⑭ R4 → **I go to school**
⑮ Why tell him this? Support
⑯ Confused → **sports hall** or **gym**
⑰ R4 → **you can do any sport**
⑱ Listing
⑲ Wrong word → **dresses**
⑳ Listing again
㉑ Repetition. Remove **As for my free time**
㉒ A feature of spoken language which is inappropriate here: remove.
㉓ Why tell him this? Support
㉔ Good phrase
㉕ Incorrect grammar; use present tense for timetabled future → **what time your flight is due**
㉖ This *must* be learnt *accurately* → **looking forward to seeing**

General comments

- This letter has a good introduction and conclusion.
- The letter sounds fluent because there are not many grammar or register mistakes.

However:

- There is no attempt to support or personalise.
- This letter is too long to be written under timed exam conditions.

Question 2
Answer B
Write a letter to a penfriend who is coming to stay, telling her/him about your home, family and school.

Dear Satomi,

I got your letter last week and I am happy you will at last manage to come.

I would like to give you a general idea① about my **family, home and school.**② My family③ is very friendly.④ I have **one**⑤ **bigger brother**⑥ who is a bit naughty, and **a smaller pretty sister.**⑦ **My home**⑧ is a **fifteen-minute walk**⑨ from the beach.

I go to **a big school.**⑩ I like it very much. There are **many activities**⑪ in my school, and I **participate**⑫ in the **music, chess and basketball activities.**⑬

In the mornings I always have **a five-minute walk**⑭ **before going**⑮ to school. **After coming**⑯ from school I study and **pass my free time**⑰ either reading or watching television. As **you would**⑱ come in the winter vacation, however, **we would**⑱ go out almost every day.

I hope you would⑲ enjoy your time staying with us.

I am waiting to meet you.⑳

Your friend,㉑

Miral

Comments

① Confused phrase → *I thought I would (let you know)/ I thought you might like to know*
② Avoid repetition of wording of title. It is formal register.
③ Repetition
④ Stating the obvious
⑤ R9 → *a(n)*
⑥ *older brother*
⑦ *a younger, pretty sister*
⑧ R1 Replace noun with person + verb
⑨ Support?
⑩ Why tell her this? Support?
⑪ Support?
⑫ R3 → *take part*
⑬ Support/personalise?
⑭ Support/personalise?
⑮ R2 → *before I go*
⑯ R2 → *after I come (home)*
⑰ Confused time phrase → *spend my free time*
⑱ Incorrect grammar: wrong use of tenses → *as you're coming in the winter vacation we'll be able to ... go out almost every day.*
   The implications of this sentence need explaining. In many countries the weather is bad in winter. Why is the weather good in winter where Miral lives?
⑲ Incorrect grammar: wrong use of tenses → *I hope you will*
⑳ Inappropriate phrase → *I'm looking forward to meeting you*
㉑ Inappropriate ending → *Love from,*

General comments

There are lots of problems with this letter.

- The beginning and ending are both confused.
- There is repetition of the words used in the title (remember titles are in formal register).
- There are problems with register and grammar.
- There is no attempt to personalise or support.

Question 3 Write a letter to a cousin you have never met before and who is coming to stay with
Answer A you, telling her/him about your home and family.

❶

How are you?❷

It was lovely to get your letter yesterday and I was so pleased to hear that you'll be coming to stay with us.❸ It is really a great feeling to know that at last you're going to meet the cousin you've never seen. Don't you think so?❹ Anyway, I thought you might like to know some more about us, apart from the picture you've seen.

We live in a five-bedroom semi. We all have our own rooms and I thought you might like to stay with me in my room. If not, there is a spare room for you to stay in. By the way, a word of warning my twin sisters love playing tricks on people. **For example,**❺ they'll try to drive you crazy by swapping their dresses every now and then. But **I'm sure that**❻ you're going to love them because they're very kind hearted. They are similar in some ways to my mum but neither of them is a good cook like her. You're going to taste many delicious **dishes which I'm sure you'll like.**❼ **By the way,**❽ my dad is not as serious as he looks in the picture you have. He's an easy-going sort of person who loves life and always likes **to say jokes**❾ and my brother takes after him. He is a great man and **I really love him so much.**❿

Anyway, I hope this gives you an idea about us and you're excited about coming.

Love,

Halima

Comments

❶ Should have **Dear ...**

❷ The first line of each paragraph should be indented.

❸ Lovely introduction

❹ Nice use of **Don't you think so?**

❺ Inappropriate register: remove

❻ R5 Remove **that**

❼ Nice support

❽ Excellent introduction to your father and personalising with the mention of the photograph

❾ Confused → **to tell jokes**

❿ → **I love him very much.**

General comments

- Generally a very good letter.
- The introduction and conclusion are appropriate and well-written.
- There are not many problems with grammar or register.
- The student has included a varied range of expressions.
- The letter contains examples of personalising and support.

Question 3 Write a letter to a cousin you have never met before and who is coming to stay with
Answer B you, telling her/him about your home and family.

Dear Jinbin,

Hi! How is life going? I really don't know what to write to my unknown cousin. Anyway I was very **happy to know❶ that❷** you're coming to stay with us in Egypt.

We live in❸ a big house with a small garden and a backyard. You'll be staying in my **small❹** brother's room and he's moving into mine.

Wait till you see my **small❹** brother. He's a complete nut roaming around the house. My advice to you is to stay out of his way, he's got all types of tricks he'll make you cry your eyes out. Although he can be a major nuisance and a **pain in the neck,❺ the house will be❻ like a graveyard❼** without him.

I have a big bedroom with a television, computer and a sound system. We could stay all night watching TV and messing with the computer, that's if we can find them under the mess.

We also live❽ near the beach so we can go swimming anytime. **Unlike England❾** it's very hot and sunny over here.

Looking forward to seeing you and hoping you will enjoy your stay with us.

Love from

Natalya

Comments

Good introduction

❶ → *happy to hear*

❷ R5 Remove

❸ Good!

❹ → *younger*

❺ Good expression!

❻ G2 Second conditional: *If he were* (past) *not here, the house would* (conditional) *be ...*

❼ Good expression

❽ No need for **also** here

❾ Contrast to create interest

General comments

- This letter is generally well-written.
- There is a relevant introduction and conclusion.
- There are not many problems with grammar or register.
- The student has included a range of expressions.

However:

- The student has not completely answered the question. The letter includes information about family and home, but does not take into account that it is being written to 'a cousin you have never met before'.
- Many opportunities for personalising have been missed in this letter.

Friendly letters: advice

Advice letters need to be written in friendly register (see page 3). These are letters written to someone who is probably about the same age as you and has asked for your help with a particular problem. Usually, these are school-related or personal problems, and include:

- not doing very well in a certain subject at school
- being overweight
- moving to a new area and feeling lonely
- being bullied.

If you had one of these problems, who would you go to for help or advice? Probably you would choose a particular friend who you feel would understand your problem and take it seriously. If possible, you would choose a friend who has had the same problem, and who you may therefore think of as being in a better position than you in terms of experience. Sometimes it is not easy to ask for help. Much depends on the relationship between the person with the problem and the friend who is asked for help.

When you write a letter of advice to a friend who has come to you with a problem, bear the following points in mind:

- You are a friend, and sympathetic to the person's situation.
- You understand the problem; you may have had the same problem or been through a similar experience yourself.
- You must make your friend feel comfortable and reassured, not intimidated.
- You must not appear to be superior in any way.

So, it would not be at all appropriate to write the following kind of sentence:

✗ *Well, you couldn't have asked a better person. Everyone knows how hopeless you are at maths. I'm an 'A' student so I know everything. You did the right thing to come to me!*

However, by far the most important point to remember is: **do not give too much advice!** There are two reasons for this. Firstly, think of occasions when someone may be giving *you* advice – for example, your father. If he spends a long time giving you the advice, you probably find that you stop listening after a while! Secondly, to avoid listing and to improve your writing style, you should follow the method explained in the previous unit about descriptive letters, and treat advice in the same way you dealt with rooms in your house, the members of your family and your hobbies. In other words, select just a few pieces of advice and then develop them.

Limit yourself to a maximum of **three** pieces of advice, and then remember to:

- personalise
- support each idea
- avoid listing.

Now look at a skeleton, or basic plan, for an advice letter.

■ Advice letters – a basic plan

Introduction

Use a short introduction so you can get to the point – in other words, the advice – quickly. The apology type of introduction is not appropriate here. Someone asking for advice obviously needs help and does not want to wait, so it would *not* be appropriate to use the following type of introduction:

> ✖ *I've been meaning to write for ages/for a long time.*

Instead, use a simple, direct introduction, for example:

It was { lovely / great } { to get your letter. / to hear from you. }

As the time factor is important, say *when* you heard from the person you are writing to. By showing that you are writing back quickly, your friend will realise your concern, which highlights the sincerity of your friendship.

yesterday/this morning/a few minutes ago

Now build the sentence up:

It was lovely to hear from you this morning, but …

The word *but* tells the reader a contrast is coming, in other words, something which is not *lovely* or *great*.

I was / I am } *sorry …*

Show your feelings.

It was lovely to hear from you this morning, but I was sorry …

… (to hear) you're { having trouble with / worried about / unhappy with/about } { your schoolwork. / being overweight. / not being fit. / bullies. }

It was lovely to hear from you this morning, but I was sorry to hear you're worried about your schoolwork.

Now reassure your friend and at the same time confirm your friendship by personalising.

Don't worry.
Try not to worry (about it).

I know { how you feel / what you're going through / what it's like } *because …*

It was lovely to hear from you this morning, but I was sorry to hear you're worried about your schoolwork. Don't worry. I know what it's like because …

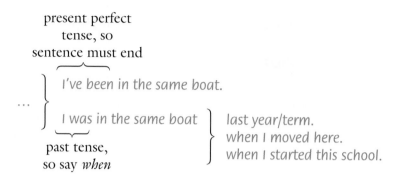

It was lovely to hear from you this morning, but I was sorry to hear you're worried about your schoolwork. Don't worry. I know what it's like because I was in the same boat (= same situation) last term.

Here is another example using the same skeleton:

It was great to get your letter yesterday, but I'm sorry you're worried about being overweight. Try not to worry about it. I know how you feel because I've been in the same boat.

Exercise 1

Identify the good points and the problems in the following introductions to advice letters.

1 'I'm sorry I haven't written for so long, but I've been busy studying and haven't had the time. Anyway, I thought I would drop you a line to give you some ideas on how to lose weight.'

2 'I've been meaning to write for ages, but I'm afraid I just haven't got round to it. It was lovely to get your letter yesterday. I thought I would drop you a line to help you organise your studying hours, as you asked me in your last letter.'

3 'How are you? I hope you're feeling better. I thought I would drop you a line to cheer you up, because I have been in the same boat before.'

4 'How are you? It was lovely to get your letter this morning, but I was sorry to hear that you're having problems with your English. Don't worry! I've been in the same boat last year.'

Exercise 2

Use a selection of the phrases studied to write the introduction to an advice letter to a friend who is being bullied.

Body of the letter

You have been asked to write a letter of advice to a friend who has to lose weight. What things do *you know* about his personal life that make him overweight?

- He loves chocolate.
- He hates exercise.
- He is a couch potato.

Begin by using personalising phrases to show how well you know him and to remind him of your friendship.

★ **Remember**

Include two or three pieces of advice *only*, and then:
- ❑ personalise
- ❑ use the selection of advice phrases (see page 37)
- ❑ support
- ❑ avoid stating the obvious.

I know …

… how much you love ⎫ chocolate
… how addicted you are to ⎬ junk food
… how much you hate exercise!
… what a couch potato you are!

or

I know you're not (exactly) the world's …

… most energetic ⎫
… sportiest ⎬ person!
… healthiest eater! ⎭

What three pieces of advice could you give your friend? There are many possibilities, for example:

■ Give up chocolate.
■ Join a sports club.
■ Take up walking.

Advice phrases

Introduce your ideas with a selection from the following **advice phrases**:

You could …
You (really) should …

You (really) ought to …
Why don't you …?

How about ⎫
What about ⎬ + verb + *ing*
Have you thought of ⎭ + noun

If I were you, I'd …
I should … if I were you.
The best thing you can do is …
It would be a good idea if you + past tense

Try ⎫
Remember ⎬ to …
Don't forget ⎭

Whatever happens, ⎫ try
Whatever you do, ⎬ remember to …
 don't forget

Try not to use the same phrase more than once – as you can see, there are many to choose from. As you have to give **two or three** pieces of advice *only*, that means you need to use only **two or three** of the advice phrases!

★ **Exam tip**
The first two phrases are the most basic ones. Impress the examiner by using some of the other phrases in this list.

Note how the sentence builds up:

I know you're not exactly the world's most energetic person, but if I were you, I'd take up walking.

I know how much you love chocolate, but have you thought of cutting down on junk food?

I know you're addicted to junk food, but you really ought to give it up.

When making your suggestions, it makes sense for the **first piece of advice** to be introduced like this:

The best
The most important } *thing you can do is …*

and for the **last piece of advice** to be introduced like this:

Whatever happens,   *try*
Whatever you do, } *remember*   *to*
   don't forget

The three pieces of advice you want to give your friend could be written as follows:

The best thing you can do is to take up walking.
It would be a good idea if you gave up chocolate.
Whatever happens, try to join a sports club.

Keep it simple

When actually giving advice, simplicity is the key. Be sure not to turn your letter into a biology lecture, especially if the topic is health, sport, smoking, the environment or any other topic most students will have learnt at school. Whatever the problem is, references to adipose tissue, gaseous exchange, eutrophication and catalytic converters are out of place and quite wrong here!

Look at the following examples to see how simple the advice you give should be:

1 Advice phrase + *eat the right things*

give up (= stop completely)
cut out (= stop completely) } *junk food*
cut down on (= reduce)   *fast food*

★ **Remember**
Do *not* list vegetables or write about vitamins, minerals, carbohydrates, protein or the digestive system here!

If I were you, I'd cut down on junk food.
Whatever happens, try to cut out chocolate.
Why don't you give up fast food?
It would be a good idea if you ate the right things.

2 Advice phrase + *take up a sport/tennis*
   do some sport
   do some exercise

Have you thought of taking up tennis?
Why don't you do some sport?
It would be a good idea if you did some exercise.

★ **Language Point**
The phrase *do some exercise* means exercise in a general sense as opposed to inactivity and is meant for someone who spends a lot of time sitting watching television or studying all the time. Do not confuse with *exercises*; these are a fixed sequence of movements performed for a specific reason, for example *warm-up exercises*.

3 Advice phrase + *take it* } *easy / gently* *at first*

don't overdo it
warm up
do some warm-up exercises

You ought to do some warm-up exercises.
Whatever happens, don't forget to take it easy at first.
Whatever you do, don't overdo it.

Notice how the phrase *don't overdo it* changes:

You really shouldn't overdo it.
If I were you, I wouldn't overdo it.
Try not to overdo it.
Remember not to overdo it.
Don't forget not to overdo it.

Give a reason

Finally, you need to give your friend a reason for carrying out your advice. In other words, you need to support your ideas in order to make them acceptable to your friend.

advice phrase   + idea   + support
        ↓   ↓
have you thought of } *+ noun / + verb + ing*   *It'll* } *help / make* *you*

Note how the sentence builds up:

I know you're not the world's most energetic person, but have you thought of taking up walking? It'll make you feel fitter.

The support phrases should also be very simple:

It'll } *help you feel fitter. / make you feel better. / do you good. / be good for you.*

It'll help you } *lose weight. / keep* } *fit. / in shape.*

It'll give you more energy.

It'll help you } *get rid of that spare tyre (of yours). / tone up those flabby muscles (of yours).*

It'll help you meet people with the same interests as you.
It'll be a good way to get to know people.

Why don't you join a sports club? It'll tone up those flabby muscles of yours and be a good way to get to know people, too.
What about taking up tennis? It'll do you good and help you keep in shape at the same time.

Exercise 3   Identify the good points and the problems in the following sentences from advice letters.

1   'You should also try to concentrate more during school hours. Another helpful piece of advice is to try to look over your past exams, find your mistakes and correct them.'
2   'I think you should make new friends and you should also get to know other people because, as you know, it is very difficult for someone to live on their own. I think you should also try to do sport, as this would give you the chance to get together with people who have the same interests as you.'
3   'You can invite students from school to one of your great parties, and I'm sure they will love it. The best thing you can do is to spend two or three weekends with them and they may take you to new places.'

Exercise 4   Use a selection of the phrases studied to write the body of a letter of advice to a friend who has moved to a new area and is feeling lonely.

Conclusion of an advice letter

As with descriptive letters, begin your conclusion with a generalisation and return to the topic in the introduction:

Well, I hope this gives you some idea what to do about …

Be positive and optimistic. Do not write:

  ✖ *Good luck!*

or

  ✖ *I hope this helps.*

Instead, write something like:

Joining a sports club/Cutting down on junk food …

… worked for	*me,* *my sister,* *my brother,* *my friend,*	*so*	*I'm sure it'll* *it's bound to* *I know it'll* *of course it'll* *why shouldn't it*	*work for you, too!*

As with the descriptive letters, try to personalise again before you conclude the letter by showing your interest. This shows that your concern for your friend is not only while you write the letter – you want to be kept informed about the situation and you also want to know if your advice has helped your friend in any way.

Do write and let me know how } *you get on.*
things go.
it goes.

To encourage your friend even more, finish with friendly encouragement:

I'll be thinking of you!

Exercise 5   Use a selection of the phrases studied to write the conclusion for an advice letter.

■ *Exam-style questions*

Question 1   Write a letter of advice to a friend who needs to take up a fitness programme.

Question 2   A friend of yours has moved away to a new area and is missing her/his school and friends. Try to make her/him feel happier, and suggest things that might help her/him to enjoy her/his new life.

Question 3   Write a letter of advice to a friend who is going for an interview, telling her/him what to avoid and making suggestions.

■ *Students' advice letters*

Read the following selection of advice letters written by different students, and the comments related to them.

★ **Note**

These are original letters written by IGCSE students and may still contain minor mistakes. In the comments column, the letter **R** refers to points in the Register unit on pages 182–5, and the letter **G** refers to points in the Grammar unit on pages 186–99. The arrow (→) points to what the text in the letter should be changed to or replaced with.

Question 1 Write a letter of advice to a friend who has been told to go on a fitness programme.
Answer A

Dear Lucas,

How are you, it was nice to hear from you yesterday. I'm sorry I **haven't written for so long** ❶ but I've been busy studying.

Anyway, when you mentioned how you needed to **regain your fitness,** ❷ in your last letter, I looked through some sports guides to get an idea of what might help you. I thought it'd be a good idea for you to start off by jogging every day for about an hour or so, but if you prefer working in groups, you ought to consider joining an aerobics class or swimming sessions. If I were you, I'd join in **swimming sessions,** ❸ they help you get fit, **they also relax you** ❹ and at the same time, it's quite fun in the water.

If you're interested, there are swimming sessions at the marina club **beside you,** ❺ twice every week at £30 per month. While you're at it **take care of your diet,** ❻ because **I know what kind of an appetite you have!** ❼ Write soon and let me know what you decide to do.

Yours,

Marc

Comments

❶ 'Apology' introduction inappropriate for an advice letter

❷ R3 and R1 → get fit

❸ Repetition

❹ R9 → they relax you, too

❺ → near where you live/next to your house

❻ → watch what you eat

❼ Personalising – good!

General comments

- This letter contains no grammar or spelling mistakes.
- The student has included some good advice with support.
- There is one good example of personalising.
- There are some nice phrases, which make this sound a very natural letter.

However:

- The introduction is not appropriate.
- More personalising is needed.

Overall, thus is an excellent answer, which is well-structured, well-written and of a good length.

Question 1 Write a letter of advice to a friend who has been told to go on a fitness programme.
Answer B

Dear Ravi,

How are you and how is life? **I'm sorry I haven't written❶** for so long but **I was very busy in a fitness program❷** and haven't had any time. **It was lovely❸** to get your letter last week. You sounded really very sad because of your strict diet and your new **fitness program❹** but don't worry and cheer up. I thought I'd **write you a letter❺** because you might like to know something about **my fitness classes which pedalled me back into shape and fitness.❻**

The best thing you can do❼ is to go carefully at first and there is no need to **overdo things because if you do you may do❽** more harm than good. Whatever happens, don't ever forget the important warming up exercises before **your fitness class begins,❾** try to stop eating fast foods and you have to give up eating sweets in order to have a good diet which will make you **loose❿** weight very fast. I should be really happy if I were you, because feeling fit has **a lot of benefits⓫** as I saw on **the BBC⓬** last night. The best thing is that it will improve your body shape, will make you sleep better and feel healthy and **moreover⓭ you will have self-discipline and team spirit.⓮**

As you see, feeling fit has a lot of benefits, I think you ought to cheer up now and be very happy because after your classes are over you'll be a fit and healthy young man. Don't forget to write and send me a picture of you in the gym.

Best wishes,

Sunil

Comments

❶ 'Apology' introduction inappropriate for advice letter

❷ This is very confusing! *Who* is getting fit?

❸ The letter could have started here.

❹ Avoid repetition of wording of title. It is formal register.

❺ Stating the obvious

❻ R1, R5 → *how the classes I joined got me fit*

❼ We were expecting to hear about the writer's classes. This is a 'jump'.

❽ Repetition

❾ R1 → *you start the class*

There are too many pieces of advice here, one after the other.

❿ Spelling → *lose*

⓫ Mixed register: *a lot of* (friendly) *benefits* (formal)

⓬ Good to mention!

⓭ R8 → *not only that*

⓮ R1 → *you'll enjoy being with other people* (who share the same interests)

General comments

- This letter has the correct structure.
- The student has included a selection of relevant advice phrases.
- The student has supported the advice.

However:

- The biggest problem with this letter is the inappropriate and mixed use of register.
- The lack of personalising makes the letter sound unfriendly, like a lecture.

Generally this is a good attempt, although marks may also be lost for a confused and inappropriate start to the introduction. The introduction and conclusion of this letter are much longer than they should be.

Question 1   Write a letter of advice to a friend who has been told to go on a fitness programme.
Answer C

Dear Yumi,

How are you?

I am sorry I haven't written for so long, but I've been busy studying and haven't had the time. I was really shocked **when I knew**❶ **that**❷ you have **put up**❸ twelve kilogrammes.

So I thought I'd drop you a line to tell you how to **reduce your weight a bit**❹.

I think that the best thing you can do is to walk. Walking is a very simple exercise but it gives good results and it won't affect your back injury. **It also can be done**❺ anywhere and at anytime. As a start you should walk for at least two hours every day. This will help you to **put down some weight**❹. I forgot to mention that you'll need some extra weights **while walking.**❻ You can use the bracelet weights that you have. **You know,**❼ the ones which you carry around your wrist like a bracelet. You should try to jog a little while walking, too.

How about **swimming?**❽ You've always loved **swimming.**❽ **Swimming**❽ will help you to get into good shape. **What's more, it won't cost you anything more than a swimming suit and going to the swimming pool once a week.**❾

Have you thought of joining a health club? You really ought to join one. I know one which has great facilities and is not at all expensive. It's called the 'Falcon Health Centre' and you can get **a membership of a month for £10 only.**❿ The best thing is that it has a steam room and a sauna room which will help you to burn the extra fats. **The centre also has aerobic classes.**⓫ Join in if you like and if your doctor **permits you.**⓬

Their exercises are very basic but they make you sweat like hell. I joined them for a while and it really **helps in giving you flexibility.**⓭

Anyway, I hope this gives you an idea about how you can get back into shape. Give my regards to your parents. Looking forward to hearing from you soon.

With love,

Tomomi

Comments

❶ → to hear

❷ R5 – remove *that*

❸ Wrong phrasal verb → *put on*

❹ R3 → *lose a bit of weight*

❺ R4 → *you can do it … too.*

❻ R2 → *while you walk*

❼ Personalising – good

❽ Repetition

❾ Good sentence

❿ R1 → *you can join for a month for only £10.*

⓫ R9 → *the centre does aerobic classes, too.*

⓬ R3 → *says you can*

⓭ R1 → *helps to make you more supple.*

General comments

- This letter contains quite a lot of advice with good support and some personalising.

However:

- There are some problems with register.
- There is not enough personalising.
- The first half of the introduction is inappropriate.

If the student had used fewer ideas and included more personalising, a shorter and more balanced letter would have been produced. This letter is much too long to be produced under exam conditions.

Question 1 Write a letter of advice to a friend who has been told to go on a fitness programme.
Answer D

Dear Jo,

It was lovely to hear from you yesterday. I'm sorry **to hear in your letter, that**❶ **you have to take up a fitness programme,**❷ I know how much you like food. Anyway, don't worry because I've been in **the same situation**❸ and I think I can help you in your "fitness mission".

Eat❹ complex carbohydrates and fibre-rich food,❺ like **whole grains, fresh fruit and vegetables**❻ to boost your energy levels. Why don't you take up walking or swimming and make them a daily routine?

They're easy, cheap and burn a lot of calories. It's better to eat your main meal earlier in the day and try not to eat within two hours of going to bed.

Listen to your body, eat when you're hungry and stop when **you feel satisfied.**❼

How about joining a fitness class? I know you're busy studying, but you could choose days to fit in with your studying programme. **Sport increases mental alertness as well as physical fitness. Sport also has psychological benefits as it makes you calmer and relaxed which means it will help you be more balanced and keen on studying. If you succeed, it gives you a sense of personal achievement, self discipline and respect.**❽ When you've finished off the fitness programme you'll **feel better and look healthier.**❾ **You'll be really happy when you get rid of your excess flab and all your tight clothes become looser.**❿

Don't forget to write to me and tell me how you are doing. I wish you all the best and I'm looking forward to hearing from you.

Yours,

Paul

Comments

❶ Poor style and wrong register

❷ Avoid repetition of wording of title. It is formal register.

❸ Register → **in the same boat**

❹ Where is the advice phrase? This sounds like a command.

❺ Register

❻ Listing

❼ Register → **you feel full**

❽ This sounds like a lecture. Why? It is full of formal register words, and so sounds as though it is copied from a book, e.g. **psychological benefits, succeed, personal achievement.**

❾ This is what your friend wants to hear, and is in friendly register – good.

❿ Good! But **excess flab** – sounds impersonal. It also confirms that your friend is fat! Better to say **the flab you think you've got** or **the flab that's worrying you so much.**

General comments

● This letter includes one or two sentences which contain supported advice.

However:

● There is a long section of inappropriately used formal register.
● The letter contains a list of unsupported advice.
● There is not enough personalising.

Question 2   Write a letter to a friend who has moved to a new area and is feeling lonely.
Answer A

Dear Anna,

How are you? Feeling better I hope. Lost that nasty flu? or is it still wearing out your nose?

I thought I'd **write back**❶ and try to **convince you**❷ that your moving wasn't as bad as you think. Try to think of all the things **that are available for you now that aren't still here**❸ in this old, **stagnant**❹ town! **For example**❺ you mentioned in your last letter that your new school has two football fields. While here we don't even have two inches of field to be proud of! And **I hope you haven't forgotten**❻ our old classroom that would've better been described as a can of sardines.

All your friends here miss you too,❼ and send their 'Hellos'. **Specially Tim.**❽ I'm sure you'll find lots of new friends there, at least ones that won't **borrow all your pocket money**❾ from you.

Anyway, write soon and tell me how you are doing in your new school, and which club you decide to join.

Love from

Linda

Comments

❶ Good. Personalising: she is replying.

❷ R3 → *make you realise*

❸ R4 → *you've got there, that we still haven't got here*

❹ Good vocabulary!

❺ Inappropriate register: remove

❻ Good use of present perfect with personalising

❼ Excellent way of referring to Anna's letter saying she missed everyone – and correct use of **too**!

❽ Giving a name is a form of personalising.

❾ Personalising with humour

General comments

● This letter has a good introduction which includes personalising.

● There are some excellent expressions and vocabulary which make it read very fluently.

● It contains plenty of personalising.

● There are not many grammar or register mistakes.

However:

● There are no advice phrases.

Question 2 Write a letter to a friend who has moved to a new area and is feeling lonely.
Answer B

Dear Samar,

How are you, I've been meaning to write to you in your new address for ages but I'm afraid I just haven't got round it. **I really miss you so much❶** and I was sorry to hear that you're very sad because you moved to **a new area.❷** That's why I thought I'd drop you a line to **cheer you up.❸**

In my opinion❹ the best thing to do when you miss your old friends is to make new friends, so why don't you **make a party❺** and invite all **the boys and girls in your area of your age❻**. Another good thing you can do is to join the nearest sports club where **you will meet❼** people with the same interests as you. If I were you, I would stop being sad because you can always **come over and see me❽** and all your all friends some time.

Love,

Mai

Comments

❶ Confused – *I really miss you* or *I miss you very much*

❷ Avoid repetition of wording of title. It is formal register.

❸ Good phrase

❹ Register → *I think*

❺ Confused phrase: *have a party* or *throw a party*

❻ R1 → *everyone your age who lives there*

❼ R6 → *you'll meet*

❽ Good point – personalising shows you want to continue the friendship, even though your friend has moved.

General comments

● This letter contains some good ideas for advice.

However:

● There is not much personalising.
● There is no conclusion.
● The introduction is the first thing the examiner reads and this one gives a bad impression..

Question 3 Write a letter to a friend who is going for an interview and needs advice.
Answer A

Dear Kinji,

It was lovely to hear from you. I'm so pleased you managed to get an interview at the Engineering College at the AUC. Well, congratulations! It must be great because you have been hunting for one for so long. Anyway I thought I'd drop you a line **to calm you down.**❶

Don't worry, **I've been in the same boat last year**❷ when I was **applying at**❸ Cairo University and I know how it feels. All you need is to **calm down.**❹ I think that the best thing you can do is to have a warm bath and **go to sleep early**❺ on the night before the big day. This will help you to relax. When you go to the interview don't panic. Take it easy and just assume you're having **a small chit chat**❻ with one of your father's friends whom you're seeing for the first time. All you really have to do is talk in a friendly polite way and keep a smile on your face. This will give a good impression.

During the interview, try to **collect yourself and to organise yourself.**❼ This will help you to answer better. Try not to rush or shout **while answering.**❽ It will show that you are nervous and will give the interviewer **a misjudgement.**❾ By the way, try not to answer 'yes' or 'no' only. **I was told so**❿ when I was in your place but I don't know why. I guess it's not polite. One more thing, try to **gain control over**⓫ your habit of yawning. I know that **you don't feel it wrong,**⓬ but the interviewer might think that you're telling him that he's boring. So just control yourself **for sometime.**⓭

Best wishes,

Nitta

Comments

❶ Nice thought – personalising

❷ Incorrect grammar: present perfect **I've been** cannot be used with definitive time **last year**. → **I was in the same boat last year**.

❸ Wrong preposition → **applying to**

❹ Repetition from introduction

❺ → **have an early night/go to bed early**

❻ Good vocabulary

❼ Repeat of **yourself**. **collect** and **organise** are in the wrong register.

❽ R2 → **when you answer**

❾ R1 → **the wrong idea**

❿ Register → **that's what I was told**

⓫ R3 → **do something about/stop**

⓬ → **you don't see anything wrong with it**

⓭ → **for a while**

General comments

● This letter has a good introduction.
● Most ideas are supported.

However:

● There are too many pieces of advice.
● There are not many examples of personalising.
● It contains too much formal register.
● There is no conlcusion.
● The student has repeated the advice phrase 'try'. Other advice phrases should have been included.

Question 3 Write a letter to a friend who is going for an interview and needs advice.
Answer B

Dear María,

It was lovely to hear from you. I'm so pleased you managed to get an interview at The State College, but I will be more pleased if you manage to get a seat there. It will mostly depend on your interview, so please, do be careful.

I know how well you speak❶ English, and how well you put your thoughts into words, but if you are nervous, **things can go wrong.**❷ So, try to relax at the interview, think of the interviewer as someone you know and respect. This will make you able to think better and will give you some confidence. **And**❸ at the same time don't over relax. You might sound bored or overconfident.

What ever❹ you do, don't rush through. Slow down and be steady, **I know that** 'rush through' **habit of yours.**❺ **If you slow down, you would**❻ be able to control what you say easily and not say anything out of place or wrong that will make you look bad.

The best thing you can do is to answer briefly, and not to blabber about unnecessary things. Don't be too brief either. Otherwise you will look hesitant **in either cases.**❼

You could always add a little humour to what you say, or just smile if you can't think of **something.**❽ It'll make the interviewer like you. And by the way, **take care of** ❾ what you wear, it gives an impression of who you are. Write soon and tell me how the interview went. **Good luck.**❿

Love,

Antonieta

Comments

❶ Personalising

❷ Good advice structure, with support

❸ Do not start a sentence with and – inappropriate here: and joins two positive sentences. Here you need but, or …, though. → *At the same time, don't over-relax, though!*

❹ One word: *whatever*

❺ Personalising

❻ G2 → *If you slow down, you will*

❼ → *in both cases*

❽ → *anything:* used with negatives and questions

❾ Wrong expression → *choose what you wear carefully/be careful what you wear*

❿ Be more positive. → *I'm sure you'll be fine./I'm sure it'll go well.*

General comments

- This letter has a good introduction.
- It contains plenty of personalising and support.
- There are some good phrases.
- There is a broad range of vocabulary.

Question 4 Write a letter to a friend who needs advice on how to study.

Dear Assem,

I've been meaning to write to you for ages,① but I'm afraid I just haven't got round to it. Anyway, **I thought I would drop you a line**② to answer some of the questions on how to organise studying for an exam, **now that you have mentioned them in your previous letter.**③

In my opinion,④ **first,**⑤ when you study you should try and find a **quiet and well-lit room.**⑥ Then following that **is your ability to set up a schedule**⑦ including your different subjects and **descions**⑧ on how to **allocate them**⑨ during the course of the week. The timetable **should also include certain hours of freedom**⑩ to **reduce your burdens**⑪ after long hours of study. You should also try to concentrate more **during your study hours,**⑫ **thus understanding the information thoroughly.**⑬ **Another helpful advice**⑭ is to try and look over your exams or homework then find your mistakes and try to correct them. **Do not**⑮ try and delay everything to **the night of**⑯ the exam, **since**⑰ that day should be used for quick revision along with more relaxation. **We can thus say that**⑱ **if you are able to**⑲ study weeks before the exam, with **carefull**⑳ planning then you feel less stress during the night of the exam.

I hope this gives you some ideas about how to organise and plan your time. Keep in touch and I look forward to seeing you soon.

Yours,

Adil

Comments

① Inappropriate introduction for an advice letter

② This is a decision made by the writer. If someone asks you a question, you are obliged to answer, you do not decide to.

③ Poor style

④ Formal register → I think

⑤ Listing

⑥ Where is the support?

⑦ R1 → make a timetable if you can

⑧ Spelling → decisions

⑨ R3 → fit them in

⑩ R1, R3, R9 → try to give yourself some free time, too

⑪ Register → help you relax

⑫ R1 → while you work

⑬ Inappropriate register → so you completely understand everything

⑭ Register: use an advice phrase.

⑮ R6: use short form → **Don't**

⑯ → the night before

⑰ Inappropriate register → because

⑱ Inappropriate register: sounds like a science experiment.

⑲ Inappropriate register → if you can

⑳ Spelling → careful

General comments

● This letter has an appropriate conclusion.

However:

● There is too much advice with no personalising.

● It contains too much formal register, which indicates the writer is not aware of different registers.

● The letter does not seem fluent, but artificial.

Friendly letters: narrative

Narrative letters need to be written in friendly register. These are letters written to a friend to describe a series of events in the recent past. The narrative letter is similar in some ways to a telephone call, when you rush in and pick up the phone to tell your friend all about something which has just happened to you: 'hot news'! You phone because what happened was **exciting**, or because you think your friend will find it **interesting**.

Before looking in detail at how to write a narrative, consider the three types of situation that involve narrative writing in the exam.

Type 1 Situations

Write a letter to a friend about something that could happen to you in everyday life, which may be exciting but which has **no serious consequences** (results). For example:

■ You get stuck in a lift.
■ You invite your friends out for coffee, but when the bill comes you find you have left your money at home!
■ You lock yourself out of your flat/house.
■ You get caught in a thunderstorm.
■ You meet a famous person in a restaurant.
■ You forget your lines during the performance of the school play.
■ A fire breaks out at your school.
■ There is a robbery at your local shop while you are there.

Can you add to this list?

As with all friendly letters in the exam, the story you write about does *not* need to be true, and you should **use your imagination** to make the narrative interesting. However, there are two points to beware of:

★ **Remember**
If you are over-dramatic, the story does not sound believable or convincing.

■ Do not be over-dramatic when you write, or the story will not sound convincing (in other words, the reader will not believe it). If you are writing about a road accident, for example, do not describe blood and bodies all over the road!
■ Do not make yourself into a hero. Do not refer to your photograph being in the newspaper, or you appearing on the television, receiving money, meeting or shaking hands with the mayor as a result of a heroic action!

Type 2 Situations

Write a letter to a friend about something you have done that is daring, unusual or not what your friend would expect you to do. As with the Type 1 Situation examples, however, there are still **no serious consequences**. For example:

■ You went sky-diving/parachute-jumping/for a hot air balloon ride. (Your friend knows you are scared of heights.)
■ You went scuba-diving. (Your friend knows about your fear of water.)
■ You went horse-riding. (Your friend knows about your fear of horses/heights/speed.)

■ You took part in a school play or concert. (This was difficult for you, because you are embarrassed about standing in front of an audience/you are not very confident about playing the piano/violin, etc.)

Can you add to this list?

Type 3 Situations

Write a letter to a friend about your happiest or proudest moment. The most effective kind of letter will be one about a simple, personal achievement. For example:

■ You won a scholarship to a well-known school/college. (This was a surprise; you never dreamt you would win it!)
■ You met a member of your family for the first time. (Perhaps they had been living abroad.)
■ A teacher who is always tough on you said something complimentary about a piece of your work/gave you a good mark for a piece of work.
■ You lost enough weight to fit into your favourite clothes.
■ You won a competition. (Perhaps a trip abroad?)

Can you add to this list?

As before, these situations should not feature you as a hero:

■ Do not write about the day you received your IGCSE results and had all A*s. Many students choose this so it must be very repetitive for the examiner to mark, and sounds as if you are showing off – especially if your English is not A* standard!
■ Most IGCSE students are not married and have not yet been to university, so do not write about your wedding or graduation day!

■ What to include in a narrative letter – a basic plan

To meet the exam requirements, your task is to understand and **combine** the features of both **narrative writing** and **friendly letter writing**. When writing a narrative letter, do not become so involved in the development of events – in other words **telling the story** – that you forget you are supposed to be writing a letter.

Narrative writing contains certain features and you should remember to do the following:

■ Write chronologically: in other words, write about the events in the same order they actually happened, including:
  – a definite beginning
  – a climax (the most dramatic or interesting moment in the story)
  – a definite conclusion.
■ Set the scene, using *wh* questions.
■ Include time sequence phrases.
■ Include connectors.
■ Include feelings and how they change during the narrative.

Friendly letter writing involves applying the techniques discussed in Section 2 Unit 1. In other words, you should remember to:

■ create interest
■ personalise
■ support
■ avoid listing.

This is more difficult to do in a narrative than in a descriptive letter. Now let's see how these features are included in a basic plan for the introduction, body and conclusion of a narrative letter.

Introduction

The most important thing about the introduction is to **keep it short**. Firstly, it is not easy to write a properly constructed narrative in 100–150 words (Core) or 150–200 words (Extended). A short introduction allows you more words to tell the story. Secondly, you are keen to tell your friend all about the incident because you think he will find it interesting or exciting, so you will not want to waste time on a long introduction. Obviously, you will contact your friend as soon as you can after the incident happened – so make sure you are not writing about something that happened three weeks or two years ago!

The main purpose of the introduction is to create interest in the story you are going to relate. Suitable introduction phrases for the narrative letter include:

I can't wait to tell you
I'm dying to tell you   } about/what/what happened (to me) ...
Wait until you hear   who/how ...

You won't believe
You'll never believe   } what happened (to me) ...
You'll never guess   who/how ...

Don't forget to say *when* the incident happened:

... this morning
... this afternoon
... just now
... a few minutes/moments ago

Body of the letter
Set the scene
Begin this part of the letter by describing what was happening before and leading up to the main event. A good way to do this is by answering some of the following *wh* questions.

■ Who were you with?
■ What were you doing?
■ Where were you?
■ When were you there?
■ Why were you there?

I was walking home from school with Sara on Tuesday ...
My mother and I had been in the city centre looking for a birthday present for Dad ...

The scene you describe should be routine and ordinary. This will provide a **contrast** with the main event and make the story more interesting. For example:

We were chatting about ⎱ *what we had for homework ...*
what we were going to do at the weekend ...
the party ...

We were listening to the radio ...
I was waiting for the bus ...
I was looking out of my window ...

Include time sequence phrases

As you develop the story, try to introduce a selection of **time sequence phrases** to give chronology (in other words, to describe events in the order they happened). There are many of these phrases, including the following:

I'd/He'd/We'd (only) just + past tense, *when ...*
We'd only just sat down at our desks, when the fire alarm went off.

The moment/minute I/he/we + past tense, *...*
The minute I walked into the room, I noticed something strange.

I/He/We was/were just about to ..., when + past tense *...*
We were just about to catch the bus, when there was a deafening noise.

Just as I/he/we was/were about to ...,
Just as we were about to catch the bus, there was a deafening noise.

As I/she/we + past tense/past continuous *...*
As I opened the door, I heard a scream.
As he was running away, we called the police.

Before + active verb (*not* the *ing* form of the verb, which is formal)
Before I shut the door, I checked I had my keys.

After what seemed like ages ...
After what seemed like ages, the lift door opened.

In the morning/afternoon/evening
All afternoon/night
By this time
In the end
For the first time in my life
It only took a moment
About ... hours later
Within no time

Avoid using common phrases like *firstly, then, after that, next* – these sound like a mechanical sequence rather than a real life experience!

Include connectors

The use of connectors such as *and*, *but*, *until* and *although* links short sentences together and helps the story to flow.

Include feelings

Another feature of narrative writing is to describe your **feelings** at each stage of the event. There could be as many as three different stages, each marked by different feelings:

- relaxed, not expecting anything to happen
- excited, frightened, amazed (depending on what your story is about)
- relieved (when the incident is all over).

This is a very simple and effective way to describe feelings:

| I was
 We were | disappointed <br> horrified <br> surprised <br> delighted <br> amazed <br> furious | to | learn <br> realise <br> see <br> find <br> discover <br> hear | that … |

Include personalising and support phrases

Personalising in narrative letters is not easy – how can you find a way to include your friend in an incident that happened when he was not there? You need to express your friend's knowledge of your character, what you would do, how you would react in certain situations and what your views are on certain topics. Here are some examples:

You know how frightened I am of {(verb + *ing*) *being alone* / (noun) *heights*}

I don't need to tell you how excited I was …
As you can imagine, I was terrified.
As you know, I can't stand heights.
You know me – I always panic in emergencies.

Another way to personalise is to involve your friend in the event by referring to his characteristics, abilities, likes and dislikes. This will be especially effective if they are in contrast to yours, as it will create interest. Look at these examples:

I wish you'd been there.
If only you'd been there.

Why do you wish your friend had been there? This requires support.

You would have {*known what to do.* / *kept a cool head.*}

If it was a good experience, something you were pleased with or proud of, for example, and would have liked to share with your friend, you can write:

It's a shame
 It's a pity } (+ past tense) *you weren't there.*

Why is it a pity? This requires support.

If, on the other hand, it was a bad or unpleasant experience and you are glad your friend did not share it with you, you can write:

It's a good thing ⎫
It's a good job ⎬ (+ past tense) *you weren't there.*
⎭

Remember to add your support.

Another way to personalise is to try to put your friend in the same situation:

I wonder what you would have done?

★ **Language Point**
❑ Notice how we can use the first half of this structure only, and **imply** the second half.
❑ *I wonder what you would have done* – if you had been there, but you were not there.
❑ For the use of the third conditional in this structure, see the Grammar unit, pages 189–91.

Concluding a narrative letter

As with the introduction, the conclusion will need to be very brief; firstly because of the number of words needed to tell the story, and secondly because you are in a hurry to tell everyone else about what happened!

Well, I must dash now – I've got to tell Sam all about it!
Well, I must go now – I want to call Sarah and tell her the news!
(Looking back) I think it was probably one of the happiest moments I can ever remember!

■ Applying the plan to a Type 1 Situation

We will now apply the basic plan to the first set of situations, which involve writing about something that could happen to you in everyday life which has **no serious consequences**. Our example situation is seeing someone famous in a restaurant.

Introduction

You'll never guess who I saw when I was at Mario's with Fumiko a few minutes ago.

★ **Remember**
Personalising phrases (underlined) included here add to the feeling of a relaxed atmosphere, as well as being good friendly letter style.

Body
Set the scene

We were sitting at <u>our favourite table</u> near the window, looking forward to a relaxing meal and trying to decide what to order. <u>You know</u> how difficult that is when everything is so delicious!

Introduce a selection of time sequence phrases, connectors and feelings

Look at this example of how these features could be joined together.

We were just about to① call the waiter, **when①** **suddenly①** we were disturbed by the noise of a large group of people coming into the restaurant. I tried to see what the fuss was about, **but②** it was impossible **because of②** the camera flashes.	① Time sequence × 3
	② Connector × 2
It wasn't until some time later,③ when③ I went to wash my hands, that I got a clear view **and④** was **amazed to see⑤** the President himself!	③ Time sequence × 2 ④ Connector ⑤ Feelings
I don't need to tell you⑥ how **excited⑦** I was. I stared **in surprise⑦** for **what seemed like ages.⑧** I decided to get his autograph **before⑧** he left, **and⑨** went to get some paper from **Fumiko.⑩**	⑥ Personalising ⑦ Feelings × 2 ⑧ Time sequence × 2 ⑨ Connector ⑩ Personalising
Just as I was about to⑪ approach the President, the whole group got up and left just as noisily as **when⑪** they had arrived. **I was disappointed to realise⑫** I had missed the chance of a lifetime!	⑪ Time sequence × 2 ⑫ Feelings

★ **Remember**

There are many different ways of writing this story. Do *not* learn this story or think of reproducing it in the exam. Your story must be original.

Conclusion

> Don't you wish you'd been there? Must dash to see if there's anything about it on the local news.

Exercise 1   Write your own letter about seeing someone famous in a restaurant.

Exercise 2   Write a letter about another Type 1 Situation – an attemped robbery at your local shop. Use the introduction below and then continue by setting the scene, using a selection of time sequence phrases, connectors and feelings, and adding an appropriate conclusion.

You won't believe what happened when I went down to the village shop yesterday evening.

Compare what you have written with a suggested answer on page 246.

Exercise 3   Write a letter about getting stuck in a lift. Write an introduction, set the scene and then use a selection of time sequence phrases, connectors and feelings and write an appropriate conclusion.

Compare what you have written with a suggested answer on page 246.

■ Applying the plan to a Type 2 Situation

We will now apply the basic plan to the second set of situations, which involve writing about something you have done that is daring, unusual or not what your friend would expect you to do. As our example, we will use doing a parachute jump.

Introduction

> *You'll never believe what I've just done!*

Body
Set the scene

> *I was having my coffee this morning and reading the local paper, when I noticed an advertisement for a free parachute jump. So I decided to go along.*

Exercise 4 Continue the narrative, using a selection of time sequence phrases, connectors and feelings and ending with an appropriate conclusion. Then compare what you have written with a suggested answer on page 247.

■ Applying the plan to a Type 3 Situation

Finally, we can apply the basic plan to the third set of situations, which involve writing about your happiest or proudest moment.

Do not begin your story by classifying it:

> ✖ *I am writing to tell you about my proudest/happiest moment.*

Put this in the ending instead, as if you are looking back over what happened and summarising it:

> ✔ *(Looking back) I think it was probably one of the proudest/happiest moments I can ever remember!*

The following plan is based on a typical Type 3 Situation – a lottery win.

Introduction

> *I can't wait to tell you my news!*

Body
Set the scene

> *I was listening to the results of the lottery on the TV when I realised I'd won!*

Introduce a selection of time sequence phrases, connectors and feelings

I can't tell you how **excited**❶ I was! **The moment**❷ I heard the news, I dashed to my bedroom to look for the ticket – **but**❸ I couldn't remember where I'd put it. **You know**❹ what a scatterbrain I am!	❶ Feelings ❷ Time sequence ❸ Connector ❹ Personalising
I was **just about to**❺ start searching my room **when**❺ the door burst open **and**❻ Mum came in with some trousers she'd been ironing. It only took **a moment**❼ for me to look at the trousers **and**❽ remember I'd been wearing them **when**❾ I bought the ticket.	❺ Time sequence × 2 ❻ Connector ❼ Time sequence ❽ Connector ❾ Time sequence
I was **horrified to realise**❿ they had been washed! **By this time**⓫ my heart was racing **because**⓬ I felt sure the ticket would be ruined.	❿ Feelings ⓫ Time sequence ⓬ Connector
In the end⓭ it turned out that Mum had checked the pockets **before**⓭ washing the trousers **and**⓮ had put the ticket in a safe place. **I have never felt so relieved**⓯ in my life!	⓭ Time sequence × 2 ⓮ Connector ⓯ Feelings

Conclusion

The prize money wasn't very much – but at least it should pay for some driving lessons … and maybe a small car? This was certainly the happiest day of my life – so far!

■ *Exam-style questions*

Question 1 You were enjoying a walk by yourself when you fell down some steps and twisted your ankle. You had to wait several hours for help to arrive. Write a letter to a friend explaining what happened. (See page 227 for a plan for this question.)

Question 2 Recently you went on a school trip to a local museum. Unfortunately, you became separated from the group and got lost. Write a letter to a friend describing what happened.

Question 3 Write a letter to a friend about your most exciting moment.

■ *Student's narrative letter*

Read the following narrative letter written by an IGCSE student in response to an exam question and the comments related to it.

> ★ **Note**
> This is an original letter written by an IGCSE student and may still contain minor mistakes. In the comments column, the letter **R** refers to a point in the Register unit on pages 182–5.
>   The arrow (→) points to what the text in the letter should be changed to or replaced with.

Question 1   Write a letter to a friend telling her/him about the happiest moment in your life.

Dear Lee,

I'm sorry I haven't written for so long, but I've been busy studying and haven't had the time.❶ It was lovely to get your letter last week and congratulations on passing your exams. I thought I would drop you a line❷ to tell you that this weekend I had **the happiest moment in my life**.❸

Two weeks ago❹ I heard that a large marathon was going to be held all round the city. One of my friends, George,❺ suggested that I could try and run the marathon which would help me to lose weight. I thought about the idea and decided to accept the challenge.

So❻ I joined the race and although I didn't win, I finished it before a lot of others. **The moment I crossed** ❼ the finish line, **I felt that I had overcome my fear** ❽ of not finishing the marathon, since **as you know**,❾ I was overweight.

Many of my friends were **attending**❿ the race and **were surprised**⓫ that I managed to run continuously without stopping throughout the entire race. That day was probably the happiest and proudest moment in my life.

Now you know all about the most exciting goal which I set myself and managed to do successfully, Take good care of yourself. I'm looking forward to seeing you soon.

Love,

Jo

Comments

❶ Inappropriate introduction

❷ Good use of friendly register

❸ Do not classify in the introduction.

❹ Correct use of time sequence phase

❺ Use of name to personalise

❻ Friendly register connector used correctly

❼ Good use of time sequence phrase and appropriate tense

❽ Good description of feelings

❾ Personalising – good

❿ R3 → at

⓫ More description of feelings – good

General comments

● This letter contains many features of narrative writing.
● It contains many of the features of friendly writing, including personalising and support.
● There are not many register or grammar mistakes.

However:

● It would lose marks due to the long and inappropriate introduction.

Friendly letters: descriptive narrative

'Descriptive narrative' letters need to be written in friendly register. These are letters written to a friend, relative or penfriend about an occasion or event. As the name suggests, descriptive narratives are a combination of descriptive and narrative writing.

The occasions you may be asked to write about can include:

■ a celebration
■ a school show
■ a sports day
■ a festival or carnival
■ a holiday.

As with other friendly letters, the main points to keep in mind are:

■ create interest
■ personalise for the reader
■ support each idea
■ do not list.

■ Basic outline

Introduction

The reason for writing a descriptive narrative is to pass on information about a particular occasion. Although the occasion may be of interest to the reader, it is certainly not as exciting as the 'hot news' in a narrative letter. As there is no sense of urgency, a descriptive narrative can have a standard introduction.

Be particularly careful to look for **hidden implications** in descriptive narrative questions. If you are asked to write a letter to your friend about sports day at your school, for example, the reader (the examiner) may expect to know why your friend was not at the sports day herself, and you should give a reason for this. On the other hand, if you are asked to write a letter to your penfriend about sports day at your school, the reader would not expect your penfriend to be at the event, as penfriends live abroad.

Look at the following examples.

■ To a friend who missed sports day you could write:

Dear Adam,
        It's a shame you missed sports day last week, but I hope you're feeling better.

In other words, he missed sports day because he was ill.

■ To a relative who missed a family party you could write:

What a pity you couldn't come to the party – but I'm glad you enjoyed your school trip to …

In other words, your relative was on a school trip at the time of the party.

▤ The same applies when writing to a friend who missed a school trip. Why did he miss it? School trips are usually fun. Think of a suitable reason for your friend to miss this trip. Having a cold, for example, would not stop him from going, whereas a broken leg may be a more appropriate excuse.

The transition sentence can be short and straight to the point:

I thought you might like to know what you missed.
I thought I'd let you know how it went.
I thought you might like to know something about …
I thought you might be interested to know something about …

Body of the letter

The starting point for the body of this kind of letter is to consider the **essential features** which go together to make the occasion and without which there would be no occasion. These will usually include the following:

▤ **People** The most important requirement for an event is *people*; it is simply impossible to have a party or hold a festival without people!
▤ **Atmosphere** People usually find an event more attractive if there is food, drink, music and so on, and this is often what creates the atmosphere.
▤ **Weather** This can also be an important factor, especially for an outdoor event, and it can add to the atmosphere.
▤ **Individual incidents** There will be a number of small, unrelated incidents which seem unimportant, but which probably add to the atmosphere and so help you to remember the occasion later. The inclusion of these small incidents help to make this letter different from a narrative letter.

At the same time, you need to remember to apply the features of friendly letter writing. In other words, you should:

▤ create interest
▤ personalise
▤ support
▤ avoid listing.

> ★ **Note**
>
> As mentioned earlier, the occasion itself is not 'hot news', because it happened some time ago – you are going over it in your memory, trying to select information that would interest your friend. Note that the result of this selection process is that the incidents you recall will not come in the order they happened. Time sequence phrases are not central in this type of letter. Another reason why there is no need to refer to time is that nothing major actually happened at the event.
>
> These are two of the factors which make this type of letter different from a narrative letter.

Conclusion of a descriptive narrative letter

The conclusion for a descriptive narrative letter should be quite short; probably only two or three lines long, and, if possible, should return to the point which began the letter.

Now you know what you missed!
Hope you'll be feeling better for Jo's party this weekend.

Let's now apply the features outlined above to four different exam-style descriptive narrative questions.

■ Putting it all together 1

Write to a relative who missed a family celebration, telling her/him all about it.

People

In order to avoid listing, select only one or two of the guests. Write about them in such a way as to create interest by giving details about their clothes, their behaviour, their personality or character. Remember to support every statement. Very often in this type of letter, the person you describe is known both to you and the person you are writing to. In other words, you have common knowledge of the person's characteristics, habits and so on. This provides an excellent opportunity for personalising.

Look at an example:

I was caught by Uncle Ken, who started giving me the usual advice about what I should study at university, and then spent half an hour telling me the same old stories we've heard so many times about his student days!

(Note the personalising phrases.)

Compare the example above with the following sentence written by a student:

✱ *Uncle Jim was there and so were Grandma and Grandad, Aunty Susan, Nina and the twins.*

The student's sentence is a boring list with no interesting details, no support and no personalising. To the examiner, this suggests that the student cannot construct a good sentence and knows only basic vocabulary.

It is always much more difficult than it seems to 'invent' characters in an exam, and so it is a very good idea to practise when you are not under pressure. Here are some ideas to start you thinking.

★ **Remember**
The people you describe do not have to be real people, but can be from your imagination.

Clothing

Someone who wears:

- clothes that are too tight, so the person bulges out of them
- clothes that are loose and shapeless – perhaps creased/not ironed
- trousers that are too short
- sleeves that are too long
- very brightly coloured clothes – bright yellow/shocking pink/brilliant orange (someone who wants to be noticed!)
- colours that do not go together – an orange shirt with a red tie, brown shoes with blue trousers, one green and one brown sock (someone who has no sense of colour co-ordination when it comes to clothes).

What do these features of clothing tell us about the character of the person who wears them?

Habits

Someone who:

- has a booming (very loud) voice which can be heard anywhere in the room (Friends and relatives try to avoid having personal or private conversations with such a person for this reason!)
- thinks he is amusing and is always telling jokes, although no one else finds them funny
- falls asleep in a chair on all family occasions (Does he snore?)
- is known to be clumsy – perhaps needs glasses but is too vain to wear them (Your mother puts her glass and china ornaments in a cupboard when this person comes to visit.)
- is a bore who is always giving you good 'advice' based on her own experience (This gives her a chance to talk about herself for hours, usually repeating stories which you have heard many times before.)
- likes to give the impression he is still a teenager – even if he is 55
- has a particular hobby (fishing? car engines? butterflies? cake making?) and can talk about nothing else
- is always talking about people who have recently died
- is permanently on a diet(!), but who helps herself to multiple slices of the chocolate cake!

Exercise 1   Try to add your own sets of characteristics and make sentences with them.

Exercise 2   Make another list about your friends. Do they have any habits which irritate you? Do not forget children!

Atmosphere

The best way to write about atmosphere is to consider the senses:

- what you hear (usually music)
- what you taste (usually food)
- what you smell (cooking, flowers)
- what you see (entertainment, dancing).

There is no point in mentioning these factors unless you can support what you write in some way. Look at some possible ways you could write support about the music at a family celebration:

★ **Remember**
Support each sentence you write.

It was really out of the ark (= old-fashioned). (So what did the young people do?)

It was deafening!

Someone had brought a karaoke machine, but luckily/sadly no one knew how to use it.

Some of the 'wrinklies' (= old people) *began singing old songs together.*

It was the best part of the evening!

We danced till we dropped.

When Alex arrived, he had brought his CDs along and volunteered to be the DJ. Then the party really livened up!

Uncle Mike's selection of music is, as you know, out of the ark, so we all went into the other room and played our own CDs.

Exercise 3	Try to think of some more examples of your own.

Look at some possible ways you could write support about the food at a family celebration:

It was much too spicy for my liking.

It was cold – and I was starving (= very hungry)!

It was my favourite! (or your friend's favourite if you want to make her jealous! Say what it was – pizza/chips/chocolate cake/something home-made.)

There was not enough food for everyone. (So what happened?)

Nobody ate anything. (Why not?)

Aunty Lena had made an enormous version of her delicious chocolate cake, and with every slice I ate, I thought how much you would have enjoyed it!

There was loads of mouth-watering food. Grandma had obviously spent the whole day in the kitchen!

Aunty Susan was happily tucking into the chocolate cake, slice by slice, forgetting about the diet she's supposed to be on!

Individual incidents

★ **Remember**
These are *minor* incidents, or small 'scenes' of **no consequence**.

Select one or two incidents to write about, for example:

■ Someone spilt coffee on the white carpet.
■ Someone tripped over while dancing.
■ A fuse blew and caused a temporary power cut.
■ A precious vase was knocked off the shelf.
■ A child pulled the tablecloth – and everything that was on it – off the table.

These are incidents which do not change the course of the evening. They do not become more important than the party itself. They may involve one or two time sequence phrases (underlined below).

I was <u>just about</u> to serve myself a second helping of gateau, <u>when</u> I accidentally knocked over a cup of coffee. It only <u>took a moment</u> for me to see that it had splashed all down the back of Julia's white dress!

Note that it is not important to attach these minor events to a specific time. If you were involved in an incident, take the opportunity to personalise.

You know how clumsy I am when I get nervous, well …

I was just getting myself a spoon when, clumsy as ever, I …

I thought I'd managed to get through the evening without causing a scene, but …

You know how careful I am …

I couldn't believe it when I looked down and saw …

Personalising in descriptive narrative and narrative letters

Personalising in descriptive narrative letters poses the same problems as for narrative letters. In our example, as your friend was not with you at the event, how can you make him feel included? Again, you will need to use phrases such as:

If you'd been there you'd have … **burst out laughing!**

I wish
If only } *you'd seen* } *the look on Grandma's face when …*
You should have seen

It's a shame
It's a pity } *you couldn't* (past tense) *make the party.* **You'd have enjoyed it.**

past tense

It's a good thing
It's a good job } *you* { *missed* *the party.* **You'd have been bored**
{ *couldn't make* *to tears.*

You can also include some of the other personalising phrases listed on pages 24–25. For example,

… as you know.
… as usual!

Possible problems

The following paragraph, written by a student in response to the question on page 63, highlights many of the problems associated with writing descriptive narrative letters.

> ✱ *Well, I arrived at the party, which was in my aunt's house, at seven o'clock. At five past seven Uncle Jim arrived. At ten past seven the food arrived. At half past seven I spilled coffee over Mary's white dress. She fainted and fell on the floor. She hit her head and had to go to hospital. It was a nice party.*

which was in my aunt's house: The person you are writing to was invited to the party himself, so he knows where it took place. Remember that you are relatives, so your aunt is probably his aunt, too. There is no need to write *my*. This whole phrase could be rewritten:

> ✔ *I arrived at Aunt Mary's party …*

at seven o'clock: Time is not central to descriptive narrative letters. It has no importance. If you mention time, then it suggests it must be important, in which case you must support your sentence by saying *why*. So, in this sentence, ask yourself: is seven o'clock an unusual time to arrive at the party? Is it early, or late for the party, and if so *why* were you early or late?

If there was a specific reason to mention the time, the time factor should be introduced in a general, casual way and this sentence could be rewritten:

> ✔ I got to Aunt Mary's about an hour before the party started, *to help her lay the table.*

On the other hand, if seven o'clock is the normal time to arrive at the party, and if there was no reason for being early or late, then you should not refer to the time.

At *five past seven Uncle Jim arrived*: another 'dead' sentence. Is it important to know *when* Uncle Jim arrived? *Why* are you mentioning this specific time in your letter? If time is referred to at all, it should be in a general way, with support:

> ✔ Uncle Jim got there soon after me *and we set up the stereo system as a surprise.*

Why is specific time mentioned in the two following sentences?

At *ten past seven the food arrived*: (Note: food does not usually 'arrive'.) Is ten past seven very early, or very late to serve the food? If not, do not refer to the time. It is not relevant or important.

At *half past seven I spilled coffee over Mary's white dress*: Is the reference to specific time necessary or important in this sentence? Surely what happened is more important. Could you really spill the coffee and notice that at that moment it just happened to be seven thirty?

She fainted and fell on the floor. She hit her head and had to go to hospital: This is not a minor incident. It *does* have a consequence. It *does* develop and become more important than the party. Therefore, it is not suitable for a descriptive narrative letter and should not be included.

★ **Language Point**
Avoid the word *nice*; it has no real meaning. Replace it with something like *marvellous* or *wonderful*.

It was a nice party: This is a 'dead' sentence. It provides no information (support). Most parties are nice. If the party was really good, or not good, for some reason, then say what the reason was. Otherwise, do not classify it at all. Take care to be logical; if your friend went to hospital as a result of it, how could you say it was a great party?

Exercise 4 Using all the information given above, write a letter to a relative who missed a family celebration, telling her/him all about it.

■ Putting it all together 2

Write a letter to a friend about a sports day that was held recently at your school.

Begin by asking yourself what factors are essential for any sports day.

- ■ **People** Try holding a sports day without people!
- ■ **Weather** This can make or break any outdoor event.
- ■ **Individual incidents** Not necessarily sporting events; this could lead to a boring list. Try to think of social events or small incidents (without consequences, of course).

■ **Atmosphere** In this case, the atmosphere is created by a combination of the other factors.

As sports day is an outdoor event, begin with the weather.

Weather

Unless you have something relevant to say about the weather, it will result in 'dead' sentences of no interest to the reader. For example, do *not* say:

✖ *The weather was nice.*

Instead, think about how the weather can *change*.

★ **Remember**
Change creates interest.

■ The day can start sunny and fine, but be wet by the time the sports day begins.
■ The day can start wet and dull, but be fine and sunny by the time the sports day begins.

How would each situation change the atmosphere of the day? Would it be more interesting/easier for you to write about sport in the rain and mud, or sport under a blue sky? Look at these phrases to describe the weather:

There was not a cloud in the sky.
The weather couldn't have been better.
The sky was overcast and threatening rain.
The weather couldn't have been worse.

People

What people are involved in a sports day?

■ the students – those taking part and spectators
■ the PE staff
■ the parents.

Parents

Let's look first at the parents. Beware of 'dead' sentences.

✖ *There were lots of parents.*

Describe the parents in a general way:

■ How were they dressed? Were their clothes too smart for the occasion? Were they trying to 'look the part' by wearing sporty clothes themselves? How would either of these situations make you feel/react?
■ How did the parents behave? Were they enthusiastic (more enthusiastic than the students perhaps)? Did they jump up and down in excitement, waving programmes and shouting words of encouragement at the top of their voices? Were they at the finishing line shouting your name to urge you on and taking your photograph?
   Or were they bored, only there because they had to be, appearing not to notice that sports day was taking place, and leaving without apparently even noticing you?
   Did they see the whole afternoon as a social event, a chance to meet other parents and discuss/compare their children? How would the different behaviour make you feel/react?

The PE staff

Now consider the PE staff. Try to make them seem real, perhaps through exaggeration.

■ Were they behaving the way they usually do in sports lessons?
■ Was there a *change* in their behaviour that may seem interesting to your friend? Are the staff normally tough on you in PE classes, shouting at you in a rude way like a sergeant major in the army? Were they more polite today, smiling at the students and their parents? Did you feel those smiles were sincere or 'plastic'?
■ Were the PE teachers well organised so that everything ran smoothly or was there confusion? Perhaps the public address system broke down.

The students

Finally, consider the students.

■ How were you and the other students feeling? Remember that *contrast* provides interest. Were you nervous, excited, confident, embarrassed?
■ How did everyone behave? Was someone showing off new sports kit or a new hairstyle? Was someone trying to get attention by pretending to faint or to have an accident?

Up to this point, the letter has mainly involved description of people and their behaviour, and creating the **atmosphere** of the day to involve the reader. Do not forget to include the food and drink aspect here, for example:

■ a refreshment tent/stall
■ dying of thirst
■ home-made cakes.

Individual incidents

A few minor incidents should be carefully included. Take care that the incidents do not become more important than the sports day itself, or you will end up writing a narrative. Here are some examples.

■ A pair of new trainers (yours?) were too big/small and fell off as you ran/gave you painful blisters.
■ Someone's parents (yours?) took part in the parents' race and came in last.
■ Someone's button (yours?) came off/the zip broke and you had to hold your shorts up as you ran along.
■ Someone wearing new kit (you?) fell over and got it covered in mud.

Other points to consider

Look again at the question: 'Write a letter to a friend about a sports day that was held recently at your school.' The question may specifically mention 'a friend in another country' or 'a penfriend' or 'a friend who missed it' or 'was unable to attend'. How would your letter be different in each case?

Firstly, consider the **introduction**.

To the friend you might write:

I'm sorry/It's a shame you couldn't make sports day last week, but I'm glad to hear you're feeling better now. I thought I'd just drop you a line to let you know how it went/what you missed.

Remember to give some reason why the friend had to miss the event.

To the penfriend you might write:

It was lovely to get your letter on Tuesday and to hear all your news. I thought you might like to/be interested to hear about my school sports day which was held last Saturday.

In the **body** of the letter to a school friend, you can refer to other students and staff by name and refer to their characteristics because the friend knows them.

Mr Roberts was his usual bossy self, ordering everyone around at the top of his voice to make sure all the parents would notice him!

Tania had put her hair up in yet another one of her fancy styles, but as she sprinted along it came down and fell all over her face! You should have seen her! She looked such a mess!

To describe the same information to a penfriend you would need to write:

Our PE teacher, Mr Roberts, was shouting instructions at the top of his voice hoping that all the parents would notice him.

One of the fashion-conscious girls in my class called Tania turned up with a new hairstyle, but as she sprinted along it fell all over her face!

To a friend you could write a **conclusion** like this:

Well, I hope that gives you some idea what you missed/what happened. I don't think you missed much, really, and anyway it won't be long till the next one!

To a penfriend your conclusion might look like this:

Well, I hope that gives you some idea about the kind of thing that happens at sports day over here. Do you have any event like this at your school? If so, I'd like to hear about it sometime.

Well, now you know about what we get up to on sports day over here. How are you getting on with your driving lessons, by the way?

Exercise 5   Using the information given above, write a letter to a friend about a sports day that was held recently at your school.

■ Putting it all together 3

★ **Exam tip**
Read the question very carefully. Here 'home town or village' means your local town or village. It does *not* say 'home, town or village'.

Write a letter to a friend about a festival or carnival that took place recently in your home town or village.

What kind of festival could you write about?

■ Avoid festivals connected to religion.
■ Avoid festivals connected to wars, victory days or any kind of politics.
■ Try to choose something cultural such as the arrival of spring, new year celebrations or a festival of flowers, for example.

Begin by asking yourself what factors are essential for any festival. (Remember that many festivals are large, perhaps even national, often outdoor public events. Carnivals also involve music and dancing in the streets.)
    Again the same list of points should be considered:

■ **Weather** This can make or break any outdoor event.
■ **People** It's impossible to hold a festival without people!
■ **Individual incidents** Try to think of small incidents (without consequences, of course).
■ **Atmosphere**.

Weather

We have already looked at how to describe the weather (see page 68) but, for this question, you should think about how the weather affects the festival.

People

■ Where have the people come from to attend this festival? Are they local people? Have they come from nearby towns/all over the country? How many of them are there? Hundreds? Thousands?

   People/visitors flocked in their hundreds

■ How do they feel?

   in a relaxed mood
   in a festive mood

■ What are they doing?

   strolling around
   wandering around

Individual incidents

Try to create the atmosphere by using the senses – what is there to see, hear, smell and taste?

■ What is there to see?

   twinkling fairy lights
   (decorated with) brightly coloured bunting (= flags used as decoration)

dancing display
colourful folk dances
traditional costumes

sideshow = a small attraction where you pay to take part in a game

stalls = small shops with open fronts (like in a market) where you can buy refreshments

tug-of-war = a sporting event where two teams pull opposite ends of a rope until one team drags the other over a line marked on the ground

float (main event) = a lorry decorated in the theme of the carnival, which drives slowly through the streets

raffle = a game where you buy a ticket with a number on. If the number on your ticket is the same as that on a prize, you win the prize.

procession = a line of people and vehicles that moves along slowly.

▪ What is there to smell, or taste?

smell of onions frying

candy floss = a type of sweet made from sugar spun round a stick

toffee apple = an apple on a stick covered with hard toffee

▪ What is there to hear?

noise of the music
marching band
traditional instruments

Exercise 6   Using the information given above, write a letter to a friend about a festival or carnival that took place recently in your home town or village.

Exercise 7   Read these articles taken from local newspapers about carnivals, and rewrite them as friendly letters.

1   The sun came out for Cranfield School's annual carnival – and so did hundreds of local residents.

The show was as spectacular as ever, with nine huge floats touring the streets of the village on Saturday afternoon, led by the Cranfield Golden Band.

This year's procession took the theme of school visits and each year group went to town with superb costumes and settings.

Among those watching was the mayor, Mr Peter Smith, who went onto the school playing fields where stalls and sideshows, rides, displays and refreshments were available.

The event was sponsored by the local emergency services.

It is hoped that up to £2000 will have been raised to benefit children of the school, with the headmaster saying the community involvement reflected 'the real spirit and essence of our carnival'.

2 Somewhere over the rainbow … the sun shone on this year's Stoke Keynes Carnival – eventually! Torrential rain and dark clouds looked like putting the dampers on the 41st annual show on Saturday but by late morning it was lights, cameras and action for the spectacular parade with a favourite films theme. Among the floats were beautifully decorated lorries dedicated to the most popular Disney films.

"Everyone really put a lot of effort into it and it looked like the weather would ruin things," said Mandy Foreman, Carnival Court chaperone, "but then the rain stopped and the sun came out and the show went on," she said.

At Riverside Valley, carnival-goers were treated to a host of attractions including tug-of-war, martial arts, fun fair and steam train rides.

Since it began, many youngsters have been Stoke Keynes Carnival Queen and Princesses.

This year's Queen, Sophie Applegate, aged 18, is now looking forward to a year representing the town at fêtes and similar events around the country.

3 There were rabbits rolling on in-line skates and dinosaurs in net stockings dancing to the rhythms of a rolling rock band.

'Having Fun', the theme of the 43rd Roses Parade, was well in evidence on a day with highs in the 70s and clear, blue skies.

Spectator Simon Barrow, 12, sprayed his five-year-old sister with crazy foam and thrilled at the passing floral whales and other motorised floats decorated entirely with roses.

Martin Jones, 23, of Stagswood, trained his camera on his girlfriend as she marched by, playing the clarinet in the university band.

The parade, featuring 54 floats and 22 marching bands, suffered the usual problems. Five floats broke down and had to be towed because of radiator and engine problems, and four spectators were overcome by the heat. A towering macerena-dancing caterpillar lost one of its hands, but rolled along with 11 others still in place.

■ Putting it all together 4

Write a letter to a friend about a holiday you went on recently.

There are several points which need careful consideration in this category.

Firstly, check the tense of the question. Are you *still* on holiday, or have you recently returned from the holiday? Secondly, is it (or was it) a school holiday? Thirdly, is the friend you are writing to from your school? If so, you must refer to the reason why he was unable to go. Lastly, does/did the holiday take place in your own country or abroad?

Exercise 8   Make a list of the differences you would need to consider if you were writing a) to a friend from school or b) to a penfriend.

■ Analysing questions

Analysing the following exam-style questions on the same topic will show how important it is to **read the question carefully** to understand exactly what is required.

You have recently been on a visit to another town. Write a letter to a friend, telling him/her what you did and saw.

---

you have recently been: This means you have returned and are now home again.

a visit: This suggests a short holiday; perhaps a weekend, a day trip or even a school trip.

another town must mean in your own country. The weather and food is unlikely to be very different from your own town, although there may be a regional speciality.

what you did and saw: Be careful not to make this a narrative in any way – they are events without consequence. Be careful not to list.

Create interest by telling the reader *why* you went.

You are on an activity holiday with your school. Write and tell a friend all about it.

---

you are on: This means you *are still* on holiday as you write your letter. Be careful of your tenses.

an activity holiday is specified. Are you in your own country or abroad? Decide on an activity you know something about, even if the question contains other suggestions or even photographs about other activities which may look more exciting. You will have more things to say if you choose a topic you are familiar with.

with your school: is your friend from the same school? If so, *why* is he not with you? Remember to include details about other students and teachers, their behaviour, appearance, etc.

all about it: But do not make it sound so marvellous or exciting that your friend feels unhappy not to be with you. Show that you miss your friend by using the third conditional phrases discussed on page 66. Show you have been thinking of him by saying you have bought a souvenir or have taken photographs to show him when you get back.

Remember to include the essential features of descriptive narrative writing:

- **Weather** If you can contrast it with weather in your own country, this will create interest.
- **People** (friends/teachers) How did they feel/behave? Could you include them in some of the individual incidents? Describe, for example, a teacher falling over, or getting on the wrong bus, misplacing her passport, locking herself out of her room.
- **Individual incidents** These may be both the activity itself and events *without* consequence that have happened until now (the moment you are writing), perhaps on the journey, or at the hotel.

■ **Atmosphere** To add to the atmosphere include details of the journey, accommodation and food, which is always important! Is the food excellent or awful? Can you combine food with a minor incident? Someone feels ill after eating too much? What did you do when not on the activity?

Try to add a little humour!

You are on a luxury holiday abroad. Write a letter to a friend telling her/him all about it.

---

you are: This means you are *still* on holiday at the time you are writing your letter.

a luxury holiday: This is clearly something special. *Why* are you on this holiday? Perhaps you won a competition? Perhaps it was a reward/thank you/present from someone for something you have achieved? Perhaps you are taking the place of a relative who was unable to go at the last moment? Did you go with anyone?

How could you include the four essential features?

■ **Weather** Probably you are on holiday somewhere with different weather from your own country. Contrast helps to create interest.
■ **People** What about people (new friends, hotel staff, local people)? Can you include them in an individual incident?
■ **Atmosphere** Describe the hotel, especially food, drink and what there is to do there: lovely views of the park (wonderful to escape from all the pollution of the city); exotic food (compare with local take-away)
■ **Individual incidents** What happened when you went:
  – to the cinema? (horror film – couldn't sleep a wink all night)
  – to the gym? (couldn't turn off the exercise machine – ache all over)
  – to the pool? (got sunburnt)
  – water-skiing? (guess who fell off!)

Exercise 9   Now try to answer the three questions analysed above, using all the information given.

■ Differences between narrative and descriptive narrative

Compare the two styles in this table.

Narrative	Descriptive narrative
While a **general occasion** or event is taking place,	A **general occasion** or event is taking place …
at one moment	over a varying length of time
a **specific** incident happens	with various incidents happening
leading to a **climax**	without consequence or climax

Sometimes it is not immediately clear from the question whether a narrative or a descriptive narrative answer is required. Look at the following topics and see how each one could be written either as a narrative piece of writing or as a descriptive narrative piece of writing.

Narrative

sports day	you broke your leg	
day trip	you got lost	
local festival	you were festival queen/king	moves from action to action
party	you fainted	in sequence, until the climax
school show	your proudest moment	
holiday	you caught a tummy bug	
rehearsals	you forgot your lines	

Descriptive narrative

Taking place over a few hours:
sports day
day trip
local festival
party
school show
Taking place over a few weeks:
holiday
Taking place over a few months:
rehearsals for a concert/show

includes description and events in the form of small 'scenes', but has *no* climax or conclusion

■ *Students' descriptive narrative letters*

Read the following selection of descriptive narrative letters written by different students in response to exam questions, and the comments related to them.

> ★ **Note**
> These are original letters written by IGCSE students and may still contain minor mistakes. In the comments column, the letter **R** refers to points in the Register unit on pages 182–5, and the letter **G** refers to points in the Grammar unit on pages 186–99. The arrow (→) points to what the text in the letter should be changed to or replaced with.

Question 1
Answer A

Write a letter to a relative who missed a family celebration, telling him/her all about it.

Dear Alessandra,

How are you? I hope you're feeling better now. I thought you might like to know **how Grandpa's 80ᵗʰ birthday party went.①**

Everybody was **dressed up②** for the party – or rather they thought they had. **Uncle Max③** came in **that awful lime green shirt of his④** with the glittery material on the collar, and Aunt Marie was wearing a huge yellow dress with frills at the sleeves and the collar. They were just a sight!

When the music started, everybody got to the dance floor and began to dance. I didn't want to dance as the only available partner was my cousin Anthony – **you know how much I hate him.⑤ To my bad luck⑥** he came up to me and offered to dance with me, so I went along dreading the whole idea. **You know how short he is⑦** – it seems he grows shorter each time I see him – he only came up to my shoulders, and he stepped **on my feet⑧** twice!

Sara and Clara, the terrible twins made such a mess when food was **laid on the table.⑨** They were hiding under the table and when **their father, Uncle Sam⑩** spotted them, they shrieked and knocked off the salad bowl.

It was fun.⑪ I hope **Grandma's 76ᵗʰ⑫** birthday party will be as good as this one or better. See you there.

Love,

Mandy

Comments

① Correct use of grammar and idiom

② Incorrect use – this phrase is usually used when someone is wearing a costume. → **smartly dressed** or **had got smart** or **in their best clothes**

③ Giving a name is a form of personalising – good.

④ Personalising – the shirt is common information shared between the writer and reader of the letter.

⑤ Personalising – good

⑥ Confused → **Unluckily for me** or **As luck would have it**

⑦ Personalising – creates a lovely mental picture. Correct use of prefixed question (G9)

⑧ Creates interest, makes it sound real, and is funny!

⑨ → **brought in**

⑩ No need for **their father**. Alessandra will know who he is.

⑪ Short sentence → **All in all, it was fun.**

⑫ Good link back to Grandad's 80ᵗʰ

General comments

- An excellent letter, using many of the features of descriptive narrative writing.
- The letter contains good examples of humour and details to create interest.
- The student has included several examples of personalising.
- The lack of register or grammar mistakes make the letter sound fluent.

Question 1 Write a letter to a relative who missed a family celebration, telling her/him all about it.
Answer B

Dear Heba,

I know you were looking **foreward**① **to be**② at Aunt Jill's birthday party, **but**③ I hope you are feeling better. **Anyway,**④ I thought I'd **drop you a line**⑤ on what **you have missed.**⑥ The same old people showed up, one by one, **Uncle Henry**⑦ being late as usual.

At the beginning, my sister and I were **at a loose end**⑧ but **finaly**⑨ **tuned into**⑩ the party atmosphere as soon as the music and dancing started. Luckily you weren't there to hear **the way they sang,**⑪ everyone trying to sing in tune but in his own way!

The buffet was quite rich, and I didn't **hesitate to go**⑫ for a second helping. **However,**⑬ Aunt Jenny decided to stick to her diet **after the sixth or seventh helping.**⑭ **As usual,**⑮ I had to **put up with**⑮ uncle Tod's criticism about what teenagers wear today, until **I got back at him**⑯ when he tripped over while trying to dance as they do. **It wasn't until**⑰ the small hours that people started to leave, wishing Aunt Jill a happy birthday. I'm sure there will be many more **partys**⑱ that you will be able to come to.

With love from

Amal

Comments

① Spelling → *forward*

② **looking forward to** should be followed by a verb + ing or a noun → *looking forward to Aunt Jill's birthday party*

③ **but** joins a negative and positive: e.g. *I am naughty* (negative) *but everyone likes me* (positive).

So it does not fit here: **you were looking forward** (positive); **I hope you are feeling better** (positive). Remove **but**, put a full stop after **party** and begin a new sentence with **I hope**.

④ Inappropriate use of **anyway**; see page 9.

⑤ **drop you a line** should be followed by **to** or a noun → **to let you know about**

⑥ Wrong tense – needs simple past → **you missed**

⑦ Personalising – they both know Uncle Henry is always late.

⑧ Good phrase

⑨ Spelling → *finally*

⑩ → **got into**

⑪ Nice detail: creates interest, and is funny.

⑫ R3 → **think twice about going**

⑬ R8 → **but**

⑭ Personalising, and gives an amusing insight into her character

⑮ Personalising

⑯ Good use of verb + preposition to replace 'formal' verbs (R3)

⑰ Good use of time phrase

⑱ Spelling → *parties*

General comments

- This is generally a very good letter.
- It includes several examples of personalising.
- The student has used a wide range of vocabulary.
- The student has created interest and included humour.
- There are not many register or grammar mistakes.

However:

- Several problems in the introduction give a bad impression.

Question 2   Write a letter to a friend about a sports day that was held recently at your school.

Dear Jennifer,

I don't know where to start. This year's Sports Day was the best one in the school's history. I'm really sorry you missed it – well, I guess I just have to blame it on your little sister, why did she have to choose this day to be sick?

You should have seen the parents – they were all dressed in these cool sports kits, with the odd parent here and there wearing jeans or regular clothes. Some pupils were showing off their tanned arms and legs but they were **a laughing stock**❶ When it came to actually **playing something**❷ – **truly speaking**,❸ they were hopeless at sport. All the Year 10 and above pupils were the most reluctant ones – you know how **embarrased**❹ they get when they are supposed to **play**❺ in front of their friends and teachers.

The Refreshment tent was packed as usual, with kids running in and out and the helpers were **tearing their hair out.**❻ The smells **drifting**❼ out of the tent were dangerously appealing – making me forget my diet. **Our very smart friend Nina**❽ managed to escape to the tent and **help in serving out**❾ pancakes. Lucky her! The best moment was when we all lined up for the obstacle race. As **Mr Bell**❿ blew his whistle, we all sprinted forward, then two Year 11 pupils bumped into each other and fell knocking over one of the obstacles. Then another pupil tripped over another obstacle and soon we were all over the playground, with the obstacles either above or under us, **rolling around with laughter.**⓫ Then came the three-legged race, which was a disaster, the cloth that held our legs together kept falling off. The last race was the parents' race with the usual parents taking part and of course the usual ones winning.

Denise⓬ came wearing her brand new sports kit and as she ran – **I don't need to tell you how BIG she is**⓬ – she toppled over and was really very angry because she had mud on her kit. I was wearing my brother's trainers – which were two sizes bigger than my shoe size, so of course they kept slipping and I had to limp all day long.

Although a lot of things happened that weren't exactly perfect, I think it was great. I really had fun. **I hope your sister**⓭ will feel well by next year's Sports Day!

Love,

Amira

Comments

Good start – but the reason for Jennifer missing sports day does not really make sense. Did *she* miss sports day because *her sister* was ill?

❶ Good vocabulary

❷ Play is always a problem word. You *play a game* (of tennis or football) but you need to *do* sport. Here, though, you need to *take part* so → *taking part*

❸ Register → *honestly* or *to tell you the truth*

❹ Spelling! Remember a double r and a double s.

❺ Again, not quite the right word. Perhaps a better word here would be *compete*.

❻ Good phrase! It means they were being driven to insanity (madness) or behaving madly due to overwork.

❼ Good vocabulary. Replaces *coming*.

❽ Personalising

❾ Good expression but wrong preposition → help *with* serving out

❿ Personalising – much more effective than saying *the teacher*, as Jennifer knows Mr Bell too

⓫ Good expression

⓬ Again, the name has a personalising effect, as does *I don't need to tell you how BIG she is* – information shared by both reader and writer.

⓭ Good attempt to return to the beginning of the letter, but still not very relevant.

General comments

- This is an excellent letter – but too long to be written in an exam. (This was set for homework.)
- It contains many examples of personalising.
- The student has created interest through the use of small, often funny incidents and lively descriptions.
- There are not many register mistakes.
- The style is very appropriate. The reader has a clear mental picture of all the events. All the features of Sports Day – sprint, obstacle race, three-legged race, parents' race, are included and are well supported in each case, often with humour.

Question 3 Write a letter to a friend about a festival or carnival that took place recently in your home town or village.

Dear Maryam,

How are you? I hope you are feeling better now. I thought you might like to know how this year's carnival in **my country** ❶ went.

There wasn't a cloud in the sky, which was quite surprising as it was overcast the day before. Every year hundreds of local people and tourists come to the place where it's held – this year there were thousands and the place was full to capacity! They were all in a festive mood and were laughing **uproariously** ❷ as they rode the merry-go-round. Some other tourists bought balloons for their children, and one child's balloon managed to escape his clutch and flew away. The other children thought it was a game and they all released their balloons into the sky.

The streamers and bunting were all around the stalls and tents. Dangerously tempting smells were drifting out from the food corner. A marching band in front **of the floats that were** ❸ in the procession **consisted of** ❹ volunteer students from all the school bands.

Everyone stood to **watch the election of the Spring Queen** ❺ – all the little girls were very pretty, and the judge took quite a time to select the little queen for this year and her two assistants. This year it was a petite blonde called Laura.

I hope this gives you an idea **about how the carnival goes in my country.** ❻

I'm eager to know how it is in yours. ❼ Please do write back and let me know.

Love,

Hoda

Comments

❶ Give the name of your town.

❷ Excellent vocabulary! But not correct register for a friendly letter → **loudly**

❸ R5 → Remove **that were**

❹ Register → **which was made up of**

❺ R1 → **see who was chosen to be Spring Queen**

❻ → **about our spring carnival**

❼ → **Do you have/Are there any special carnivals in your town?**

General comments

- This is an excellent letter.
- The introduction is simple and direct.
- It includes a variety of incidents to help create interest.
- It refers to a number of features associated with carnivals.
- It contains good vocabulary, and not many register mistakes.

Section 3 focuses on the new topic of formal writing. Unit 1 introduces the type of exam questions which need to be answered in formal writing, together with some basic rules related to formal register. It then describes a variety of features for you to include when you write in formal register, using examples relevant to exam topics. Units 2–4 focus on specific phrases and expressions used for making suggestions, giving your opinions, and putting forward your views and arguments.

UNIT 1 | Basic tools

Apart from friendly letters and certain cases in school magazine articles, everything you write in the exam, including compositions, summaries and the answers to the reading comprehensions, requires **formal register**. Formal register is (among other things) the language of textbooks and for this reason it is usually less of a challenge for students. Some general rules apply to formal writing.

1 When writing formally, it is *not* appropriate to include the following:

- contracted or short forms of verbs

  - ✖ It's
  - ✔ It is

  - ✖ I'm
  - ✔ I am

  - ✖ Won't
  - ✔ Will not

  - ✖ Hasn't
  - ✔ Has not

- words or phrases that belong to the friendly register

  - ✖ It'll do you good.
  - ✔ It will benefit you.

- slang words or phrases

  - ✖ guy/bloke/dude
  - ✔ man

  - ✖ You need to chilla.
  - ✔ You should relax.

  - ✖ He's well safe.
  - ✔ He's a very good person.

- humour – most of the topics are of a serious nature, or factual
- exclamation marks
- personal style.

2 When giving your opinion or point of view, details about how the situation affects *you personally* are *not* appropriate. When giving your opinion about the provision of cycling lanes, for example, it would not be appropriate to explain your reasons with reference to your own situation by mentioning that you have a bike, or to include information about what time of day you ride it or for what reason. In other words, the style should be **impersonal**.

■ The tools for formal writing

Before considering the different types of composition you may be asked to write using formal writing, and the different writing techniques involved, we must first examine the tools needed to produce formal writing. These include:

- time fixer phrases
- phrases for introducing points
- phrases for joining points
- phrases for adding support
- phrases for making generalisations
- formal language structures
  - suggestion
  - opinion
  - views and arguments

Time fixer phrases

When writing formally, it is often good style to begin the introduction with a time fixer, such as one from the selection below:

Nowadays
These days
Until now

Every day/week/year
Recently
For many years

In the past
Ten years ago
In the last few/five/days/weeks/months/years
Since + specific time/noun

Look at these examples:

Thirty years ago, nearly all children went to single sex schools.

For many years, environmentalists have been warning about the effects of global warming.

Nowadays, most teenagers own a mobile phone.

If there has been a *change* in the situation you are writing about, two time fixers can be used to show contrast and create interest.

Thirty years ago, nearly all children went to single sex schools. These days most schools in this country are mixed.

Introducing points

As discussed in the units on friendly letters, listing is considered to be poor style. In formal writing also you should remember to limit the ideas, opinions or suggestions to a maximum of three.

Look at the following examples showing how to introduce points chronologically, using the language of formal register.

In the first place,
Firstly,
The main
The most important } *point/reason*
The first

Secondly,
Another point …
Another reason …

Thirdly,
In addition …

Finally,
Lastly,
The last point …
The final reason …

To sum up,
In conclusion,

Joining points

In formal writing, there are certain ways to join points together, or add more points of the same kind.

■ When joining *similar points*, use the following addition words:

Furthermore,
Moreover,
Besides,

Regular exercise is beneficial for health. Moreover, it may result in weight reduction.

(Both sentences are *positive*.)

Smoking can seriously damage health. Furthermore, it is an anti-social habit.

(Both sentences are *negative*.)

■ When joining *contrasting points*, or beginning a new paragraph that introduces an opposite opinion, use the following concession words:

However,
Nevertheless,
On the other hand,
Although …,

Note: each of the above phrases *begins* a sentence.

Tourism represents a significant contribution to the national economy.
However, it is argued that large numbers of tourists can damage the
environment.

(The first sentence is *positive*, and the second sentence is *negative*.)

Adding support

In formal writing, as mentioned above, it is *not* appropriate to personalise, because you are not writing for a reader who knows you. The style is **impersonal** throughout.

This means that support in formal writing is factual, and can be introduced in many ways, including the following:

This means that …
As a result, …
This may lead to …
This may result in …
Consequently, …
Therefore, …
because …
, which means that …

Generalisations

Sometimes a minor modification (change) can make a big difference to your sentence. Some statements can sound very dull. For example:

Tourists drop litter.

Sentences can be modified by the use of various generalisations. You can use these on their own, or in combination throughout a sentence.

■ One of the simplest ways is to use one of the following generalisations, at the *beginning* of the sentence. This makes it more acceptable to the English ear. Your sentence will also sound more convincing.

Almost all
The vast majority of
A large number of
Most
Many ⎫ tourists drop litter.
Some
A few
Not many
Hardly any

In almost all cases,
In the majority of cases,
In a large number of cases,
In most cases,   } tourists drop litter.
In many cases,
In some cases,
In a few cases,
On the whole,

Look at these examples:

Almost all teenagers enjoy watching television.
The vast majority of teenagers enjoy watching television.
In many cases, pollution is the result of ignorance.

These phrases can add focus to a dull statement (as above) or can replace exact figures, numbers and percentages (see below).

Look at this example from a summary passage which includes the following sentence:

A study shows that 95% of teenagers spend five hours a week watching television.

A summary must not contain figures or percentages or specific numbers. Therefore, a generalisation could be used to express the same information:

The vast majority of teenagers enjoy watching television.

★ **Note**

Generalisations are also very useful for writing summaries of reading passages that contain figures, numbers or statistics.

■ **A frequency word**, such as *generally*, *usually*, *often* or *sometimes* can also be used as a generalisation to achieve a similar effect.

Teenagers often watch television.
Generally, teenagers enjoy watching television.
Teenagers generally enjoy watching television.

■ Modifying the **verb** can generalise your sentence and make it more informative.

Replace the basic verb with the verb *tend*:

In many cases, pollution tends to be the result of ignorance.

If the subject is a person, you can use the phrase *have a tendency to*.
This suggests that whatever follows in the sentence is this person's habit.
For example:

Women have a tendency to spend more time at home than men.

My brother has a tendency to shout.

The following examples show how generalisations can be combined:

Almost all Italians have a tendency to nap (= have a short sleep) in the afternoon.

In most cases, teenagers have a tendency to feel self-conscious (= shy, embarrassed).

Without generalisations, the above sentence would look like this:

Teenagers feel self-conscious.

Compare this with the modified sentence and notice the difference. The sentence with generalisations is much more fluent and more likely to make a good impression on the examiner.

★ Exam tip

In this case, the use of generalisations has increased the number of words in the sentence by *seven*. This can be very useful in summaries if you do not have the required number of words.

Formal language structures

The most important tools needed for formal writing are the formal language structures themselves.

In the exam, the question will usually contain a **function word**, for example: opinion, views, arguments or suggestions.

One of the most effective ways to study formal writing is through learning various phrases associated with selected language functions. For example, consider these ways of making suggestions:

In order to reduce pollution, the government should increase tax on petrol.

(This is a simple structure in terms of grammar.)

Surely it would be a good idea if the government increased tax on petrol.

(This is a more advanced structure, using the second conditional with the past tense.)

It is high time the government increased tax on petrol.

(This is an advanced structure, using the phrase 'it is time' with the past tense.)

All the phrases listed in this unit use formal register. Some are more advanced in structure than others, but this does not mean that they are better or more formal than those with a simpler structure. The key is to use what you feel comfortable with.

★ **Remember**
Any structure that you intend to learn specifically for exam purposes must be learnt thoroughly, through practice, until you are confident that you can reproduce it accurately. This takes time.

In the remaining units of this section, we examine in detail the formal language structures we have been referring to, under the headings:

■ Suggestions
■ Opinions
■ Views and arguments.

We will then apply them to a range of typical exam composition questions (Section 4).

Suggestions

There are several ways of introducing, or putting forward, a suggestion in formal register, including the following structures and phrases. Here each one is followed by an example sentence relevant to an exam topic.

1 (Surely) + subject + could/should

(Surely) an advertising campaign could help/promote awareness of ...

2 I (would) suggest + verb + *ing*

I (would) suggest introducing laws to deal with the problem of deforestation.

3 I (would) suggest + that + subject + should

I would suggest that drivers should use unleaded petrol.

4 It would (clearly/surely) be a good idea if + subject + past tense

It would be a good idea if
- we had { better sports facilities / a cinema club } at school.
- students were made aware of the importance of good study habits.
- the public were better informed about the dangers of pollution.

5 Subject + have a responsibility ...

Television companies (clearly) have a responsibility ...

... to show
... to broadcast
... to screen
... to transmit
} programmes unsuitable for children late in the evening.

Schools (clearly) have a responsibility to make students aware of the dangers of smoking.

6 It is (high) time (that) + subject + past tense

It is high time that schools introduced classes to inform students about the dangers of smoking.

Exercise 1 Make sentences putting forward suggestions, using the following prompts:

1 Schools/promote awareness/dangers of smoking
2 I/introduce laws/problem of pollution
3 I/drivers/take a more difficult driving test
4 It/children/made aware/importance/good eating habits
5 Tourists/responsibility/respect the places they vist
6 It/time/doctors/give more advice on health

Opinions

There are several ways of giving your opinion in formal register:

In my opinion,
In my view,
Personally,
It seems to me that ...
As far as I am concerned,
As I see it,

I think
I feel   } that ...
I believe

Many people   } think
              } feel   } that ...
              } believe

The following examples show how the above phrases can be used:

In my opinion, sport is very important for our health.

In my view, single sex schools allow students to concentrate fully on their studies.

In many cases, sentences which begin with giving an opinion continue by making a suggestion. Look at the following examples:

Personally, I feel that sport should be part of every school timetable.

It seems to me that we should judge a person by his actions and not by his appearance.

As far as I am concerned, It is high time we began to respect the environment.

As I see it, schools have a responsibility to educate children about the dangers of taking drugs.

Many people believe that schools have a responsibility to motivate students.

Exercise 1   Make sentences which begin by giving an opinion and continue by making a suggestion, using the following prompts:

1 Judge a person by his actions and not by his appearance.
   (**As far as I am concerned**, + should)

2 Educate children about the dangers of taking drugs.
   (**As I see it**, + it is high time schools)

3 Take steps to reduce the negative aspects of tourism.
   (**Personally, I feel that** + countries could)

4 Preserve the environment for future generations.
   (**In my opinion**, + schools have a responsibility)

5 Part of every school timetable
   (**As far as I am concerned**, + sport should be)

6 Seatbelts prevent serious injuries in car accidents.
(opinion + **could**)

7 Ring roads built around major cities.
(opinion + **would be sensible if**)

8 Make students aware of the problems caused by pollution.
(opinion + **have a responsibility**)

★ **Remember**

Include details about *whose* opinion (underlined in these examples) is being expressed to make the sentence more interesting.

A large number of <u>parents</u> **believe that** *schools have a responsibility to motivate students.*

In many cases, <u>teenagers</u> **feel that** *it would be a good idea if parents listened to their point of view.*

The vast majority of <u>scientists</u> **believe that** *it is high time we began to respect the environment.*

Exercise 2   Use a variety of generalisation, opinion and suggestion phrases to form sentences from the following prompts:

1 generalisation + **parents** + opinion + **good idea if** + *schools motivated children*
2 generalisation + **teenagers** + opinion + **high time** + *parents listen to their point of view*
3 generalisation + **people** + opinion + **have a responsibility** + *begin to respect the environment*
4 generalisation + **people** + opinion + **high time** + *government reduced the price of petrol*
5 generalisation + **students** + opinion + **should** + *responsible members of society*

Emphasise or develop your opinion 1

When you are confident about using the above selection of opinion phrases, you could try to emphasise or **develop your opinion**. As opinions are closely linked to the way you *feel* about something, you can use sentences containing verbs of **feeling** to express your reaction to something. Use verbs such as:

amaze
annoy (= less than angry)
bore
depress
embarrass
frighten
infuriate (= make you very angry)
shock
upset (= make you feel unhappy)
worry

Here are some examples:

People who have no respect for the environment annoy me.

People who are cruel to animals infuriate me.

Photographs of children with incurable diseases upset me.

By turning the verbs into adjectives you can produce a slightly more formal sentence in the following way:

I find people who have no respect for the environment annoying.

I find people who are cruel to animals infuriating.

I find photographs of children with incurable diseases upsetting.

Exercise 3 Now try to make some sentences of your own. What annoys you? Make a list, using the structures in the examples and referring to the topics in the Database of topic-related vocabulary and ideas (pages 231–44).

Exercise 4 How do you feel about people who watch TV all day? Use the verbs of feeling and the structures given in the examples. Make a list of other topics you feel strongly about. Refer to the topics in the Database of topic-related vocabulary and ideas (pages 231–44).

Emphasise or develop your opinion 2

Another way to develop your opinion is to express your attitude by using the phrase *the way*. Look at the following examples:

1 verb + *the way* + noun
   Sentences constructed this way can be *positive*:

   I like the way documentary programmes teach us about wildlife.
   I love the way classical music relaxes you.

   Sentences constructed this way can also be *negative*:

   I object to the way teenagers are treated like children.

2 *one thing/what I like about* + noun + *is the way*
   Sentences constructed this way can be *positive*:

   What I like about mobile phones is the way they make communication easy.

   Sentences constructed this way can also be *negative*:

   One thing I dislike about parents is the way they never stop talking about studying.

3 *what/one thing that* + verb + *about* + noun + *is the way*

   What irritates me about TV is the way the programmes are repeated.

   One thing that infuriates me is the way some people waste paper.

Exercise 5   Now look at your answers to exercise 4 and rewrite them using the different constructions given in the examples above.

Exercise 6   Use the following prompts and the structures outlined above to produce a wide variety of sentences, positive and negative. For example:

teenagers/smoke

I object to the way teenagers *smoke to look cool.*

One thing I dislike about teenagers *is the way they smoke to look cool.*

One thing that annoys me is the way teenagers *smoke to look cool.*

1 people/are cruel to animals
2 computers/never do what you want
3 teachers/make lessons interesting
4 cars/pollute the environment

Emphasise or develop your opinion 3

Another way to develop personal opinion, is to use an adjective + infinitive:

It is	difficult easy frightening hard interesting upsetting	to	believe … hear … imagine … think … see … realise …

It is upsetting to think that many children have Aids.

In other words, I think or In my opinion it is upsetting to think that many children have Aids.

Exercise 7   Use the following prompts to make similar sentences.

1 Some people cannot read (hard/imagine)
2 Crime is on the increase (upsetting/hear)
3 Travelling broadens the mind (easy/understand)
4 Pollution is destroying the environment (frightening/realise)
5 Revision is important (easy/see)

Views and arguments

There are several ways of putting forward views and arguments in formal register, including:

1 One of the main arguments ⎱ in favour of
The main argument ⎰ against (something) is that …

2 Some people (would) argue that …

3
Many people ⎰ think
⎱ feel   that …
⎱ believe

4 It can be argued that …

The main argument against tourism is that large numbers of visitors tend to spoil the natural beauty of a place.

In phrases **1** to **4** above, you are putting forward points of view which are well known, but which you may or may not agree with. Phrases **5** to **8**, however, express your own, personal point of view. For this reason, some of these phrases can also be used for giving opinions.

5 Personally, I would argue that …

6 I am ⎰ very much ⎱ in favour of …
⎱ strongly   ⎰ against …
⎱ opposed to …

7 It seems to me that …

8
I ⎰ think
⎱ feel   that …
⎱ believe

I am strongly opposed to the use of illegal drugs.

It seems to me that more people are becoming environmentally friendly.

Exercise 1 Use the following prompts and the phrases given in **1–4** above to produce sentences expressing views and arguments.

1 modern technology/damaging our planet
2 windmills/environmentally friendly
3 team sports/cause aggression
4 competitive team sports/spirit of co-operation

Exercise 2   Use the following prompts and the phrases given in **5–8** above to produce sentences expressing views and arguments.

1 television/mislead and misinform
2 appearance/personality
3 passengers/seatbelts
4 breakdown of social values/increased crime

Giving details about *who* is involved in the controversy can make the sentence more interesting. Compare these two examples:

Some <u>people</u> would argue that boys and girls are happier when educated separately.

Some <u>teachers</u> would argue that boys and girls are happier when educated separately.

Exercise 3   Use the following prompts and include details about whose view is being expressed to make more views and arguments sentences.

1 competitive team sports/violence (psychologists)
2 mixed schools/mixed society (teachers)
3 regular exercise/health (doctors)
4 tourism/national economy (the government)
5 poverty/crime (sociologists)

PRODUCING FORMAL WRITING

Section 4 examines the techniques for producing different types of formal writing, incorporating the features and expressions introduced in the previous section. Each of the four units focuses on a particular type of formal writing and includes clear, easy-to-remember plans so you can be sure to answer a question in a full and relevant way.

As noted in Section 2, when answering a writing question in the exam, you should aim to write four paragraphs. You are usually asked to write between 100 and 150 words (Core) and between 150 and 200 words (Extended). This means that each paragraph should contain 25–40 words (Core) and 40–50 words (Extended). On the basis of ten words to a line (for average-size hand-writing) this means you need to write about three or four lines (Core) and four or five lines (Extended) in each paragraph.

UNIT
1

Compositions

This unit shows you how to apply the basic tools of formal writing (introduced in Section 3) to the different types of composition you may be asked to write in the exam, and covers the following categories:

- Opinions and suggestions
- Views and arguments
- Problems and solutions
- Projects

Opinions and suggestions

There are usually several key words or phrases in the exam question that indicate the type of answer and the range of phrases the examiner is expecting you to write. Read the question carefully. Does it contain one of the following underlined phrases?

- give your <u>opinion</u>
- say whether you <u>agree or disagree</u>
- say what you <u>think about</u>
- give your <u>view</u>

If so, then the phrases the examiner certainly expects to see will include those for giving opinions, as outlined in Section 3.

Writing an opinion composition

Every composition should be planned (see Exam hints for the writing exam, pages 224–30). In an **opinion composition**, only *one* viewpoint is expressed. Use the following basic plan for every opinion composition.

1 General introduction – explain the importance of the subject you have been asked to write about. Put forward your **own opinion**.
2 Support – explain the **first** reason for your opinion.
3 Support – explain the **second** reason for your opinion.
4 Conclusion – summarise and write your opinion. Include a suggestion, if possible.

★ **Remember**
Opinion is often linked to suggestion.

Expanding the plan

First paragraph

This is a general introduction which explains the importance of the subject. Put forward your own opinion. Make sure you include the features of formal writing outlined in Section 3:

■ Time fixers
  nowadays/these days/recently/until now/in the past/
  twenty years ago/in the last five years

■ Generalisations
  nearly all/many/a large number of/several

■ Opinion phrases
  I think/I feel/I believe/As far as I am concerned

Second paragraph

Support – explain the **first** reason for your opinion. Introduce it with one of the following phrases:

Firstly,/In the first place,/First of all,

Third paragraph

Support – explain the **second** reason for your opinion. Introduce it with a phrase like:

Another reason

Fourth paragraph

Conclusion – summarise and write your opinion. Include a suggestion, if possible. Make sure you include the following:

■ Phrases to introduce points

  To sum up,/In conclusion,

■ Opinion phrases

  In my opinion,/I believe (that)/Personally,/In my view,
  I am very much in favour of/I am strongly opposed to/I am against

■ Suggestion phrases

It would be a good idea if + past tense

■ Support phrases

because/as/since

When asked about a topic, you may not be sure exactly what your opinion is, because you can see good things and bad things about it. In an opinion composition it is important to write about *either* the good things *or* the bad things, but not both. (If you include both, then you would be writing a views and arguments composition – see pages 98–107.)

So, before you start writing your answer, make a list of points in favour and a list of points against. If there are two or three points in favour, for example, and only one against, choose your opinion to be in favour, because you will have more opportunity to include support.

Example question

Now look at the following *opinion* composition, based on a question from a past exam paper, and the example answer that follows.

Zoos are cruel to animals and should be closed down. What do you think?

Consider the points in favour of and against zoos.

In favour
Zoos could:

■ save animals from extinction
■ provide a safe breeding environment
■ offer day trips
■ offer educational experience
■ provide employment for local people
■ need less space than a safari park.

Against
Zoos might:

■ cause wild animals to suffer away from their natural environment.

In this case, as there are more points in favour of zoos, you would take this as your opinion.

★ **Remember**
   ❏ You only need two (or maximum three) points, so choose the most relevant, or the most important, or the ones you can support easily.
   ❏ Use as much relevant vocabulary as possible.
   ❏ Use the basic plan as outlined above.
   ❏ Never dive directly into the topic. Always begin *outside* the topic itself, to set the context, then move in to introduce the exact topic under consideration. Here the topic is zoos, so begin with the wider issue of conservation, endangered species, etc.

★ **Remember**
Refer to the Database of topic-related vocabulary and ideas on pages 231–44. Before the exam, make sure you are familiar with the contents. Add your own ideas.

Example answer

Paragraph 1

General introduction explaining the importance of conservation.

Nowadays, (time fixer) *a significant number* (generalisation) *of naturalists* (say who) *have been campaigning against zoos* (explain what the problem is), *arguing that* (views and arguments) *it is cruel to keep wild animals in cages, away from their natural environment.* However, (joining points – contrast) *like many other people,* (generalisation) I *believe that* (opinion) *zoos have a positive role to play.*

42 words

Paragraph 2

Explain the first reason for your opinion.

First of all, (introducing point) *many species* (generalisation) *of animal are in danger of extinction because their natural habitat is disappearing, due to deforestation* (support). *Some, like the elephant,* (example) *are hunted for their ivory or the tiger for their skins. Therefore, if animals are kept in captivity they can breed in safety, which will prevent the species from dying out* (support).

56 words
Total: 98 words

Paragraph 3

Explain the second reason for your opinion.

Another reason (joining points – addition) *for keeping animals in captivity is that it gives many of us a chance to see animals from all round the world without having to travel* (support). *A trip to the zoo is an example way to spend a day out because we can enjoy ourselves and learn about animals at the same time* (support).

55 words
Total: 153 words

Paragraph 4

Conclusion.

To sum up, (introducing point) *in my opinion* (opinion) *zoos should not be closed down* (suggestion) *because they are beneficial both to humans and to animals* (support).

22 words
Total: 175 words

Exercise 1   Using the plan and information above, write your own answer to the following *opinion* composition question.

Zoos are cruel to animals and should be closed down. What do you think?

■ Student's composition: opinion/suggestion

★ **Note**
This is an original composition written by an IGCSE student and may still contain minor mistakes.

Read the following opinion/suggestion composition written by a student in response to an exam question. The comments on the right show how the student has constructed the answer using the features discussed in Section 3.

Question 1 Do you agree or disagree with the idea that it is important to keep Antarctica untouched?

For many years, ① man has been looking for the best ways to exploit nature and benefit from its resources. However, **in most cases** ② these exploitations have resulted in harming the environment and **many species.** ②

To begin with, ③ animal species living in Antarctica **tend to be** ④ more rare due to the scarcity of this special habitat. **Many people believe that it would be senseless to destroy their only habitable home.** ⑤ This will lead to their extinction and **consequently a huge disturbance in nature would arise.** ⑥

Another reason ⑦ to prevent oil companies from invading Antarctica is that it is almost impossible to obtain the oil without adversely affecting the environment. **Furthermore,** ⑧ the amount of oil produced would not be worth the effort.

To sum up, in my opinion oil companies **should be** ⑨ prohibited from drilling for oil in Antarctica **because this would completely destroy wildlife there.** ⑩ **Surely we have a responsibility** ⑪ to protect it?

Comments

① Time fixer

② Generalisation × 2

③ Introducing first point in list

④ Generalisation

⑤ Opinion

⑥ Support

⑦ Introducing second point in list

⑧ Joining points – addition

⑨ Introducing point + opinion + suggestion phrase

⑩ Support

⑪ Suggestion phrase

■ Views and arguments

There are usually several key words or phrases in the exam question that indicate the type of answer and the range of phrases the examiner is expecting you to write. Read the question carefully. Does it contain one of the following underlined phrases?

■ put forward your <u>views and arguments</u>
■ put forward your ideas <u>and arguments</u>
■ put forward your opinions <u>and arguments</u>
■ outline your opinions <u>for and/or against</u>
■ set out your arguments <u>for and/or against</u>.

If so, then the phrases the examiner certainly expects to see will include those for putting forward views and arguments, as outlined in Section 3. See page 94 for information about how much to write in the exam.

Writing a views and arguments composition

Every composition should be planned (see Exam hints for the writing exam, pages 224–30). In a **views and arguments composition**, the word 'argument' indicates that you must show both points of view. Use the following basic plan for every views and arguments composition.

1 General introduction explaining the importance of the subject you have been asked to write about.
2 Put forward **one side** of the issue being argued – for example, the argument in favour.
3 Put forward **the other side** of the issue being argued – for example, the argument against.
4 Conclusion – put forward your personal opinion.

Expanding the plan

First paragraph

This is a general introduction which explains the importance of the subject. Put forward your own opinion. Make sure you include appropriate features of formal writing as outlined in Section 3.

■ Time fixers

nowadays/these days/recently/until now/in the past/
twenty years ago/in the last five years

■ Generalisations

nearly all/many/a large number of/several

■ Opinion phrases

I think/I feel/I believe/As far as I am concerned

Second paragraph

Put forward one side of the issue being argued – for example, the argument *in favour*. Make sure you include the following:

■ Views and arguments phrases

One of the main arguments in favour of … is that
Some people (would) argue that …
It is a fact that …

■ Addition phrases

Furthermore,/Moreover,/What is more,/Besides,

■ Support phrases

which/this/which means that/this means that/as a result/consequently

★ **Remember**
There is no right or wrong answer.

Third paragraph

Put forward the other side of the issue being argued – for example, the argument *against*. Make sure you include the following:

- Concession phrases (for contrast)

  On the other hand,/However,/Nevertheless,

- Views and arguments phrases

  *One of the main arguments against ... is that
  It can be argued that ...
  It has been said that ...*

- Addition phrases

  Furthermore,/Moreover,/What is more,/Besides,

- Support phrases

  which/this/which means that/this means that/as a result/consequently

Fourth paragraph

Conclusion – put forward your personal opinion. Remember that opinion is often linked to suggestion. Can you put forward a suggestion? Make sure you include the following:

- Phrases to introduce points

  To sum up,/In conclusion,

- Opinion phrases

  *In my opinion,/I believe (that)/Personally,/In my view/
  I am very much in favour of/I am strongly opposed to/I am against*

- Suggestion phrase

  It would be a good idea if + past tense

- Support phrases

  because/as/since

Example question 1

Now look at the following *views and arguments* composition, based on a question from a past exam paper and the example answer that follows.

★ **Note**

In some exam questions of this kind, as in the one here, you are given a list of comments that people have made related to the topic. These are given to help you by providing you with ideas, but you are usually free to use ideas of your own as well.

There is a plan to build a wind farm in your area to provide electricity for the local population. Put forward your views and arguments concerning the project.

a 'This will really benefit us all – we'll have a reliable electricity supply at last.'
b 'I think it's outrageous and dreadful. It will be an eyesore for miles around!'
c 'The amount of electricity these things will generate is just not worth all the disruption it will cause.'
d 'Well, it will look nice, won't it? All those windmills, I know they're the modern kind, but it reminds me a bit of Holland.'
e 'It will enable us to have new small industries, and that means jobs. That's good, isn't it?'
f 'People say they are environmentally friendly and all that, but they do make a noise – it's an awful swishing sound. I certainly don't want to hear that when I'm out enjoying the countryside.'
g 'In other areas where they've put these things motorists have had accidents watching the windmill blades instead of the road. They can be rather hypnotic.'

If you have studied the Database of topic-related vocabulary and ideas (pages 231–44), and are familiar with the topic, it is very possible that you will have your own ideas ready. If so, do not waste time reading the comments given. Your own ideas will be more original, and will already be in your own words.

However, if the topic is one you feel unsure of, then you will need to read the comments. If this is the case, remember to carry out the following steps:

1 Read each comment and mark with a tick or a cross whether it is in favour (positive) or against (negative) in meaning.
2 Make two headings, one *In favour* and the other *Against*.
3 Rewrite each comment in your own words, remembering to change the comments from friendly into formal register where necessary.
4 Number the comments in order of importance; you may not need to use them all.

Now read the comments given in the windmills composition carefully and apply the steps outlined above.

a) 'This will really benefit us all – we'll have a reliable electricity supply at last.'
Is this point *in favour* or *against*?
(It is *in favour*. Mark with a tick: ✔)

b) 'I think it's outrageous and dreadful. It will be an eyesore for miles around!'
Is this point *in favour* or *against*?
(It is *against*. Mark with a cross: ✖)

c) 'The amount of electricity these things will generate is just not worth all the disruption it will cause.'
(This point is *against*. Mark with a cross: ✖)

d) 'Well, it will look nice, won't it? All those windmills, I know they're the modern kind, but it reminds me a bit of Holland.'
(This point is *in favour*. Mark with a tick: ✔)

e) 'It will enable us to have new small industries, and that means jobs. That's good, isn't it?'
(This point is *in favour*. Mark with a tick: ✔)

f) 'People say they are environmentally friendly and all that, but they do make a noise – it's an awful swishing sound. I certainly don't want to hear that when I'm out enjoying the countryside.'
(This point is *against*. Mark with a cross: ✖)

g) 'In other areas where they've put these things motorists have had accidents watching the windmill blades instead of the road. They can be rather hypnotic.'
(This point is *against*. Mark with a cross: ✖)

Now make a heading **In favour** and go back to the points marked with a tick. Rewrite them in your own words, one by one. It is important to remember that many of the comments given are people's actual spoken words – this means they are in informal register. When you rewrite the comments, make sure you change them into formal register. Then number them in order of importance.

In favour

a) 'This will really benefit us all – we'll have a reliable electricity supply at last.'
1 *A reliable supply of electricity will be beneficial to everyone.*

d) 'Well, it will look nice, won't it? All those windmills, I know they're the modern kind, but it reminds me a bit of Holland.'
3 *They will be attractive.*

e) 'It will enable us to have new small industries, and that means jobs. That's good, isn't it?'
2 *A reliable electricity supply will allow small industries to be established, which will be good for the local economy.*

Now make a heading **Against** and go back to the points marked with a cross. Rewrite them in your own words, one by one. Then number them in order of importance.

Against

b) 'I think it's outrageous and dreadful. It will be an eyesore for miles around!'
1 *They will be ugly.*

c) 'The amount of electricity these things will generate is just not worth all the disruption it will cause.'
3 *There will be a great deal of inconvenience for nothing.*

f) 'People say they are environmentally friendly and all that, but they do make a noise – it's an awful swishing sound. I certainly don't want to hear that when I'm out enjoying the countryside.'
2 *They cause noise pollution.*

g) 'In other areas where they've put these things motorists have had accidents watching the windmill blades instead of the road. They can be rather hypnotic.'
4 *They can distract drivers and cause accidents.*

Now, refer to the Database of topic-related vocabulary and ideas for additional information. This may be particularly useful in the introduction and conclusion.

In favour

Wind farms:

- are environmentally friendly, no dangerous fumes, no air pollution
- are more attractive than a conventional power station
- provide a reliable source of electricity
- make small industries possible, which …
- … create employment in the area.

Against

Wind farms:

- are ugly, eyesores, spoil the natural beauty of a place
- may put tourists off, reduce tourism – bad for the economy
- encourage noise pollution, may disturb local wildlife
- are distracting, especially for motorists
- may cause pollution by blowing dust and dirt around
- need large area of land – may be used for farming.

Refer back to your plan. Never dive directly into the topic. Always begin outside the topic itself, to set the context, then move in to introduce the exact topic under consideration. Here the topic is windmills, so begin with the wider issue of power generation.

Example answer 1

Now look at an example answer to the *views and arguments* question on page 101.

Paragraph 1

General introduction explaining the importance of the subject.

Until now, (time fixer) *power generation has relied on natural resources, such as coal, gas and oil* (examples). *As these supplies begin to run out, scientists have been investigating alternative methods of producing electricity, such as windmills* (link to main topic).

34 words

Paragraph 2

Introduce one point of view.

One of the main arguments against windmills is that (views and arguments) *they are an eyesore, and spoil areas of natural beauty. This may lead to a reduction of tourism, which would be bad for the local economy* (support). *Moreover,* (joining points – addition) *many people* (generalisation) *are concerned that the windmills are not only a distraction to motorists, but that the noise they make may disturb local wildlife* (support).

60 words
Total: 94 words

Paragraph 3

Introduce the opposite point of view.

On the other hand, (joining points – contrast) *the main argument in favour of windmills is that* (views and arguments) *they will provide a much more reliable power supply to remote areas and consequently small industries will be established which will provide employment for local people* (support) *and at the same time* (joining points – addition) *boost the economy* (support).

47 words
Total: 141 words

Paragraph 4

Conclusion.

In conclusion, (introducing point) *I believe that* (opinion) *it would be a good idea if* (suggestion) *plans for the windmill farm went ahead, as they pose no threat to the environment* (support) *in terms of air pollution and they would certainly be more attractive than a conventional power station* (support).

44 words
Total: 185 words

Exercise 2   Using the plan and information given above, write your own answer to the following *views and arguments* composition.

There is a plan to build a wind farm in your area to provide electricity for the local population. Put forward your views and arguments concerning the project.

Example question 2

Now look at another *views and arguments* composition, based on a question from a past exam paper, and the example answer that follows.

The governors of your school have decided that all students should take part in competitive team sports. Set out your arguments for and/or against compulsory competitive team sports.

- all students – That means everyone.
- compulsory – That means there is no choice, you must take part.
- competitive – That means playing to win, not just for fun or keeping fit.
- team sports – That means games like football, volley ball and hockey.

The exam contains comments for you to use. The question says 'you are free to use ideas of your own'. In this example, we will use our own ideas. List each factor under positive and negative headings.

★ **Remember**
- ❑ Every word in the question is there for a reason.
- ❑ Make sure you have read every word before you begin.

In favour

Compulsory competitive team sports should be encouraged because:

- they prevent students from becoming unfit due to laziness
- sport should be part of the timetable/makes you fit/gives you more energy/a healthy mind in a healthy body
- team games encourage the idea of working together, co-operation
- they encourage social interaction.

Against

Compulsory competitive team sports should not be encouraged because:

- when people are forced to do things, they are not enthusiastic participants
- students who do not like sport may weaken the team/may be bullied or even socially isolated
- too much emphasis on sport can result in obsession with winning, which can result in aggressive behaviour.

> ★ **Remember**
> Never dive directly into the topic. Always begin outside the topic itself, to set the context, then move in to introduce the exact topic under consideration. Here the exact topic is sport in schools, so begin with the larger issue of health.

Refer back to the plan on page 99.

Example answer 2

Now look at an example answer to the question on page 104.

Paragraph 1

General introduction explaining the importance of the subject.

Nowadays, (time fixer) *due to the media and awareness campaigns, the vast majority of people* (generalisation) *realise the importance of exercise, and the benefits it can have on health* (explain the importance of the issue and the effect it has). *In an effort to promote this idea, a large number* (generalisation) *of schools want to make participation in team sports compulsory* (link to main topic).

46 words

Paragraph 2

Introduce one point of view.

One of the main arguments against (views and arguments) *anything compulsory is that when a student is forced into something, he will not be an enthusiastic participant, and this may weaken the performance of his team* (support). *Consequently, he could become unpopular, isolated socially, or even become a victim of bullying* (support).

47 words
Total: 93 words

Paragraph 3

Introduce the opposite point of view.

On the other hand (joining points – contrast), *many people* (generalisation – can you say *who* exactly? Teachers? Doctors?) *would argue that* (views and arguments) *sport makes us fit and gives us energy. In order to* (support) *have a healthy mind in a healthy body, sport should be* (suggestion) *a compulsory subject on every school timetable. Furthermore* (joining points – contrast), *it is a fact that* (views and arguments) *team sport encourages co-operation and promotes social interaction* (support).

52 words
Total: 145 words

Paragraph 4

Conclusion.

To sum up (introducing point), *in my opinion* (opinion) *it would be a good idea if* (suggestion) *team sports were made compulsory in schools to establish healthy habits early in life, and to prevent students from becoming unfit due to laziness* (support).

37 words
Total: 182 words

Exercise 3 Using the plan and information above, write your own answer to the following *views and arguments* question.

The governors of your school have decided that all students should take part in competitive team sports. Set out your arguments for and/or against compulsory competitive team sports.

Exercise 4 Use the prompts given below to write a full plan and then an answer to the following question.

The government are planning to build an airport near your area. Write a letter to a local newspaper, setting out your views and arguments about the issue.

1 why important	poor transport/ decrease in tourist industry
2 views and arguments against the proposal	(+ support) noise pollution/disturb local people/ (+ support) loss of farmland/drop in crop yield
3 views and arguments in favour of the proposal	(+ support) encourage tourists/improve economy/ (+ support) more jobs
4 conclusion + opinion	good way to boost the economy

Now compare your answer with one written by a student, on the next page.

■ *Student's composition: views and arguments*

★ **Note**
This is an original letter written by an IGCSE student and may still contain minor mistakes.

Read the following views and arguments composition written by a student in response to this exam question. The comments on the right show how the student has constructed the answer using the features discussed in Section 3.

Question 2 The government are planning to build an airport near your area. Write a letter to a local newspaper, setting out your views and arguments about the issue.

Dear Sir,

For many years, ❶ transportation has been a major problem in this town **which has resulted in a decrease in the tourist industry,** ❷ **leading to financial difficulties.** ❸ For this reason, as we are all aware, the government decided to build an airport on the outskirts of the town.

One of the main arguments against ❹ the scheme is that it will cause a lot of noise pollution, **which would disturb a significant number of people** ❺ in the nearby rural area. **Moreover,** ❻ building an airport requires a vast area of land, **which would mean the loss of farm land,** ❼ since agricultural land will be abused. Therefore a drop in crop yield would definitely be the effect of such action.

On the other hand, ❽ many people **believe** ❾ that our town does not lack any resources and is beautiful to the foreign eye, **so it would be senseless** ❿ to miss an opportunity to facilitate the entry of tourists to our town. **This will not only improve the economy** ⓫ but will **also provide more jobs** ⓫ for our unemployed citizens. At a later stage, it would be easy to restore the farmland by purchasing fertilisers that would increase the crop.

Personally, ⓬ the plan seems to be an efficient way to **boost the economy of our town, making it a prosperous one,** ⓭ and in the end the most important factor to consider is the welfare of our people.

Yours faithfully,

Jane Smith

Jane Smith (Miss)

Comments

❶ Time fixer

❷ Why this is important

❸ Effect

❹ Views and arguments

❺ Support

❻ Joining points – addition

❼ Support

❽ Joining points – contrast

❾ Opinion

❿ Suggestion

⓫ Support × 2

⓬ Opinion

⓭ Support

■ Problems and solutions

Problems and solutions compositions are, basically, a mixture of the other types of composition. Many of the phrases here are ones you have already met. You will need to include opinions and suggestions. The main difference is that the introduction will probably be longer and more detailed.

There are usually several key words or phrases in the exam question that indicate the type of answer and the range of phrases the examiner is expecting you to write. Read the question carefully. Does it contain one of the following underlined phrases?

■ What can be done to <u>overcome</u> …?
■ Ways of <u>solving the problem</u>
■ How can the <u>problem be solved</u>?

If so, then the phrases the examiner certainly expects to see will include those for giving opinions and making suggestions. See page 94 for information about how much to write in the exam.

Writing a problems and solutions composition

Every composition should be planned (see Exam hints for the writing exam, pages 224–30). Use the following basic plan for every **problems and solutions composition**.

1	General introduction to the topic, explaining what the problem is, what is causing it and what the results will be.
2 + 3	Put forward suggestions for overcoming the problem. Support your suggestions.
4	Conclusion – explain that you are sure the problem can be overcome.

Expanding the plan

First paragraph

Introduce the topic and explain what the problem is, what is causing it and what the results will be.

■ Begin with a time fixer.

Nowadays,/These days,/More than ever before,/Recently,

■ Explain what the problem is. There are several possible ways to do this, including:

a) Traffic / Tourism / Shortage of water } has become } a major / a serious / a global problem.

b) There is a } serious / worldwide / global shortage of …

c) There has been a } noticeable / marked } increase/rise in / decrease in } awareness. / the number/ amount of …

d) We are running out of time/trees/water/natural resources.

■ Explain the reason for the problem.

This is
$\begin{cases} \textit{due to} \dots \\ \textit{because of} \dots \end{cases}$

The reason for this is ...

■ If there is more than one reason, link them with addition phrases.

Moreover,/Furthermore,/Besides,
not only ... *but also* ...
both ... *and* ...

For example:

Windmills are an eyesore. Windmills are bad for the local economy.

(two negative ideas)

Windmills are **not only** *an eyesore* **but also** *bad for the local economy.*

Windmills are **both** *an eyesore* **and** *bad for the local economy.*

■ Explain what the consequences (result, effect) will be.

$\begin{cases} \textit{This} \\ \dots \textit{which} \end{cases}$ will $\begin{cases} \textit{result in} \dots \\ \textit{cause} \dots \end{cases}$

This means that ...
... which means that ...

... if we do not protect the environment, future generations will suffer.
... unless we protect the environment, future generations will suffer.

Second and third paragraphs

■ Make suggestions about how to overcome the problem.

+ past tense

Clearly it would be a good idea if
It is about high time
$\begin{cases} \textit{we organised a campaign.} \\ \textit{we took positive action.} \end{cases}$

■ Remember to support your suggestions.

It would be a good idea if we set up a campaign
$\begin{cases} \textit{to make people aware of} \dots \\ \textit{so that people are aware of} \dots \end{cases}$

If we organised a campaign, people would $\begin{cases} \textit{be} \\ \textit{become} \end{cases}$ *more aware* ...

Fourth paragraph

■ Make your conclusion short. Do not repeat what you have already written. Try to be positive and confident about your suggestions – but do not repeat them! Explain that you are sure the problem can be overcome.

I am sure
I feel confident } that ...

... if these {
measures are taken ...
ideas are taken into consideration ...
suggestions are put into practice ...
rules are applied ...
laws are brought into force ...
}

... the {
water shortage
problem of { pollution / smoking / bullying }
negative aspects of { tourism / science }
}

... will soon be {
overcome
a thing of the past
reduced
improved
}

... and ... the world will be a { better / safer / healthier } place for { everyone / us all } to live in.

Exercise 5 Using the plan and information above, write an answer to the following *problems and solutions* composition.

Violent incidents at football matches are on the increase. What can be done to overcome the problem?

Now compare your answer with the suggested answer given on pages 248–9.

Exercise 6 Use the prompts given below to write a full plan and then an answer to the following *problems and solutions* question.

Many countries in the world are suffering from severe shortage of food. What measures can be taken to solve this problem?

1 problem   worldwide shortage of food
    cause (1)   destruction of natural environment/pollution
    result (1)   less land for farming
    who says?   environmentalists
    cause (2)   overpopulation in some countries
    result (2)   less food per person

2
3 } suggestion + support {
share food with countries that have a surplus
share technology to help developing countries
inform about dangers of pollution
}

4 conclusion

Now compare your answer with the answer written by an IGCSE student on the next page.

Student's composition: problems and solutions

★ **Note**

This is an original composition written by an IGCSE student and may still contain minor mistakes.

Read the following problems and solutions composition written by a student in response to this exam question. The comments on the right show how the student has constructed the answer using the features discussed in Section 3.

Question 3 Many countries in the world are suffering from severe shortage of food. What measures can be taken to solve this problem?

*Nowadays,*❶ *due to the mass media and global communication we are more than ever aware of* **the problem of worldwide food shortage which is on the increase.**❷ *This hopeless situation* **has been caused,**❸ *environmentalists inform us, by destruction of the natural environment and pollution* **which have led to**❹ *less farming land.* **Furthermore,**❺ *overpopulation in many countries* **has meant**❻ *a substantial reduction in food per person.*

It would seem to me that❼ *total commitment is required to eradicate this problem for good. If we bury our heads in the sand, the lives of many innocent people will be at risk. How many people must die of starvation before we take action?*

Surely it would be a good idea if❽ *countries with a surplus of food were encouraged to distribute it to those with none.* **It is high time**❾ *we shared our technology with developing countries* **to help them make better use of their land.**❿ **Furthermore,**⓫ *we have no alternative but to inform others of the dangers of pollution and reduce it.*

In my opinion,⓬ *the difficulties are* **not insurmountable**⓭ *provided that we act together.*

Comments

❶ Time fixer

❷ Explain the problem

❸ Explain the reason

❹ Consequences

❺ Joining points – addition

❻ Consequences

❼ Opinion

❽ Suggestion

❾ Suggestion

❿ Support

⓫ Joining points – addition

⓬ Opinion

⓭ Positive outlook

▉ Projects

Sometimes the question asks you to write about a **project**. Before we look at how to write the composition, consider what the projects involve. There are three types:

1 Awareness projects

   These are usually carried out at school. As their name suggests, these projects aim to inform people and make them more aware of certain facts or circumstances. They do not involve raising money. Topics in this category include:

   ▪ the environment
   ▪ conservation
   ▪ smoking.

2 Raising money within the school, for the school

   These projects aim to collect money to:

   ▪ improve the school facilities
   ▪ buy equipment for the labs (laboratories), books for the library, more computers, a sports hall or a swimming pool, for example.

3 Raising money for a good cause or charity

   These projects aim to collect money for:

   ▪ a charity, such as Cancer Research
   ▪ victims of a natural disaster: earthquake, drought, floods, famine
   ▪ victims of war
   ▪ a local amenity: health centre, library, hospice (= nursing home for the terminally ill).

When writing about projects, keep the following points in mind:

▪ The projects should involve as many students as possible.
▪ You should include the benefits to the students, such as building self-confidence and team work.

Now let's look at the types of project in more detail, taking into account the points given above.

Project 1a Awareness of the environment

This aims to make students aware of pollution, and teaches them to respect the environment. At school, this means, for example, not dropping litter.

How can you involve as many students as possible?

▪ Organise a 'design-a-poster' competition throughout the school, where everyone designs a poster showing the theme of the project.
▪ How can you motivate everyone? Choose a winner from each Year group. The winning posters will be put up round the school – and locally in the town library, for example, or on the supermarket noticeboard. One of the students may become famous!

■ Arrange for someone from the local environment group to come and give a talk. To avoid this being boring, make sure the person gives out stickers, leaflets, paper hats or paper flags. You could hand out a questionnaire and whoever answers the questions correctly wins an environment T-shirt.

■ Arrange to go on a trip to the town refuse collection department. Find out what happens to your rubbish after you throw it away. Meet a refuse collector (the person who collects the rubbish bags).

■ Let students discover what a landfill site is. (It is a very large, deep hole or pit dug to obtain clay for brick making, or minerals, then filled up with compressed rubbish over a long period of time. Eventually, after several tonnes of rubbish have been dumped, a large hill is formed.)

■ Hand out rubbish bags and rubber gloves to each Year group and make them responsible for clearing up certain parts of the school grounds.

■ Take some groups out to clear up a local park or beach. Make sure the local newspaper photographer is there to record their efforts. Another chance to become famous.

■ Arrange for your school to decorate a float (see page 72) in the local festival/parade. Some students could design the float, others take part on the float, and others walk behind it waving banners about pollution/ litter/the environment. Again, make sure the school magazine photographer is there.

■ Older Year groups could research the topic and put up a display in the reception for visitors to admire.

What are the benefits to the students?

■ They learn a great deal about the environment from first-hand experience (they do it themselves).

■ When they are actively involved, the subject makes more of an impression on students than simply reading or being told about it.

■ They will remember it because they had fun learning about it.

■ As future citizens they will use their knowledge to behave in a more responsible way.

Project 1b Awareness of conservation

This aims to teach students about conservation of natural resources. At school, this means looking at recycling.

How can you involve as many students as possible?

Use many of the ideas outlined for the awareness of the environment project above, including:

■ Posters
■ Speakers
■ Visits – this time to a recycling factory. Let the students discover what happens to a soft drink can after it is thrown away.
■ Decorate a float in the recycling theme.
■ At school, put out containers round the grounds: one for empty soft drink cans, one for glass and one for paper. See if your school can fill more containers than it did last year.
■ Put up a display in reception.

What are the benefits to the students?

The same as those mentioned for the awareness of the environment project above.

Project 2 Raising money to improve school facilities

Many ideas should spring to mind here, for example holding a cake sale or having a jumble sale. (A jumble sale is when people bring in old but respectable clothes, toys or unwanted items from home to be sold very inexpensively.) Remember, though, the important factor is how to involve as many people as possible.

One idea would be to put on a **school concert or play**:

How can you involve as many students as possible?

Consider how many people are needed for a concert or play:

- the actors
- people to design and make the costumes
- people to design and make the scenery
- people to put make-up on the actors
- musicians to perform the music
- backstage crew – lighting, sound
- people to produce posters for advertising
- people to design and produce programmes
- people to make and sell refreshments at the performances
- people to make recordings/take photographs.

Clearly, a very large number of students can be involved in this project! With such a variety of skills required, there should be something to suit or interest everyone.

What are the benefits to the students?

There are many. Putting on a production takes months of practice.

- It means missing lunch break or staying on after school. This requires dedication, sacrifice and patience.
- Working together teaches teamwork and the spirit of co-operation.
- You also feel that, however small the part you play, you are important; this increases self-esteem (= having a good opinion of yourself); this, in turn improves your self-confidence.
- You understand that achievement comes as a result of hard work.
- Working as a group develops your social skills.
- It is an experience you will never forget; it becomes part of your personal development.
- You feel a sense of pride that your effort contributed to the new swimming pool, for example.
- You have fun and enjoy yourself.

Another idea would be to organise a **sponsored event**.

Again, this usually involves everyone at school. Sponsored swims are often popular. They are quick and easy to organise. Each student can swim either a maximum number of lengths of the pool (40, for example), or for a maximum length of time (an hour, for example). Each student takes home a sponsor form for parents to fill in, agreeing to pay the young person whatever amount of money they choose for every length their child swims. Ideally, parents should also pass the form to their friends and colleagues to complete.

On the day, there is a great deal of cheering and noise! Teachers count off the lengths as the students swim, and stamp the form when each student finishes, certifying the number of lengths swum. Parents then multiply the number of lengths by the amount per length promised, and send the money to school.

What are the benefits to the students?

Again, there are many. Most were mentioned in the notes about putting on a school concert or play and include the following:

- pride to be doing something worthwhile
- increased self-confidence and self-esteem, because your effort is important
- development of social skills
- awareness that effort is required for achievement.

Project 3 Raising money for a good cause

Putting on a play or holding sponsored events are the projects most likely to be successful. The benefits to the students will be the same as those mentioned above. It will develop in the students a sense of charity, and the importance of giving.

Now you have all the ideas, and are aware of the kind of points the examiner expects you to include.

Writing a project composition

See page 94 for information about how much to write in the exam.

Introduction

The **introduction** should start outside the actual topic. If your project is concerned with raising money for a new X-ray machine for your local hospital, for example, your introduction could start with health.

Begin in the same way as usual for formal compositions, using a time fixer.

| These days, Nowadays, | } | due to thanks to as a result of | } | awareness campaigns ... documentary programmes ... the media ... |

| we people teenagers | } | are better informed about are very aware of are kept up to date about | } | the importance of | } | health ... protecting the environment ... conserving natural resources ... |

These days, as a result of awareness campaigns, we are better informed about the importance of health.

Nowadays, thanks to documentary programmes, people are very aware of the importance of protecting the environment.

Go on to explain what the problem is:

- a lack of equipment at the health centre?
- inadequate sports facilities at school?
- a lack of respect for the environment among schoolchildren?

Go on to explain what has caused the problem:

- lack of funds?
- increase in the local population?

Then explain what the consequences are:

This means that ...
... which means that ...

Body

Now move on to the **body** of the composition:

Our school project involves ...
Bearing this in mind, we have chosen ... as our school project. This involves ...

Then continue by using the ideas previously outlined. Remember to include:

- how the students are involved
- the benefits to them.

Conclusion

The **conclusion** should be short and relevant:

We hope you will come along and support us.
Please give generously.
Every little helps.
No amount is too small.

When writing about a good cause, try to make your composition relevant to the reader. If it is to do with health, for example, remember to point out that none of us knows when we may need medical help.

When you practise writing these compositions, you will find it is easier to write about the project in the past tense, as if it is finished, especially when you come to write about the benefits to the students. It is hard to say what these are if the project has not started!

■ *Exam-style questions*

Question 1   You want to collect money for a special project. Write a feature for your local newspaper, describing your project and persuading the readers to give money to it. You may choose one of the following projects or any you are interested in.
- Support your local hospice
- Computers for schools!
- Public swimming pool for our town

Question 2   Write an entry for the competition advertised below to win a computer for your school.

> If your school is involved in a project that you believe is interesting, we want to hear about it.
>
> The type and size of school does not matter, and nor does the nature of the project, whether it is improving the school environment, for example, or raising money for charity or producing a play.
>
> To enter, you must write a description of your project in about 200 words giving details of your aims, methods and the people involved.

Question 3   Write a short article for your school magazine suggesting how the school can raise money for facilities or equipment, for example the library/new computers/sports equipment. Write about 150–200 words.

Formal letters

Sometimes the letter you are asked to write may not be to a friend. You may be asked to write to a group or society, asking for information of some kind, or you may be asked to write an application for a job.

As an IGCSE student, you are probably still at school or college, and would only be looking for an evening or holiday job. This may involve being a receptionist, a tour guide, or someone who helps organise play activities for children. It is important to remember that this kind of job is not your career. You want the job for the money, the experience and something to fill your time.

For these reasons, the language in a job application letter (that you write in an exam) should be formal, but not over-formal. Do not include information about previous employment experience or qualifications. Write simply about yourself as you are now. Answer the points made in the advertisement, remembering to create interest if you can. This may involve **contrast**: if you want to join a singing group, for example, you may mention that your voice is not exceptionally good. Modesty is important.

Look at this example, based on a question from a past exam paper:

You are looking for a holiday job and you see this advertisement.

PLAYGROUP HELPERS

The Village Playgroup looks after children aged 5–10 while their parents are at work and during the school holidays. Playgroup helpers are needed to organise indoor and outdoor activities and to take part in children's games and outings.

Helpers must:
• be able to supervise meals and make snacks
• accompany children on day trips to local places of interest.

The ability to speak another language would be an advantage.

Applications from students will be considered.

Write a letter of application explaining why you think you would be suitable.

Where did you see the advertisement? You probably saw it locally (it is a *village* playgroup), perhaps:

■ on the noticeboard in the public library
■ in the local newspaper (*Citizen, Herald, Smallville Times*)
■ in the village newsletter
■ in the Post Office window.

Begin your letter by referring to the job, saying where you saw it and when. You may want to give your age and explain your situation:

Dear Sir/Madam,
        I was interested to see your advertisement for playgroup helpers in this week's *Citizen*.

I am revising for my IGCSEs.

I have just finished taking my IGCSEs.

I have been under a lot of stress revising and would welcome a complete change from academic work.

I would like to put my energy into something completely different from studying.

You may want to mention any languages you have been studying. Be careful not to list the languages (one is enough) or to give the impression that you are brilliant at it. Instead, say something like:

I have a working knowledge of Russian.

Russian was one of my IGCSE subjects, but my spoken experience is limited.

When writing about your qualities and abilities, try not to start by boasting:

> ✖ *I am good at …*

> ✔ *I enjoy*

> or

> ✔ *My friends tell me that I am good at …*
> ✔ *My teachers tell me …*
> ✔ *My music/sports/cookery teacher is usually pleased with my work/efforts.*

★ **Remember**
Create interest through contrast.

Although I do not enjoy cooking, I regularly prepare a variety of snacks for my neighbours' children when I babysit for them each week.

Although I am not/do not consider myself to be a particularly sporty person, I have successfully organised fun races for local children on several occasions.

Perhaps your parents both work and it is your responsibility to look after a younger brother or sister (or both!) when you come home from school. You may have accompanied a class of younger children from your school on a day trip to the zoo/theme park, etc.

As with all compositions, do not attempt to answer everything, just pick out one or two points and expand them to create interest. Do not try to sound wonderful at everything: be modest.

Finish off with something like:

I should be grateful if you would send me an application form and any other relevant information/details.

Then the formal:

I look forward to hearing from you.

Yours faithfully,

Sign the letter with your first and family name, then write it underneath the signature in capital letters, with your status in brackets:

Susan Mendes

SUSAN MENDES (Miss)

Example application letter

This job application letter was written by a student. The comments show how the student has written the letter using the features discussed in this unit.

Dear Sir,

     I was very interested to read your **advertisement for a play-worker** ❶ on the **notice-board in the public library** ❷ **yesterday.** ❸

     I am seventeen year old ❹ and am currently **studying for my IGCSEs** ❺ which will end on the 17th June. I am under a lot of pressure right now and feel **I need a break after the exams.** ❺ I am good at handling children and **although** ❻ I am not particularly keen on sports, **my friends tell me I am good at organising games and children's activities.** ❼

     I used to go baby-sitting twice a week for our neighbour's children and usually prepared snacks for them. I took a course in cookery last year at the Food and Health Centre. ❽

     I should be grateful if you would send me an application form and any other relevant details.

     I look forward to hearing from you.

Yours faithfully, ❾

Maria Leal

MARIA LEAL (Miss)

Comments

❶ States what the job is

❷ States where she saw the advertisement

❸ States when she saw the advertisement

❹ States age

❺ States situation

❻ Creates interest through contrast

❼ States qualities and abilities

❽ Further supports the application. Two modest examples

❾ Appropriate ending

Exercise 1   Look at the advertisement below (based on a past exam question) about joining a music group. Using the student's letter above and the examples and the notes given on the next page, write a letter describing yourself, explaining why you want to become a member of the group and asking for more details.

Do you enjoy singing?

Would you like to learn about and perform
music from different cultures?

Does the idea of taking part in a concert interest you?

If so, why not come along and join:

THE CIVIC MUSIC GROUP

Workshop every weekend

Points to consider

- Your style should be formal with no short forms and no slang. However, it should not be over-formal – you want to join the local music group, not an international academic institution!
- Select one or two points from the advertisement and expand them to create interest. Be modest. Use contrast to create interest.
- Remember to start by saying what the advertisement is about and where you saw it:

  I was interested to read your advertisement in last week's Citizen for new members to join the Civic Music Group.

- When you are describing yourself you should write about your character and relevant qualities, not a physical description. Why are you suddenly interested in joining the group? Here are some ideas to start you thinking.

  - Have you recently moved to the area and would welcome an opportunity to meet people with the same interests?
  - Do you finally have some free time, having just finished your exams, and want to relax, expand socially? Have you been too busy until now?
  - Are you under stress because most of your time is spent revising? Do you want to make the most of your limited available free time? Would the Civic Music Group help you relax and unwind? Give you something worthwhile to do?
  - Do you enjoy singing even though you do not have the best voice in the world? Create interest through contrast.
  - Do you go to an international school/live in a cosmopolitan society and have friends from other cultures?
  - Would you like to learn something about people from other cultures because you never meet them?
  - Will your own cultural background be of interest to/enrich the group?
  - Have you always wanted to take part in a concert?

- Remember to ask for more information:

  I should be grateful if you would send me an application form and any other relevant information/details.

- Then the formal ending:

  I look forward to hearing from you.

- Sign the letter with your first and family name, then write it underneath the signature in capital letters, with your status in brackets.

★ **Remember**
In this kind of letter, you do not know the person you are writing to: so your letter should *not* include personalising.

Exercise 2 Now try to write the letter to the Civic Music Group several times, using the suggestions given above in different combinations and also using your own ideas.

Use of descriptive narrative in formal letters

Some letters may require 'descriptive narrative' treatment. Look back to Section 2, Unit 4 for the features of descriptive narrative writing.

In exercise 3 you are going to write to the manager of a hotel you stayed at recently to inform him that you lost a personal item while you were there.

■ Writing to a hotel manager means:

- no short forms
- no slang
- no personalising.

■ What did you lose? Spend some time thinking about this. Consider its size and value and why it is important. Many students will write about an expensive item – so, be different! Why not choose something with *sentimental* value, which would have no real appeal to a thief – for example:

- a digital camera with photos of your 82-year-old grandmother who you had travelled to visit for the first time
- a mobile phone (with the number of an old friend)
- a special souvenir or gift.

■ Don't forget to say which room you were staying in.
■ How did you lose/forget the item? This is the narrative part. Create the circumstances.
■ When did you realise you no longer had it?
■ You are hoping to have the item returned, so be diplomatic, not rude. Do not write in an accusing tone:

- Do *not* suggest the item was stolen, say *you misplaced* it.
- Do *not* suggest the staff are dishonest. On the contrary, make it clear that you feel certain they would have handed the item in if they had found it.
- Do *not* make any other complaints about the hotel.

■ Decide what you want the manager to do with the item if he finds it.

- forward it to you?
- keep it for someone to collect?
- telephone you with the information?

Exercise 3 Using the information given above, write a letter to the manager of a hotel you stayed in recently, to inform him that you lost a personal item while you were there. Then compare your answer with the one written by a student on the next page.

■ *Student's formal letter*

Read the following formal letter written by a student in respose to this exam question, and the comments related to it.

★ Note

This is an original composition written by an IGCSE student and may still contain minor mistakes. In the comments column, the letter **G** refers to points in the Grammar unit on pages 186–99.

The arrow (→) points to what the text in the letter should be changed to or replaced with.

Question 1 Write a letter to the manager of a hotel you stayed in recently to inform him/her that you lost a personal item while you were there.

Dear Sir,

    I am writing to inform you① that during my stay in your hotel last week I unfortunately **misplaced an important personal item.**②

    I was staying③ in Room 1042, **having a great time,**④ **when**⑤ I decided to buy something for my grandmother. I looked in all the shops trying to find something for her. The selection was marvellous, **but**⑥ I wanted something memorable. In the end I found a unique photo album, the shape of dolphins, she happens to adore them. Another customer wanted to buy it and since it was the last one, I convinced him to leave it for me.

    On walking back to my room I stopped at the Oasis Pool to meet a friend of mine. Then I went to pack and **completely forgot**⑦ about the present **I had bought.**⑧ **It was not until**⑨ I unpacked my bag at home this morning that I realised **I must have**⑩ left it at the pool.

    Although it is inexpensive, it is of special value to me and would make an old lady happy. It may be in the lost property office as one of your **honest**⑪ staff may have found it.

    If so, I should be grateful if you would forward it to the above address.

    Thank you for your co-operation in this matter.

    I look forward to hearing from you.

Yours faithfully,

Ola Kassem

OLA KASSEM (Miss)

Comments

① Correct use of formal register. *Let you know* is friendly register and would not be appropriate here.

② As a rule, do not repeat the word used in the question. Here, the student changed *lost* to **misplaced** and included **important**. Good!

③ Narrative: setting the scene

④ This is friendly register → **I was having an enjoyable stay ...**

⑤ **when**: time sequence: usually introduces a *sudden* contrast. Here, **and** would be better.

⑥ G5 and G4 Wrong use of **but**: *but* joins a positive to a negative sentence. Here both parts of the sentence are positive. Use **and**.

⑦ Nice word partners

⑧ Correct use of past perfect

⑨ Time sequence phrase

⑩ Deduction – good grammar point

⑪ No need to mention this

School magazine articles

What is a school magazine?

Many IGCSE ESL students have never heard of a school magazine until they read the exam question.

■ A school magazine is usually produced once a year (but is not to be confused with a Year Book), and is printed on good quality paper, often with colour photographs.

■ It contains information about new and retiring members of staff, news about school clubs and societies, sport, school trips both at home and abroad, exchange visits with language students, exam results and, of course, original contributions written by students of all ages.

■ Articles for a school magazine are mainly written by students for students: in other words for people about the same age as you and with almost the same education, background, culture, ideas and outlook on life as you. It is like writing to a large number of friends all at once!

The right approach

When writing a school magazine article, bear in mind the following.

■ Do not give the impression that you are an expert and the readers know nothing.

■ Be enthusiastic. Whatever you write must be something you are enthusiastic about and firmly believe in because contributions to the school magazine are voluntary. No one approaches you and asks you to write an article. This enthusiasm should show through in your writing.

■ Be convincing. If you want your article to be printed in the magazine, it must be written in a convincing way because not every contribution is automatically included. Usually an editorial committee, which consists of students and one or two members of staff, reads everything and selects the best.

■ Be interesting. Remember that most of the readers are at school with you and know the things you know, so be careful not to give them a biology lesson, for example, if you write about smoking or keeping fit. To avoid doing this, you have to present information from a different, more interesting angle.

■ Personalise. Emphasise any points you have in common with your readers (attitude to parents, school work, friends, for example). Try to replace *I* whenever possible with *we*. This has the effect of personalising the article, and making the reader feel involved.

Register in school magazine articles

The register (or **level** of language) used in a school magazine article can vary. Much depends on how serious the topic is. Some topics can be treated in a light-hearted way and can be written in **informal** (friendly) register. Other topics are more serious and will need **formal** register. Sometimes the language needed may fall halfway between the two registers.

◼ Format of a school magazine article

School magazine articles can be divided into the following different sections:

- ◼ Title
- ◼ Introduction
- ◼ Body
- ◼ Ending

Let's look at each stage in detail, beginning with the title, introduction and ending, and then looking at different types of body separately.

Title

Always give the article a title, and underline it. Make it **interesting**. From the very beginning, show the examiner that you know exactly what you are doing. Try to think of an effective, interesting title. Compare the two following titles:

How to Prepare for Exams

Exam Nerves Cure

From these titles, which article would you prefer to read? Not many teenagers about to take multiple IGCSEs would bother to look at an article with the first title. How much advice have you been given about how to prepare for exams? Certainly your teachers, your parents, older brothers and sisters and perhaps even friends have all passed on their own tips, hints and advice. The title sounds dull, boring and uninspiring. There is no suggestion that an article about such a serious subject might be treated in a light-hearted way. Most readers would probably turn the page as quickly as possible!

The second title, on the other hand, looks more interesting. Perhaps you have exam nerves (most students do, although not many of them admit this in public), and it is nice to know you are not alone. It is always interesting and reassuring to find people who are in the same situation and how they are dealing with it. Could there be something to calm you down in this article? Is there really a cure for exam nerves? Clearly, there is more chance of the reader being attracted to an article with the second title. This means the second title is more effective. (It is interesting to note, however, that both articles *could* contain almost the same ideas!)

Unfortunately, good titles do not always jump into your mind just when you need them. You will find, though, that with practice, titles will come to you more easily than you may think. Read as many English newspapers or teenage magazines as possible and take note of the titles. Look at some more titles and why they are successful.

Summer Holidays Loom

This is interesting because the word 'holidays' usually means something to look forward to, something positive, the idea of freedom and happiness. The word 'loom' usually gives the feeling of something very large, unknown and unpleasant, dark and threatening, always in the distance but coming slowly closer. Clouds *loom* in the sky. Exams *loom*; you cannot escape from them! So how could a holiday *loom*? This is a good title because it does *not* explain to the reader exactly what the article is about, unlike *How to Prepare for Exams*, and this makes it interesting. In other words, it is an effective title because it creates interest through contrast.

What could an article with this title be about? We all know that, after the first few days, long holidays can become really boring. This article could be to encourage readers to take up a sport or a fitness programme, read a particular book, become involved in charity work and so on, in order to get some benefit from the holiday.

TV: The Teenager's Viewpoint

This is interesting because the letters *T* and *V* have been used as an abbreviation for *television* and then repeated in the extended title.

TV – A Teenage View

This is another variation of the same technique.

Introduction

An effective introduction often starts with a question to involve the reader and encourage him to continue reading. Look at some examples and why they are successful.

Are you one of the many students with exam nerves?

■ The use of the word *you* makes this personal, and the reader automatically relates to himself.
■ The use of the phrase *one of the many* suggests that the reader is not alone and gives a feeling of belonging and familiarity.

An introductory question can often concern a topic such as bullying, academic performance or being overweight, which a student may prefer not to discuss or admit to in public, and this makes it very personal indeed.

Are you a secret TV addict?

You probably know the kind of person who says that TV is rubbish and a waste of time, but who then goes home and watches it every evening. Or friends who say they are far too busy studying to watch TV, but talk about all the characters in every programme!

Another advantage of using a question in the introduction is that it gives no indication of the content of the article. In the example above, the article could be about:

■ informing the reader about the dangers of watching too much TV
■ informing the reader about the educational benefits of watching TV
■ warning readers that too much time in front of the TV screen will affect their schoolwork/exam grades
■ suggesting readers spend their time on more useful hobbies such as sport and reading.

Creating interest in this way makes the reader want to read on to find out what the article *is* about. This makes it a successful introduction.

Are you a self-confessed couch potato?

A *couch potato* is someone who lies on a couch (= sofa, settee), usually in front of the TV and usually with a box of chocolates, a container of popcorn or other fattening snack, for hours without moving.

This introduction is successful for the same reasons as mentioned above.

Try to think what the following examples of possible introductions could be about, remembering that, to be effective, there should be several possible meanings.

Are you so busy working that you have no time for sport?

Do you long to finish your homework quickly so you can collapse in front of the TV screen?

Are you fed up with all the arguments you have heard against television?

Are you dreading the thought of the long, boring holidays?

Transition

Introductions using questions are often followed by a **transition sentence**, which acts as a link between the introduction and the body of the article by preparing the reader for what the article is about. If the topic is of a serious nature, it also marks the beginning of the **formal** language. Here are some introductions from magazine articles, using the question technique. The transition sentences are underlined.

Look, no stress!! Don't we all wish we could say this every day of our lives – and mean it? <u>Nowadays stress seems to be the one word that's on everybody's mind.</u>
(An article on stress)

Looking dull and stressed? Well, don't worry. <u>You need not spend the entire evening in the bathroom.</u>
(An article on health or beauty)

Want to experience the joys of the countryside? <u>There's nothing to beat a canal holiday to take you closer to nature.</u>
(An article about canal holidays)

What does the term 'working woman' evoke? Are women's attitudes changing? Is feminism outdated? <u>Two studies highlight the issues at stake and the changing role of today's women.</u>
(An article about the two studies and their content)

There is no law that prohibits driving while fatigued, <u>but should we take the risk?</u>
(An article on road safety)

Ending

A school magazine article ending should be fairly short and use the same personal style and register as the introduction and transition.

The purpose of the ending could be:

■ to summarise the article
■ to express your own opinion
■ to leave the reader with something to think about.

If the topic of the article can be treated in a light-hearted way, then the style and register will be the same throughout.

If the topic (and, therefore, the body) of the article is serious (and, therefore, formal and impersonal), the ending will be in contrasting style, similar to the introduction and transition, and linking to them. The ending will be direct and personal and will try to involve the reader again.

Look at the endings of the articles outlined in the rest of this unit.

Body of magazine article
Before you begin

The basic ideas for a serious (formal) or a light-hearted (informal) article will be the same, but will need to be adapted to the question according to register. It will be helpful to consider each topic and the different phrases associated with different register *before* the exam. (Refer to the Database of topic-related vocabulary and ideas on pages 231–44.) Before you begin, decide whether you can treat the topic in a light-hearted way or not. It is often *easier* to write a serious article, but *more interesting* to write in a light-hearted way.

■ Types of school magazine article questions

There are several types of school magazine article questions you may be asked to answer in the exam, including the following:

1 Giving your view or opinion/putting forward arguments *for* and *against*
2 Dealing with problems and solutions
3 Giving advice/making suggestions
4 Narrative – sometimes referred to in the question as *an account*

Let's look at each type of article in detail.

1 Giving your view or opinion/putting forward arguments *for* and *against*

Clearly, the instruction words are the same as those used for formal writing and the topics will often be of an apparently serious nature. This type of question involves 'sandwiching' a formal body between an informal introduction and ending. Look at the kind of question that has or could come up:

■ the effects of modern science
■ the effect of cars on the environment
■ single sex schools
■ tourism
■ compulsory competitive team sports at school
■ the importance of appearance.

Let's look at a question based on a past exam paper.

Write an article for your school magazine about the effects of tourism on your country, putting forward your ideas and arguments.

For the **body** of this type of article, begin by writing the first three paragraphs of a views and arguments composition.

★ **Remember**
❏ How much to write in the exam.
❏ Refer to the Database of topic-related vocabulary and ideas to make sure you know all the pros and cons of tourism – and add any of your own ideas.

First paragraph

General introduction explaining the importance of the subject. Make sure you include the following:

■ Time fixers

nowadays/these days/recently/until now/in the past/twenty years ago/in the last five years

■ Generalisations

nearly all/many/a large number of/several

Second paragraph

Put forward *one* side of the issue being argued; for example, the argument *in favour*. Make sure you include the following:

■ Views and arguments phrases

One of the main arguments in favour of … is that
Some people (would) argue that …
It is a fact that …

■ Joining points – addition

Furthermore,/Moreover,/What is more,/Besides,

■ Support phrases

which/this/which means that/this means that/as a result/consequently

Third paragraph

Put forward the other side of the issue being argued; for example, the argument *against*. Make sure you include the following:

■ Joining points – contrast

On the other hand,/However,/Nevertheless,

■ Views and arguments phrases

One of the main arguments against … is that
It can be argued that …
It has been said that …

■ Joining points – addition

Furthermore,/Moreover,/What is more,/Besides,

■ Support phrases

which/this/which means that/this means that/as a result/consequently

From composition to school magazine article

To turn a views and arguments composition into a school magazine article, follow the three steps below.

1 Add a school magazine article introduction without a clear explanation of the topic (to get the reader's attention).

Have you ever been a tourist? Did you consider yourself a menace?

2 At the end of the introductory paragraph, insert the transition sentence to prepare the reader for what is to come.

Do we really want to be flooded with tourists?
Perhaps it's time we stopped to consider the negative aspects of tourism.

3 After the formal controversy paragraphs, write a school magazine article ending.

Next time you go abroad remember to behave the way you would like to see tourists behave here.

Exercise 1   Using the information above, write an article for your school magazine about the effects of tourism on your country, putting forward your ideas and arguments. Then compare your answer with that written by another student and the teacher's comments on page 134.

2 Dealing with problems and solutions

Let's look at a question based on a past exam paper, which deals with the apparently serious topic of pollution.

Many students hope to have their own cars one day but young people are well aware of the problems which cars cause the environment. Write an article for your school magazine explaining how drivers can reduce the impact the car has on the environment.

Is there any way to make this serious subject more interesting?

Look again at the clues in the question: 'Many students hope to have their own cars one day…' Most young people consider being able to drive and owning a car to be an important milestone in their lives. Why? It represents freedom and independence and you can go where you like when you like without relying on parents or public transport. This is the positive, optimistic side of driving.

On the other hand, as the young people in your school are educated and intelligent, they must be 'aware of the problems which cars cause the environment'. This means you must be extra careful not to make your article sound like a lesson or a list of boring facts which the reader has heard before, just as you have, from the teachers at school.

It is important not to begin with anything negative, threatening, pessimistic or too serious. In other words, do not begin with a formal introduction. Do not launch into an attack on cars! If your introduction in any way suggests that cars are bad or that driving should be banned, this will not correspond with the feelings and attitude of the young readers. They may even feel annoyed by the article – *what position are you in*, they may ask, *to point out the bad things about cars?* In other words, readers will not be encouraged to continue reading.

Your task is to make the article factual, but readable and convincing at the same time – to point out the facts in an acceptable way to fellow students.

Now carry out the following steps to write the article.

Step 1

Before you begin, it will help if you list your real feelings a[nd] other words, from a young person's point of view. These a[re] to be shared by most young people. For example:

I don't care if car exhaust causes air pollution; I want to drive:
- *so I can visit my friends whenever I want*
- *because I can't afford public transport*
- *because I'm fed up relying on Mum and Dad to take me everywhere*
- *because I want to be independent.*

My brother drives and so do my parents, so why shouldn't I?

All we hear about these days is the environment.

Step 2

Make sure you begin with a school magazine article introduction. Try to write something the reader can identify with. This may be the complete opposite of the theme of the article, as shown by the list of real feelings above. The introduction of the article may be something like this:

How many of you are counting the days until you can drive?

How many of us are nearly reaching driving age?

Are you looking forward to getting behind the wheel of your very first, very own car – or even taking your Dad's out for a run?

Be honest. How often do you daydream about being at the wheel of an open-topped sports car when you should be revising your Business Studies?

This involves the readers and makes them want to continue reading.

Step 3

Now that you have the readers' attention, you can slowly bring them back to reality by beginning to introduce the serious side of the topic, using a transition sentence:

… but have you ever stopped to consider the down side of driving?

… but how often do we stop to think of the damage cars are doing to the world we live in?

Step 4

Look again at the instruction words in the question. Decide which format of formal writing is required (problems and solutions/suggestions) and plan out the paragraphs.

Step 5

Write an ending to the school magazine article.

So when you do actually get behind you own steering wheel, remember to consider the environment. Happy driving!

Exercise 2 Many students hope to have their own cars one day but young people are very aware of the problems which cars cause to the environment. Using the information and basic plan above, write an article for your school magazine explaining how drivers can reduce the impact their car has on the environment.

3 Giving advice/making suggestions

Most of the topics you may be asked to give advice about are well-known to students. For example, most of the students reading the magazine will already know everything there is to know about healthy eating. The key is to find a light-hearted approach to the topic, as this will make a more interesting and more readable article. Possible topics include:

- how to study for exams
- the benefits of sport
- the benefits of healthy eating
- the dangers of watching too much TV
- how to improve the school
- the benefits of discipline at school
- the benefits of school uniform.

Let's look at a question based on a past exam paper.

★ **Exam tip**
See page 94 for information about how much to write in the exam.

Write an article for your school magazine giving advice and suggestions on the best way to revise for exams.

- Begin with an introduction suitable for a school magazine article but without a clear explanation of the topic (to get the reader's attention).
- Write a transition sentence or two to prepare the reader for what is to come.
- The two or three serious paragraphs should include advice phrases and include the kind of support you would put in a friendly letter. Try to include *we*, for personalising, and perhaps refer to teachers, other students or relevant incidents which may add humour.
- The ending should return to the school magazine article style.

Exercise 3 Using the information above, write the article. Then compare your answer with that written by another student and the teacher's comments on page 135.

4 Narrative

You may be asked to write a narrative (or account) about the following:

- a holiday you have been on recently
- a school trip you went on recently
- a place you visited recently.

Most students go on school trips with the intention of having fun and without much thought for the educational purpose. An account of a school trip or holiday will be very successful if it is written in a humorous, almost conversational style, as if you are actually telling your friends about it. The style of writing should be the same as your mood on the trip.

Do not worry if this seems impossible for you to achieve. Remember that accounts of trips are, basically, descriptive narrative style and, at the same time, school magazine articles. You should include:

■ an introduction which sets the scene by giving an indication of:
  – the weather, the time of year …

  > … *on a cold Saturday morning in November*
  > … *on the last day of the summer term*

  – the number of students (and teachers)
  – the type of transport
  – the general mood or atmosphere
■ a selection of small, probably amusing incidents with no consequence – in other words, interesting but not important
■ a serious section describing the things you saw/places you visited
■ references to members of staff and other students to personalise
■ an ending which says how enjoyable/successful the trip was.

Exercise 4   Using the information above, write an account of a school trip you went on recently. Then compare your answer with that written by another student and the teacher's comments on page 137.

■ *Students' school magazine articles*

Read the following selection of school magazine articles written by different students in response to exam questions, and the comments related to them. The comments in questions 1 and 4 show how the student has written the answer using the structure discussed in this unit.

★ **Note**

These are original articles written by IGCSE students and may still contain minor mistakes. In the comments column, the letter **R** refers to points in the Register unit on pages 182–5, and the letter **G** refers to points in the Grammar unit on pages 186–99. The arrow (→) points to what the text in the article should be changed to or replaced with.

Question 1   Write an article for your school magazine about the effects of tourism on your country, putting forward your ideas and arguments.

A problem called tourism ①

When was the last time you travelled abroad? ② **Did you follow the rules of the place and respect the environment?** ② **If you didn't, then you ought to give it some thought.** ③

Recently, ④ **there has been a great increase in the tourist industry,** ⑤ which has led to various environmental and social problems in **a large number of** ⑥ countries.

It has been argued that ⑦ the tourist industry is one of the largest in the world, yielding a profit that is often enough to support a whole country's economy. **Furthermore,** ⑧ it provides jobs for many young people, **leading to** ⑨ a decrease in the levels of unemployment, **which is the reason for** ⑨ many crimes in society.

On the other hand, ⑩ tourists seem to spoil the beauty of the sites they invade due to littering as well as the fumes pumped out from their cars which leads to the pollution of the place.

Besides, ⑪ some tourists do not respect the cultures and traditions of the places they visit and as a result influence the community and change its habits.

Whenever you travel abroad bear in mind that the way you behave reflects the society you are from – and **you don't want people to think we don't care about the environment, do you?** ⑫

Comments

① Good title – makes you wonder how tourism can be a problem.

② Nice, school magazine article introductory questions

③ Unclear transition → **If not, bear these points in mind next time you go abroad.**

④ Time fixer

⑤ Explaining the problem

⑥ Generalisation

⑦ Controversy (views and arguments) phrase + first point in favour

⑧ Introduction of second point in favour

⑨ Support phrases

⑩ Controversy (views and arguments) phrase + first point against

⑪ Introduction of second point against tourism

⑫ School magazine article ending

General comments

- This is a very good article.
- There is a good introduction using questions to involve the reader.
- The subject is treated in a serious way.
- The student has included a good views and arguments section, with good use of support and formal register.
- The ending contains informal register and addresses the reader directly.

Question 2 Write an article for your school magazine giving advice and suggestions on the best way to revise for exams.

If you have been FILLING BUCKETS with your own sweat at hearing the word 'Exam', GET A GRIP OF YOURSELF! A solution has been found. You will not have to worry about exams any more after reading this page.❶

'Studying' is the keyword.❷ All of us, or at any rate, most of us **study** before exams, but how well we **study** is important. To **study,**❸ **you should be in a state of concentration,**❹ so try to find a quiet, well-lit room to work in. **While you are at it,**❺ you might as well **get rid of** ❻ your mp3 player – it will not help you with grammar!

The best thing you can do is **revision. Revise**❼ your notes every week and ask your teacher if you find anything that is not clear. You might also consider making a **revision timetable, it could be very helpful in sorting out your time.**❽

If I were you, I would not only stick to my notes, but also use other references like course books and exercise books. That will **help in increasing**❾ your knowledge.

If you take some of this advice, you might actually be going into the exam with a smile on your face!❿

Comments

There should be a title, underlined.

❶ Excellent introduction

❷ Short, simple and direct

❸ study: repetition

❹ R1 → you should concentrate

❺ **While you are at it**: good expression = at the same time

❻ R3 **get rid of**: friendly register, phrasal verb. Good

❼ **revision. Revise**: repetition

❽ Weak support – of course a timetable helps to sort out time.

❾ Grammar → **help to increase**

❿ **If you ... face!** Lovely ending. Nice idea – sure to appeal to other students. Good use of exclamation mark to indicate how unlikely this would be

General comments

- This is an excellent article.
- It has a very good introduction, which is effective because it does *not* make clear what the article is about. It is direct and addresses students personally. The use of capital letters (as if shouting) gets the reader's attention.
- The student treats the subject in a light-hearted way to appeal to student readers.
- The student has used good expressions and vocabulary.
- There is a very good ending, using humour to make the reader relax after all the serious advice about studying.

Question 3 Write an article for your school magazine suggesting how to improve school.

Imagine how it would feel if you could change school rules to ones you like! It would be great, but we all know that it is not likely to happen. School rules could be changed and improved, **though,** ❶ to suit students a little, without being overdone. ❷

Take the old grey and white school uniform, common in a lot of schools, but a bit dull, I must say. Students get bored wearing the same clothes for three quarters of the year … who wouldn't? **It would be nice** ❸ if students were allowed to come in whatever they wish as long as it is decent.

Hairstyles, too! We are not allowed to have our hair cut in any way we like. **I think that should be changed.** ❹ How can a haircut affect our schoolwork?

How about ❺ a second recess instead of just one for the whole day? Students are humans, too! They need to have a break every now and then, and not just sit on chairs learning their heads off!

Anyway, these rules should be considered. Even though changing school rules is very limited, some changes might add more life and excitement to school.

Comments

There should be a title.

❶ R8: Use of **though** to replace **but**

❷ Excellent introduction

❸ First suggestion. G2: Correct use of second conditional tense

❹ Second suggestion

❺ Another advice/suggestion phrase

General comments
- A very good article.
- The introduction is direct and easy for students to identify with.
- The subject is treated in a light-hearted way.
- The suggestions are sensible and expressed with respect, which shows the student understands that the article may be read not only by other students, but also by teachers at the school.
- There are not many mistakes of any kind.

Question 4 Write an article for your school magazine about a school trip you went on recently.

Year 11 Trip to Manton Theme Park (1)

After a month of boring revision, followed by another month of tough exams, I can say that most of us needed a good day out. We were lucky because **the weather** (2) on that day was really **hot and sunny.** (2) After a very long and sticky **coach journey,** (3) 32 excited pupils and four anxious teachers finally arrived at the theme park.

As you can imagine, because it was so hot, the water rides had by far the longest queues, so having waited for ages and climbed into the long log thing, we were really **in the mood for a bit of fun.** (4) Due to this fact, when we floated past **Mr Brown and Mrs Smith,** (5) who were still waiting patiently in the queue, we soaked them both with water. **Unfortunately for them the water was rather green and dirty!** (6)

By lunchtime we were starving, but had to face more queues, whether for burgers or pizza and anything cold to drink. We were not surprised to see that **Miss Green** (7) had sensibly brought along sandwiches and a flask of tea and seemed to have enough to share with Mr Brown (who had recovered from the soaking). The most popular ride was The Trojan, a roller coaster which climbs up steeply and then drops you into a deep hole. **Sally** (7) found out that after a meal is perhaps not the best time to try this ride, as **it made her quite sick, and many others complained of headaches.** (8)

The rest of the afternoon was great fun, eating ice-cream, laughing together and going on as many rides as we could. Soon it was time to leave, but as we climbed back onto the coach we realised that **Sarah and Julie were missing!** (7) + (8) After a quick panic, and several calls to mobile phones they were found safe and sound – they had gone to the wrong car park and couldn't find the coach.

After half an hour, the coach left for London with 32 exhausted pupils and four relieved teachers, after a really good day out.

Comments

1. Appropriate title
2. Description of the weather
3. Description of the journey
4. Description of the atmosphere
5. Personalising
6. Humour
7. Personalising
8. Minor incident

General comments

- This is a good descriptive narrative school magazine article.
- The trip is obviously a fun one at the end of the school year, and has been treated in a light-hearted way, using a mixture of formal and friendly register.
- The student has included minor incidents to create interest and personalising to appeal to the student readers.
- There is description of the weather, the journey and the atmosphere.
- The introduction and ending are well written, with the ending referring back to the introduction.

Book reviews

Sometimes one of the composition questions in the exam involves writing a review, usually of a book. A book review has an almost standard layout in English.

◼ How to write a book review

Begin by writing the title of the book and the author as a heading and underline it.

For example:

'Oliver Twist' by Charles Dickens

Introduction

A book I read recently and enjoyed was … (book title) by … (author), …

Next give the **type** of book: romance, drama, thriller, crime, horror, science fiction, classic, contemporary (= modern).

Then **set** the book geographically and historically (in time); for example:

Geographically

- in rural France
- in suburban New York
- in the suburbs of Cairo
- on a remote/desert island
- on a distant planet/star
- in the foothills of the Himalayas

Historically

- at the turn of the last century
- before/after the First World War
- in the twenty-third century
- before/after the revolution
- in pre-historic times
- in the early 1800s
- in the late 50s

… a classic romance set in pre-industrialised (= before the industrial revolution) rural England.

Paragraph 1: the storyline

Do *not* tell the story. Take one sentence to compare how the situation at the end of the book is different from how it was at the beginning of the book.

The novel traces/outlines/sketches/follows/the life of … (character), a … (define), who …

The novel traces the life of Christina, an orphan who, after spending many years living with her aunt, finds herself transported to a man's world when she moves in with her uncle and two cousins, Mark and William.

Paragraph 2: the characters

Begin with a general statement about the characters:

*There are many well-drawn/strong/convincing characters, such as …
(character's name), a (define using the character's occupation/age/
personality/role played), who … and … (repeat for another character).*

*The novel contains a variety of well-drawn characters, such as Tom, the stable
boy who shows that moral values and compassion are more important than
social position, and William, whose imagination and free spirit often cause
tension between him and his traditionally-minded father.*

Then move on to select one particular character to describe slightly more
fully. This may be the central character in the book.

By far the most interesting/appealing to me was … (character's name, etc.).

Why do we like a certain character in a book or film more than another? It is
usually either because this character reminds us of ourselves in the way he (or
she) reacts, or because the character is totally the opposite of us, someone we
would like to be (if we dared!). It could also be because of the situation this
particular character is in. It is important to explain the connection you feel
with the character at this point. Look at the following examples:

*By far the most appealing character to me, though, was …, because I was
able to identify with him, especially the way he felt when/about …*

*The character that made the most impression on me was … because I was
able to relate to her, especially when/the way/how she …*

*By far the most interesting character to me, though, was … . I admired the
way he dealt with the situation when …*

The character I most admired, however, was … because	*he*	*represents*	*justice.*
The character I admired most, however, was … because	*she*	*symbolises* *stands for*	*freedom.* *compassion.*

Paragraph 3: memorable incident

This is the most difficult paragraph in the book review. *It is a good idea to
choose a suitable incident before the exam.* Here are some tips about how to
make your choice.

■ Remember that the reader may not be familiar with your selected novel. In
 other words, your reader may not have read the novel you are reviewing.
 Therefore, the incident should have a relevance of its own.
■ Do not include reference to a large number of characters. As each character
 needs to be defined, and this takes time and space, including too many
 would be confusing to the reader.

  ✖ *Mary, Jack's younger sister, decides to take revenge on her step-sister, Jane,
   whose husband John is blackmailing Mark, Mary's husband …*

■ Do not refer to earlier events that the reader will not be aware of.

✖ *James wants to help Rachel because of what her father had said/done to him.*

Can you be sure that the reader knows *what* it was that Rachel's father had said or done to James? If not, you will need to explain it and there is neither space nor time to do so in the exam. Begin this section with a phrase such as:

One of the most memorable moments in the novel was when …
One of the incidents I shall never forget was when …
One of the incidents which made a lasting impression on me was when …
I think one of the best parts in the book is when …

Paragraph 4: recommendation

In the final paragraph, you should give your overall opinion of the book and support your opinion. Do *not* say:

✖ *I liked the book.*
✖ *It was a nice book.*
✖ *You should read the book.*
✖ *I think you will like this book.*

Who exactly do you think the book is suitable for? Teenagers? All age groups? Romantics? Those with a sense of adventure? *Why* do you think the book is suitable for that particular group of people?

Anyone with a taste for adventure would certainly enjoy the fast moving action of …

The use of imagination in this novel would definitely …   }   *appeal to a wide range of ages.*
cross the age barrier.
close the generation gap.

The description of rural settings and the weaving of complicated relationships make this novel a must for all romantics.

This novel, as with all classics, has a message of relevance today.

What is the message?

The triumph of good over evil.
The power of love.
The importance of friendship.
Happiness cannot be found through wealth alone.
The mystery of life.

Exercise 1   Using the information given above, write a review of a book you have read recently, saying why you enjoyed it.

READING

Section 5 sets out the different tasks which you will find in the reading exam. Unit 1 includes examples of each type of exam question, to enable you to familiarise yourself with them, together with hints on how to approach the questions and suggested answers. Unit 2 then looks in detail at the techniques you need to summarise a reading passage, and explains the importance of skim reading. The techniques are applied to fully worked examples of four different types of summary and exercises are included to give you practice and build your confidence.

Overview

The reading passages are found in Parts 1 and 2 of Paper 1 (Core) and Paper 2 (Extended). In the reading part of the exam, Core candidates will have four texts to answer questions from, and Extended candidates will have five texts.

■ Exercises 1 and 2

The texts for exercises 1 and 2 are the same for both levels, but there are more questions to answer for each text in the Extended syllabus. The texts are usually taken from a brochure or an advertisement or a pamphlet.

Answering the questions

- Read the introduction to the exercise. Look at the passage. Notice the title, the illustrations and the headings to understand what the text is about and how the information is arranged. Do not read the text.
- Read the first question and underline the key word(s). In a continuous passage, the answers come chronologically (the answer to question 3 comes after the answer to questions 1 and 2). Sometimes an answer may appear in the introduction to the passage. In a passage with headed paragraphs, you will need to refer to the relevant paragraph.
- Skim read (see Unit 2) to find the answers. Ignore any vocabulary you do not understand. Sometimes a date or name will be referred to in a question and will be easy to find in the text. Your answers should be brief – sometimes just one word. Complete sentences are *not* required.

Look at an example Exercise 1 question from a Core level reading paper on the following pages.

WITH THE SEA ON YOUR DOORSTEP, A LARGE FLEET OF BOATS TO CHOOSE FROM, AND A TEAM OF EXPERIENCED INSTRUCTORS, THE OUTDOOR ACTIVITIES CENTRE IS THERE JUST FOR YOU!

COURSES AVAILABLE:

DINGHY SAILING

Our boats are chosen carefully to provide a wide range of safe and exciting learning opportunities. Instructors will take you through the basics of rigging, launching and sailing.

CATAMARAN SAILING

For those with little or no experience, this course is a good introduction to this fast and exciting form of sailing. If weather conditions are favourable, students should be able to handle a catamaran single-handedly during the course.

Cost for each course (age 16 years and over):
£165 non residential
£180 residential

CANOEING & KAYAKING

The Outdoor Activities Centre is the ideal venue for kayaking. With the sea close at hand, our one-day course will introduce the skills of kayaking at sea. There will be an opportunity to try a variety of different canoes and kayaks and to take part in a short kayak sea journey.

WINDSURFING

Our centre runs a JUNIOR WINDSURFING CLUB on Monday and Wednesday evenings during the summer season and is open to anyone until they are 18 years old. Aimed at those who already have some windsurfing experience (level one certificate), this club aims to give young windsurfers the opportunity to progress within a safe and exciting environment.
Cost: £7 per session or £6 per session if four sessions are booked in advance

SKIING AND SNOWBOARDING

This centre has three ski slopes – each surface is easy to ski on and soft to fall on. The slopes have ski lifts, are floodlit and are situated inside a hangar, offering an ideal learning environment whatever the weather.

FIRST AID COURSES

Our first aid courses are ideal for anyone concerned with outdoor sports. Our trainers are also sports instructors so they make sure that the first aid training given is always relevant for your sport or situation.

Exercise 1	Read the advertisement about courses at the Outdoor Activities Centre, and then answer the questions below.

  a How long does it take to complete the introduction to sea kayaking course? ☐1

  b Who can join the Junior Windsurfing Club? ☐1

  c How much does it cost someone staying at the Centre to learn to sail? ☐1

  d How can a junior windsurfer save money? ☐1

  e Why wouldn't a skiing lesson at the centre be cancelled in bad weather? ☐1

  f What other useful experience do the first aid instructors have? ☐1

  [Total: 6]

a) <u>How long</u> does it take to <u>complete</u> the <u>introduction</u> to the <u>sea kayaking</u> course?

Underline key words. Refer to the paragraph on 'canoeing and kayaking'.

d) How can a <u>junior windsurfer</u> <u>save money</u>?

Refer to the paragraph on 'windsurfing'.

■ Exercise 3

This uses different texts for each level, and requires you to transfer information from the passage onto a form.

- The answers may not come chronologically.
- Do not read the passage.

Answering the questions

Look at the following example of an Exercise 3 question from an Extended level paper.

Exercise 3	Read the article about a special educational residential course in Toronto, Canada. Imagine you are Kim, and complete the form on the following page (page 145).

Kim Jones is 16 and attends ABC International School, 321 Town Road, Antananarivo, the capital of Madagascar (situated in the Indian Ocean, and the world's fifth largest island). The school's email address is ABC@education.org.mg, and its office telephone number is 867300 (putting code 261 before it if dialing from outside Madagascar). In an emergency, when the school is closed, the school secretary, Ms Smith, may be contacted on 867324. Kim's school has recently been lucky to win an *amazing* prize in a competition. The prize is for a group of students (plus two of their teachers) to visit Toronto, Canada, to attend a Special Educational Residential Course – entirely free of charge. They will be staying at the Course Centre during their visit.

Twenty students at Kim's school (including Kim) – ten boys and ten girls – will attend the course, and they will be accompanied by their teachers Ms A. Roma and Mr V. Zachariah. The students will be accommodated in pairs, with boys and girls occupying separate accommodation blocks. The course will last for four days, from Monday 17 July until Thursday 20 July inclusive, but because of the long journey involved the group will need to arrive one day before the start of the course, departing after breakfast on 21 July. They will fly out from Madagascar's main airport, and the number of the flight they have booked is MM001. The daily programme for the course will begin at 8.15 each morning. At the weekend, lunch is served at 1.00 pm, but is one hour earlier on all other days. The course finishes each day at 4.00 pm and then there is a relaxation period of one hour, and study preparation of one and a half hours before dinner.

There are facilities available for the group to relax, and there will be one afternoon of a choice of organized activities. In Kim's group most of the students are interested in drawing and painting, and table tennis and/or performing plays; the rest enjoy swimming and going for long walks. At the course Centre there is a swimming pool (but it is open on Saturdays and Sundays only). One of the days of the course will involve a tour of the historic sights of Toronto, with a packed lunch provided; transport by bus can be supplied if requested. Eleven of the students in the group are strict vegetarians, and one of them is seriously allergic to wheat. Just over a third of the group speak Malagasy as their 'main' language when they are back at home with their families; the main languages spoken by the others are (in alphabetical order): Afrikaans, Arabic, Dhivehi, French, Greek, Kreol, Mandarin, Setswana, Spanish, Turkish and Urdu. All the students in Kim's group are used to talking to their teachers and to each other in English at school, and they are all studying it for an IGCSE examination.

So that everything will run smoothly, the Course Centre organizers need Kim's school to give them some information before arrival, and the task has been given to Kim.

Read the form very carefully and make sure you provide the *exact* information needed.

1 If the form asks for 'block capitals' you must write in **capital letters**. Check where they are to be used. In this example, it says 'in this section'.

2 If the form asks for a postal address 'including country', make sure you include the country – it may be separate from the address in the text.

3 With telephone numbers, check whether you should include a **code**.

4 When you need to choose dates or times, check the information carefully. Sometimes the answer may seem obvious, but further information later in the text may change the answer. For example, the form asks for 'Duration of stay (give dates)'. The text reads:

The course will last for four days, from Monday 17 July until Thursday 20 July inclusive, but because of the long journey involved the group will need to arrive one day before the start of the course, departing after breakfast on 21 July.

In this example, if you wrote your answer as *Monday 17 July to Thursday 20 July*, you would be wrong. According to the information which follows these dates, the correct answer should be *Sunday 16 July to Friday 21 July*.

5 If the form asks you to tick (✓), then tick.

6 If the form asks you to circle, then draw a circle round the answer.

Finally, if the form asks you to 'delete as necessary', this means you should cross out all the answers except the correct one.

TORONTO COURSE CENTRE – INFORMATION SHEET
Complete all sections, and send to us at 1550 Helligan St., Toronto, Canada

1

Section A   (Use block capitals in this section.)

Name of person completing this form ....

Name of organization..

2

Postal address (including country) ....

....

3

Contact telephone number out of hours (in emergency) ....

4

Duration of stay (give dates) ....

Student accommodation required:

number of female rooms ....

number of male rooms ....

Section B
To help us plan your leisure time

5

Tick the **three** activities at the Centre most suitable for your group during your stay

Art ☐   Basketball ☐   Dance ☐   Drama ☐   Pottery ☐   Swimming ☐   Walking ☐

Suggest one other activity not listed above

....

Which one language should the tour guide use with your group during your tour of Toronto?

Arabic ☐   English ☐   French ☐   Spanish ☐   Other (please state) ....

Section C
To help our catering staff

6

For each meal, circle the better start time to suit your group
  Lunch: 12.00   13.00
  Dinner: 17.45   18.45

Specify any special dietary requirements...

....

Section D
Write **one sentence** of 12–20 words to tell us what you are most looking forward to during your time in Toronto.

....

....

[Total: 8]

■ Exercises 4 and 5

Exercise 4 at both levels requires you to read a text and make notes from it. At Core level, the text for exercise 4 is used for the summary writing in exercise 5. At Extended level, the text for exercise 4 is different from the text to be summarised in exercise 5.

- The headings for making notes are given to you.
- The answers may not come chronologically.

Answering the questions

Look at the following example of an Exercise 4 question from a Core level paper.

Read the introduction to the exercise so you know what the passage is about. Then, before you read the article, look at the *question* on page 147 to learn what points you need to find. Code the points *a*, *b*, *c*, or *1*, *2*, *3* and mark them next to the passage as you read it. (This has been done for you on this example.)

Exercise 4   Read the article below about the effects of the El Niño storms on sea lions, and then complete the note-taking exercise which follows. (Sea lions are large seals that live in the Pacific Ocean, but can move on land.)

SEA LIONS SEEK REFUGE FROM EL NIÑO

In a normal winter, this is the slow season for the Friends of the Sea Lion Marine Mammal Centre at Laguna Beach, California – a time to prepare for the busy weeks of spring and summer, when the bulk of the youngest of the sad-eyed creatures come ashore in need of nurturing, food and rest. But this is an El Niño winter and it seems nothing is as it should be, on land or at sea.

a
a
Around this time last year, the Centre had seven sea lions to care for and eventually release. Today there are 73, most of them weak and underweight young pups that have been beached and battered by the storms of El Niño.

c
c
c
Filled to capacity, the Centre stopped taking in new sea lions on 4 February and eventually closed its gift shop because it needed the space for its overflowing population. The Centre's office has been converted into a special care unit, housing 13 of the smallest and weakest pups. To answer the telephone, the staff members sometimes have to push a sea lion off it first!

a
Often when the sea lions come in they have to be wrapped in blankets because they are cold and skinny. Once they begin recovering, they can be moved into the pools.

b b
b
El Niño, the huge body of warm water in the Pacific that has altered weather conditions around the world, has harmed the sea lions and their cousins in several different ways. It has made the winds and the waves worse, the ocean currents stronger. And the waters off California are five degrees warmer than normal, so much of the fish population that the sea lions rely on has left the area in search of colder waters.

a | To feed their pups, the mothers have had to spend more time and energy searching for food. In a normal year about 1500 seals and sea lions end up on the beaches of California. This year the prediction is for at least twice that number.

But last Sunday, El Niño did not seem so big and bad. Last Sunday was a release day. The Centre released four pups back into the ocean, including the first two taken in during this long season of storms. The Centre's staff and volunteers loaded the sea lions into pet carriers and drove them to a beach a little farther away than normal. The beach that the Centre usually uses to

c | release the animals is under water, another victim of El Niño.

The cages were carried across the sand by about a hundred beachgoers and put down a few yards from the roaring surf. As the young sea lions disappeared under a big wave and bobbed up again a few moments later, everyone cheered from the beach.

You are preparing to give a short talk to your class about the effects of El Niño.

On the notepad below, make **two** short notes under each heading as a plan for your presentation. Do not use complete sentences. (An example is given under the first heading.)

---

a   **Effects of El Niño on the sea lions**

- *weak pups* ....
- ....
- ....

b   **Effects of El Niño on the weather and ocean**

- ....
- ....

c   **Effects of El Niño on the Sea Lion Marine Mammal Centre**

- ....
- ....

[Total: 6]

You may find more points than you are asked for. Only give the number asked for. When you find the answer, try to rewrite the meaning in your own words if you can, as this shows the examiner that you have *understood* what you have read. Your answers should be short and should not be complete sentences. For example, you read:

> To feed their pups, the mothers have had to spend more time and energy searching for food.

Your answer for 'Effects of El Niño on the sea lions' might be:

Hard for mothers to find food for pups.

You read:

> The beach that the Centre usually uses to release the animals is under water, another victim of El Niño.

Your answer for 'Effects of El Niño on the Sea Lion Marine Mammal Centre' might be:

(Have to) drive further to put seals back in sea.

Now look at an example of an Exercise 5 question from the same Core level reading paper.

Exercise 5

Imagine that you have made your presentation to the class in exercise 4. Now your teacher wants you to follow this up with a summary for homework.

Look at your notes in exercise 4 above. Using the ideas in your notes, write a summary about the effects of the El Niño storms.

Your summary should be one paragraph of no more than 70 words. You should use your own words as much as you can.

[Total: 4]

The following unit looks in detail at how to answer questions that involve writing a summary.

Summaries

Before we begin to look at how to approach a summary, it is important to understand what a summary is and to realise that we use summaries in many everyday situations.

Imagine you are reading an article in a magazine in your own language. As you seem very interested in it and because I cannot understand your language, I ask you what it is about. Of course you are not going to translate the whole thing, so your brain quickly sorts out what bits I might find interesting, and reorganises them so that you can then pass on the information using words I can understand immediately. The words you choose and the way you express the ideas contained in the article are, in fact, your summary. As a result, I am better informed, without having to take the time and make the effort to work through a passage in a foreign language.

Imagine you went to see a popular film at the local cinema. Later, you want to tell your friend about it. Again, you pick the parts you think will appeal to your friend and also give him an idea of the basic story of the film. In other words, you summarise it for him. This may even save your friend from having to go to the cinema himself; if your summary does not make the film sound interesting to your friend, then he may decide not to go and watch it!

We do exactly the same thing when telling someone about a conversation we have had with someone else. We certainly do not repeat the conversation word for word exactly as it happened, nor do we always use the words used in the actual conversation. We also select *what* we say depending on *who* we say it to. Do you tell your mother everything your friend said to you at a party? I doubt it!

A summary allows you to understand quickly and easily a passage which may be long and may contain difficult or specialised vocabulary.

■ How to approach a summary question

Stage 1

- **Read the question**. What exactly do you need to summarise? How many words do you have to use? Look at any pictures or headings for clues about the content of the passage.
- As you read, **underline the key words** in the question. For example, from the exam question 'Write a summary about the cause and extent of the flooding', you would probably identify *cause* and *effect* as key words.
- **Code the key words** if there is more than one. Choose whichever coding method you prefer: either *a, b,* or *1, 2,* or the first letter of the key word(s). In the above example, and depending on which coding method you choose, *cause* will be coded *a* or *1* or *c*; *extent* will be coded *b* or *2* or *e.*

Stage 2

- **Skim read the passage** paragraph by paragraph. Pick out relevant points and **underline** them. At the same time, use your code to identify each point at the side of the text so that you can find it easily. Continuing with the above example, every time you found a reference to *cause* in the passage, you would write *a* or *1* or *c* next to the text. Every time you found a reference to *extent* in the passage, you would write *b* or *2* or *e* next to the text. See pages 146–7 for an example of where this has been done.

■ Sometimes the points related to each key word can be scattered throughout the passage. Coding in this way helps you to locate the relevant points easily.

Stage 3

■ On a blank page of the exam question paper (or underneath the summary text if there is space), **write a heading for each key word** you are looking for (if there is more than one).
■ Take each of your underlined points and **rewrite it in your own words** under the relevant heading.
■ Do not try to translate each word and replace it with another. Instead, try to write down what you *understand* from the sentence.

Stage 4

■ Group together any points that are similar, and then number the points according to how important you think they are, with 1 for the most important.

Stage 5

■ Compare how many points you have found with the number of words asked for in the question. If there are too many points:
   – check that no idea has been repeated
   – try to connect similar ideas
   – drop any point that seems unnecessary, or that you do not fully understand.
■ If you do not have many points, consider using generalisations and time fixers.

Stage 6

■ Write your summary.

■ What is skim reading?

The passages to summarise in the exam may be long and there is not enough time to read every word, so you must be good at skim reading. You do this all the time in your own language. Imagine looking at a noticeboard to find out which room to go to for your physics class. There are many other notices on the board, but your eye quickly skims over most of them, deciding they are not what you are looking for, until it sees the relevant notice. In the same way, you should be able to look *quickly* at a paragraph and decide what it is about and whether it is relevant. *Many paragraphs in the passage will not contain any points relevant to the key words in the question.* Skim reading allows you to recognise and quickly pass over paragraphs which contain no relevant points so that you have more time to concentrate on relevant paragraphs.

Skim reading is a skill which needs to be practised *before* the exam.

■ Different types of summary

Not every summary is the same. This unit looks at four different types of summary:

- standard summary
- relationship summary
- history summary
- structure summary.

■ Standard summaries

Worked example of a standard summary

Let's work through a standard summary question adapted from a past exam paper.

Stage 1

First **read the question** and **underline the key words**.

Read the following article ('Hitting the right button') about boys and computers. Then write a summary of the article explaining how computers can help boys. Your summary should be one paragraph of no more than 100 words. You should use your own words as much as you can.

Take time to analyse the question carefully before you begin to read the passage. The question does *not* ask you to write a summary of the whole passage, but to summarise certain points *only*. Look carefully at the **key words**.

- *computers*: the passage may refer to other things which help boys. These should *not* be included in your summary.
- *help*: the passage may refer to computers being a *bad* influence on boys. This should not be included in your summary.
- *boys*: the passage may refer to girls, or how computers help girls. No reference to girls should be included in your summary.

Hitting the right button

It has been found that in some countries, achievement in some subjects at school is not always as good for boys as it is for girls. It is possible that using computers may be a way to solve this problem.

Many boys seem to have a natural liking for computers, but it can often be hard to leave the screen and concentrate on work the teacher wants them to do.

As computers are becoming more and more important in the world of education today, it is natural to assume that computers can help greatly with boys who do not do well at school and need to raise their general educational standards. There is growing research that shows studying ICT (Information Communications Technology) is very motivating for boys in particular. Many boys appear to be more confident than girls in using it, and they tend to use computers more frequently, especially at home.

Researchers at universities now think that it could be a really good way of re-engaging under-achieving boys in the learning process, and teachers have indicated that it does work. They have found that, although lots of boys do not seem to like writing in the classroom, when they use a computer they are more willing to compose longer pieces of writing and use different styles. The issue of unintelligible handwriting is no longer a problem, either, as the neatness and presentation standards rise when boys use a computer to print out their work.

Many boys welcome the 'hands-on' approach of computers. However, researchers and teachers need to be careful that boys don't just 'cut and paste' things that they have found on the internet, but haven't read, and hand it in as a completed assignment. Some boys over-estimate how good they are and think they can do things without any effort. They need to develop proper research skills and make their written work more structured. Indeed, everyone needs to understand how to use computers to get the best results. They should always be clear about the aims and outcomes of the classroom work they are being asked to do. If they don't see the point, then they are less inclined to make an effort.

Some boys take short cuts, or look at internet sites they haven't been asked to look at. They may not plan or think carefully about their work, or they may try to finish their work quickly. This tendency is not going to be completely cured by using computers. One way to get boys to concentrate properly on the work they have been asked to do may be to encourage them to use their computers at home. However, they also need to be set tasks that are interesting and relevant to them.

As in all things, the interaction between the student, the teacher and the computer is crucial.

Stage 2

Begin by skim reading the passage, paragraph by paragraph, looking for anything that relates to *how computers can help boys.* Underline any relevant point you find and mark it at the side of the text.

It has been found that in some countries, achievement in some subjects at school is not always as good for boys as it is for girls. It is possible that using computers may be a way to solve this problem.

As you look quickly at this paragraph, you should notice generalisation words, such as *some countries, some subjects* and also *this problem.* These words tell you that this paragraph is a general introduction to the topic and does not contain anything relevant to the question. There is no need to waste time reading it in detail. Now read on:

Many boys seem to have a natural liking for computers, but it can often be hard to leave the screen and concentrate on work the teacher wants them to do.

In this paragraph, you see the words *boys* and *computers,* but nothing connected to *helping* boys. This is just an extension of the introduction. Now read on:

As computers are becoming more and more important in the world of education today, it is natural to assume that computers can help greatly with boys who do not do well at school and need to raise their general educational standards. There is growing research that shows studying ICT (Information Communications Technology) is very motivating for boys in particular. Many boys appear to be more confident than girls in using it, and they tend to use computers more frequently, especially at home.

As you skim read this paragraph you should quickly see the key words *computers can help greatly with boys*. These are definitely relevant, so they should be underlined. At the same time, you should indicate at the side of the text wherever you find a relevant point. Here, for example, you could write the letter *h* (for 'help') at the side of the text, next to the relevant point.

Continue skim reading the paragraph, looking for any more relevant points. You see the words *very motivating for boys*. Perhaps you do not understand the word *motivating*. If it means something *positive*, it will be a relevant point. Read the previous sentence again. *Motivating* is a result of ICT, which is an example of how computers *help* boys. So *motivating* is something *positive* connected to *computers* and *boys*. It *is* a relevant point. Underline it, and mark it at the side of the text.

You also see the word *confident*, which clearly refers to boys and in a positive way. What are boys confident about? Read the sentence again. Boys are more confident *in using it*. Make sure you understand what 'it' refers to – here it is ICT, so this *is* another relevant point. Underline it, and mark it at the side of the text. Finally, in this paragraph we see the positive words *they tend to use computers more frequently, especially at home*. Who does *they* refer to? Read the sentence again. The answer is *boys*, so this is a relevant point. Underline it, and mark it at the side of the text. Now read on:

> Researchers at universities now think that it could be a really good way of re-engaging under-achieving boys in the learning process, and teachers have indicated that it does work. They have found that, although lots of boys do not seem to like writing in the classroom, when they use a computer they are more willing to compose longer pieces of writing and use different styles. The issue of unintelligible handwriting is no longer a problem, either, as the neatness and presentation standards rise when boys use a computer to print out their work.

This paragraph contains both positive and negative ideas. As you skim read you notice the phrases *under-achieving boys, boys do not seem to like writing, unintelligible handwriting* and *a problem*, which are all negative. It seems there is nothing about *helping boys* here. However, you also find contrasting, *positive* ideas, *connected to computers*, introduced by *although*, such as *when they use a computer they are more willing, longer pieces of writing, different styles* and *neatness and presentation standards rise when boys use a computer*. The 'problem' is described as *no longer a problem*. All of these phrases are clearly relevant, and should be underlined and marked at the side of the text. Now read on:

> Many boys welcome the 'hands-on' approach of computers. However, researchers and teachers need to be careful that boys don't just 'cut and paste' things that they have found on the internet, but haven't read, and hand it in as a completed assignment. Some boys over-estimate how good they are and think they can do things without any effort. They need to develop proper research skills and make their written work more

★ **Remember**
Relevant points can often come together in the same paragraph.

★ **Remember**
❑ Underline each point.
❑ Mark each point at the side of the text (see pages 146–7 for an example).

structured. Indeed, everyone needs to understand how to use computers to get the best results. They should always be clear about the aims and outcomes of the classroom work they are being asked to do. If they don't see the point, then they are less inclined to make an effort.

As you skim read, you notice that this paragraph also includes the words *boys* and *computers*. The first sentence tells us that boys like (*welcome*) computers, which is something *positive*. The next sentence begins with the word However, and this indicates a *contrast* with the previous sentence. In other words, it indicates something *negative*. Just by looking at the text, without even reading it, you can see the negative words *don't* and *haven't*. Skim reading the paragraph, you find more negative ideas: *teachers need to be careful* (this is a warning), *without any effort* and *less inclined to make an effort*. None of these ideas relates to computers *helping*, so there are no relevant points here.

Now read on:

> Some boys take short cuts, or look at internet sites they haven't been asked to look at. They may not plan or think carefully about their work, or they may try to finish their work quickly. This tendency is not going to be completely cured by using computers. One way to get boys to concentrate properly on the work they have been asked to do may be to encourage them to use their computers at home. However, they also need to be set tasks that are interesting and relevant to them.

The beginning of this paragraph also contains negative ideas. You can see *haven't, may not plan* and *not going to be completely cured by using computers*. As you skim read you notice *concentrate properly* and *encourage*, both positive ideas and connected to *using computers at home*. This is a relevant point. Underline it and mark it at the side of the text.

Now read on:

> As in all things, the interaction between the student, the teacher and the computer is crucial.

Clearly there is nothing relevant to the question in this short, final paragraph.

Having now read the complete passage, underlining the relevant points and marking them at the side of the text, it is time to move on to the next stage.

Stage 3

The next stage of the summary task involves explaining the points you have found using your own words, in order to show that you understand what they mean.

Go back to the first point you underlined and read it again. What do you *understand*? Now try to write the point in your own words.

■ **ICT is very motivating for boys**
This could be rewritten as:

    ✔ *boys are more interested in things which involve using computers*

■ **boys appear to be more confident than girls in using ICT**
This could be rewritten as:

    ✔ *boys are confident about using computing technology*

★ **Remember**
Not every paragraph will contain relevant points.

★ **Remember**
Do not try to translate each word and change it with another. This will sound very artificial. Instead, write down what you understand from the original phrase or sentence as a whole.

- boys use computers more frequently, especially at home
  This could be rewritten as:

  ✔ *boys often use computers at home*
    (in other words, from choice, because they enjoy it)

- boys are ... more willing to compose longer pieces of writing
  This could be rewritten as:

  ✔ *boys are happier to write more*

- use different styles
  Some points, like this one, will be very simple and will not need to be changed into your own words.

- unintelligible handwriting is no longer a problem
  Is there a word that you don't understand? Does the rest of the sentence makes sense without the difficult word? If so, ignore it.
    This could be rewritten as:

  ✔ *they do not need to worry about (bad) handwriting*

- neatness and presentation standards rise when boys use a computer
  Try to remove abstract nouns to show you understand them.

  ✔ *using a computer encourages boys to try harder to make their work look good*

- one way to get boys to concentrate properly ... may be to encourage them to use their computers at home
  This could be rewritten as:

  ✔ *using computers at home could improve boys' concentration*

Stage 4

The next step is to group any points that are similar, and then number the points according to how important you think they are, with 1 for the most important.

1 *boys are more interested in things which involve using computers*
3 *boys are confident about using computing technology*
2 *boys often use computers at home*
5 *boys are happier to write more*
6 *boys do not need to worry about (bad) handwriting*
4 *use different styles*
7 *using a computer encourages boys to try harder to make their work look good*
8 *using computers at home could improve boys' concentration*

Stage 5

Now consider the number of points you have and the number of words the question asks you to write.

- In an Extended paper, candidates are asked to write 'no more than' a certain number of words (usually 100). It is important to count the number of words you write carefully, as the examiner will count up to the number of words asked for in the question and then cross through the rest. You will not lose marks for writing more words than required. However, you *will* lose marks if you include any *points* in the extra words, as they will not be read.

■ In a Core paper, candidates are asked to write 'about' a certain number of words. You will need approximately ten lines to write 100 words.

■ In this summary, you have found eight points: eight points in ten lines is comfortable.

■ If you had found ten points, you would need to combine ideas, or perhaps select some less important points to drop at this stage to avoid writing more words than asked for.

■ If, on the other hand, you had found only four points, you would need to use generalisations and joining points to reach the required number of words. Do not include your own ideas or other irrelevant material in an attempt to make more words.

You will be given a maximum of 4 marks for finding relevant points (one mark for each point) and a maximum of 4 marks for the way you write your summary. However, if you write 100 words and do *not* include any relevant points, you will not be given any marks for language!

Stage 6

Now write the summary. Your summary should *not* contain:

■ any kind of introduction

■ any direct speech (words inside speech marks " " said by people in the passage)

■ repetition of words or ideas

■ exact figures, numbers or statistics

■ anything that is not clearly stated in the passage, especially your own ideas, even if you cannot find many points in the passage.

Consider the different ways you could express your points and link them to the next points:

★ **Remember**
There are many possible ways to write your summary.

1 The majority of
   Many
   Most
} boys tend to be interested in something if it involves (using) computers,

2 because they often } choose to spend (their free) time on computers } in their free time
                       use computers   outside the classroom
                                                                           at home

3 and they are } confident about using
                 not frightened by
                 not afraid to use
} computing technology.

4 (Using) Computers give(s) boys confidence because they do not need to worry about their handwriting.

5 This means they are } happy
                         keen
} to write more

6 *and makes them keen to use a variety of styles*

7   to   ⎱ *make their work look good.*
          ⎰ *give their work a better appearance.*
            improve the appearance of their work.

8 *Giving boys work to do on the computer at home may improve their concentration.*

Example answers

There is no correct answer for a summary. Once you have grouped the similar points together, you can choose the order in which they should be included. Look at two possible versions of our example summary:

First version

Grouping the ideas in the order given above: (1,2,3) (4,5,6,7) (8)

The majority of boys tend to be more interested in something if it involves computers, because they often choose to spend their free time on computers and are not afraid of computing technology. Computers give boys confidence because they do not need to worry about their handwriting. This means they are happy to write more and makes them keen to use a variety of styles to improve the appearance of their work. It has been suggested that giving boys interesting work to do on the computer at home may improve their concentration.

(92 words)

Second version

Grouping the ideas in the following order: (4,5,6,7) (1,2,3) (8)

Computers tend to give boys confidence because they do not need to worry about their handwriting. This means they are happy to write more and as a result they are keen to use a variety of styles to make their work look better. Most boys tend to be more interested in something if it involves computers, because they often choose to spend their free time on computers and are confident about using computing technology. It has been suggested that giving boys interesting work to do on the computer at home may improve their concentration.

(94 words)

Exercise 1   Write a summary of the article explaining how computers can help boys (see pages 151–2), grouping the ideas together in the following order: (2,3,1) (8) (4,5,6,7).

Then compare what you have written with the suggested answer on page 249.

■ 'Relationship' summaries

In a 'relationship' summary you are asked to trace the *development of the relationship*, often between a person and an animal. In this kind of summary, many students make the mistake of including irrelevant facts by concentrating on the events that take place instead of the *significance* of those events.

Any relationship you have with a friend, your father or your sister involves give and take and sacrifice. If you want to develop a friendship with someone, you are willing to do things for this person that you would not consider doing for anyone else; you may even change the way you dress or the way you speak in order to please this person. Likewise, in these summaries, you should look for the way the person's life *changes* and what sacrifices the person makes for the sake of the animal.

Whenever *a change takes place*, you will need to include sentence structures such as:

To begin with, ... but then ...
In the past ... but now ...

At first ... but as the relationship (has) }
developed
intensified
strengthened
grown/(grew)

To illustrate change, you will need to show comparison between:

■ where the animal lived at the beginning and end of the relationship
■ feeding arrangements at the beginning and end of the relationship
■ attitude towards the animal at the beginning and end of the relationship.

Worked example of a relationship summary
Stage 1

Read this question based on a past exam paper and underline the key words.

★ **Remember**
Underline the key words in the question before you begin.

Read the following article and write a summary of the development of the relationship between Rocky and Michael. Your summary should be one paragraph of no more than 100 words.

Rocky the owl

The helpless baby owl was delivered in a small cardboard box lined with an old towel. She was only about 20 minutes old and was no bigger than a hamster, but I knew that in less than a year this untidy, off-white bundle of feathers would grow into one of the largest and most powerful birds on earth.

Young chicks are often brought to my owl rescue centre, but this unexpected arrival was a completely new experience, for it was a European eagle owl. With a wingspan of almost two metres, these are the largest owls in existence. Adult females, larger than males, stand nearly 70cm high and need lots of food. Unlike a standard owl diet of mice and voles, these eagle owls will eat dogs, foxes and even small deer in the wild. It was clear that this chick was going to be quite a handful.

Whenever very young chicks are brought to the centre, we try to place them with other families as quickly as possible. Despite their wise image, owls are not the cleverest of birds – to be brutally honest, they are surprisingly dim. A female never knows how many youngsters she has in her family. It's essential that young owls are adopted by their own species, for they take the identity of their foster parents. This process is called 'imprinting' and it happens during the first few weeks of an owl's life.

The baby eagle owl that was brought to me had been abandoned by her mother immediately after she was born and none of my contacts had a breeding pair of eagle owls at the right stage to take on such a young chick. Most owl keepers do their best to avoid this situation because once an owl becomes used to humans, it is then too tame to release. With no alternative, I had to hand-rear the chick, and so began our unique relationship.

Although eagle owls are nocturnal mammals, spending the daytime sleeping, I persuaded the chick to eat during the day and sleep at night. Every two hours I had to cut up food and feed the owlet thin slivers of meat small enough to swallow whole. Within six days I had been completely accepted as 'mother'.

It is impossible to work out the gender of a young owl as there are no external differences between the sexes. Any name we choose is not always appropriate. The name of Rocky was chosen for no special reason, but it has proved to be entirely unsuitable as we now know beyond doubt that she is female.

Inside her cardboard box, Rocky went everywhere with me. For the first two weeks she dozed endlessly on a bed of towels. But as she grew bigger and stronger she began to explore. The edges of the box became torn and ragged as she pecked at the cardboard. Whenever she was hungry, which was most of the time, she would call me with a frantic, asthmatic sounding wheeze that couldn't be ignored. At about

this time her eyes opened fully and developed their full colour. Eagle owls are the owners of probably the most hauntingly beautiful eyes in the animal kingdom. Rocky's huge orange and black orbs are much more magnetic and dramatic than any human's could ever be.

Lecturing is a big part of my job and I often give talks to conservation groups. Rocky, now a seasoned traveller, has accompanied me on hundreds of car journeys, up and down the highways and byways of Britain perched on her own log on the back seat of my car. People in passing vehicles watch in wonder as they realise that the giant owl peering at them is very much alive.

As time goes on our relationship grows and intensifies. Rocky was presented to me seven years ago and in owl terms she is still a youngster – the oldest surviving owl on record lived to a ripe old age of 68. Hopefully, she will be with me for many years to come. Imprinting is for life and cannot be reversed. But despite our mutual affection I would have preferred Rocky to have grown up naturally in the wild where she could have soared freely in the wide blue yonder.

I am supposed to be a dispassionate naturalist who views animals with an objective eye, but I would be less than honest if I said that Rocky was just another owl to me. Quite simply she is unique, the tamest animal I have ever met. When we are alone the mutual trust is so great that she gently nibbles my nose and ears, then carefully preens my hair. She will even sleep on my lap. Every morning, before anyone else is up, we call to each other using the low, mournful 'oo-hoo' call of eagle owls. The conversations are long and repetitive, and although I will never fully understand the meaning of them, the companionship they signify has enriched my life.

Stage 2

Begin by skim reading the paragraphs, looking for the points which show the development of the relationship.

> The helpless baby owl was delivered in a small cardboard box lined with an old towel. She was only about 20 minutes old and was no bigger than a hamster, but I knew that in less than a year this untidy, off-white bundle of feathers would grow into one of the largest and most powerful birds on earth.

Here we see the word *helpless* describing the owl at the beginning of the relationship, and note that it arrived in *a small cardboard box*. These are two features which may change as the relationship grows, so should be underlined. Now skim read the next paragraph.

> Young chicks are often brought to my owl rescue centre, but this unexpected arrival was a completely new experience, for it was a European eagle owl. With a wingspan of almost two metres, these are the largest owls in existence. Adult females, larger than males, stand nearly 70cm high and need lots of food. Unlike a standard owl diet of mice and voles, these eagle owls will eat dogs, foxes and even small deer in the wild. It was clear that this chick was going to be quite a handful.

Clearly, this is a descriptive paragraph about eagle owls in general. There are no relevant points here. Now read on.

> Whenever very young chicks are brought to the centre, we try to place them with other families as quickly as possible. Despite their wise image, owls are not the cleverest of birds - to be brutally honest, they are surprisingly dim. A female never knows how many youngsters she has in her family. It's essential that young owls are adopted by their own species, for they take the identity of their foster parents. This process is called 'imprinting' and it happens during the first few weeks of an owl's life.

This is another paragraph continuing the description of owl habits. There are no relevant points here, so read on:

> The baby eagle owl that was brought to me had been abandoned by her mother immediately after she was born, and none of my contacts had a breeding pair of eagle owls at the right stage to take on such a young chick. Most owl keepers do their best to avoid this situation because once an owl becomes used to humans, it is then too tame to release. With no alternative, I had to hand-rear the chick, and so began our unique relationship.

Here the word *abandoned* again describes the condition of the owl at the beginning of the relationship. *With no alternative* tells us that Michael does not really want the owl at this stage. The fact that he has to hand-rear the chick is something which may change later. Here, too, is the first mention of the quality of the relationship – *unique*. These points should be underlined. Now read on:

> Although eagle owls are nocturnal mammals, spending the daytime sleeping, I persuaded the chick to eat during the day and sleep at night. Every two hours I had to cut up food and feed the owlet thin slivers of meat small enough to swallow whole. Within six days I had been completely accepted as 'mother'.

Here we see the owl's natural routine being changed; it has to stay awake during the day. We also see how much Michael is willing to do for the owl (cutting the food into small pieces for the owl to swallow whole; feeding the owl every two hours). These points should be underlined – *but* remember these are *examples* of Michael's *dedication*. Examples should not be included in a summary. Being accepted as a '*mother*' is an important step in the relationship. Now read on:

It is impossible to work out the gender of a young owl as there are no external differences between the sexes. Any name we choose is not always appropriate. The name of Rocky was chosen for no special reason, but it has proved to be entirely unsuitable as we now know beyond doubt that she is female.

This paragraph contains general information which is not relevant to the relationship, especially as the name was chosen for *no special reason*. Now read on:

Inside her cardboard box, Rocky went everywhere with me. For the first two weeks she dozed endlessly on a bed of towels. But as she grew bigger and stronger she began to explore. The edges of the box became torn and ragged as she pecked at the cardboard. Whenever she was hungry, which was most of the time, she would call me with a frantic, asthmatic sounding wheeze that couldn't be ignored. At about this time her eyes opened fully and developed their full colour. Eagle owls are the owners of probably the most hauntingly beautiful eyes in the animal kingdom. Rocky's huge orange and black orbs are much more magnetic and dramatic than any human's could ever be.

Again, the *cardboard box* is mentioned. While in the cardboard box Rocky goes everywhere with Michael; could this situation *change*? There is a comparison between *for the first two weeks* and *but as she grew bigger and stronger*. There is also a reference to feeding; already the situation has *changed*; now the owl calls him when she is hungry and cannot *be ignored*. Notice that the description of her physical beauty is *not* relevant to the development of the relationship. Underline the relevant points. Now read on.

★ **Remember**
Remember to skim read.

Lecturing is a big part of my job and I often give talks to conservation groups. Rocky, now a seasoned traveller, has accompanied me on hundreds of car journeys, up and down the highways and byways of Britain perched on her own log on the back seat of my car. People in passing vehicles watch in wonder as they realise that the giant owl peering at them is very much alive.

We learn that the owl still goes on trips with Michael; but what has *changed*? Underline the relevant points. Now read on.

As time goes on our relationship grows and intensifies. Rocky was presented to me seven years ago and in owl terms she is still a youngster - the oldest surviving owl on record lived to a ripe old age of 68. Hopefully, she will be with me for many years to come. Imprinting is for life and cannot be reversed. But despite our mutual affection I would have preferred Rocky to have grown up naturally in the wild where she could have soared freely in the wide blue yonder.

This paragraph contains direct reference to the growth of the relationship. There is also reference to future hopes. Notice phrases referring to the *quality* of the relationship – *mutual affection* and the regret Michael feels because Rocky can never be free. Does he feel guilty about this? Underline the relevant points, then skim read the final paragraph, still looking for the key features which show development of the relationship.

I am supposed to be a dispassionate naturalist who views animals with an objective eye, but I would be less than honest if I said that Rocky was just another owl to me. Quite simply she is unique, the tamest animal I have ever met. When we are alone the mutual trust is so great that she gently nibbles my nose and ears, then carefully preens my hair. She will even sleep on my lap. Every morning, before anyone else is up, we call to each other using the low, mournful 'oo-hoo' call of eagle owls. The conversations are long and repetitive, and although I will never fully understand the meaning of them, the companionship they signify has enriched my life.

In this final paragraph, we find more quality of relationship words such as *unique* and *mutual trust*. Notice that they call each other in the mornings *before anyone else is up*. What does this tell us about the relationship? Underline the point here, but remember that *examples are not used* in summaries. How does Michael summarise their relationship and how has this changed his life?

Stage 3

On a blank page of the exam question paper (or underneath the summary text if there is space), go back to each point and rewrite the idea *in your own words*.

Here are the points which you should have underlined in the passage, in the order in which they appeared.

The helpless baby owl was delivered in a small cardboard box (paragraph 1)

abandoned by her mother
once an owl becomes used to humans, it is then too tame to release. With no alternative, I had to hand-rear the chick, and so began our unique relationship. (paragraph 4)

I persuaded the chick to eat during the day and sleep at night. Every two hours I had to cut up food and feed the owlet thin slivers of meat small enough to swallow whole.
Within six days I had been completely accepted as 'mother'. (paragraph 5)

Inside her cardboard box, Rocky went everywhere with me. For the first two weeks she dozed endlessly on a bed of towels. But as she grew bigger and stronger she began to explore.
Whenever she was hungry, which was most of the time, she would call me with a frantic, asthmatic sounding wheeze that couldn't be ignored. (paragraph 7)

now a seasoned traveller
perched on her own log on the back seat of my car (paragraph 8)

As time goes on our relationship grows and intensifies.
Hopefully, she will be with me for many years to come.
Despite out mutual affection I would have preferred Rocky to have grown up naturally in the wild where she could have soared freely. (paragraph 9)

she is unique
mutual trust
Every morning, before anyone else is up, we call to each other
the companionship has enriched my life (paragraph 10)

★ **Remember**
Picking out points shows the examiner *your reading comprehension skills only*. To get full marks you have to show the examiner *what you have understood*, and to do this you must express the points in an alternative way.

In a relationship summary, the main feature is how things change. The passage will probably be written in chronological style (like a story, describing events in the same order that happened): to compare, you will have to take points from early on in the relationship and show how they have changed from points taken later in the passage.

Exercise 2 Group together points which show how the relationship changed or developed. Then write out the points in your own words, before comparing with the suggested answer on pages 249–50.

★ **Remember**
There is no 'right' answer. There will be many different ways of expressing *what you understand*. The important thing is not to translate word for word but to give the main idea. If your sentence includes one or two words from the original sentence, do not waste time trying to re-phrase them; leave them as they are but *do not copy whole phrases*.

Stage 4
Number the points according to how important you think they are.

Exercise 3 Now number the points made in exercise 2 according to how important you think they are, before comparing with the suggested answer on page 250.

Now look at the number of points and the number of words asked for (not more than 100). If you think you have too many words in a point, now is the time to reduce them. Look at the words underlined in the following point.

The owlet was <u>all alone in the world</u> and Michael dedicated himself to <u>preparing her food and feeding her</u>. Soon Rocky learnt to call him <u>every time</u> she wanted food. At first <u>the owl was sleepy</u> most of the time, but as she <u>began to grow</u> she became more demanding and more of a responsibility <u>for Michael</u>.
(57 words)

Notice how the words underlined above have now been removed or replaced by fewer words in the paragraph below.

★ **Remember**
Summaries do not need an introduction.

As the owlet was <u>orphaned</u>, Michael dedicated himself to <u>feeding her</u>. Soon Rocky learnt to call him <u>when</u> she wanted food. At first <u>Rocky slept</u> most of the time, but as she <u>grew</u> she became more demanding and more of a responsibility.
(42 words)

Exercise 4 If any of your points seem too long, remove some of the words. Then compare with the suggested answer on page 250.

Exercise 5 Now write your summary. When you have finished, compare it with a suggested answer on page 250.

■ 'History' summaries

Another type of summary is the 'history' summary, where you may be asked to *outline the history* of something, for example a sport or a hobby. When attempting a history summary, you should be looking for *events* that resulted in *change*, and how the first attempt to do something was different from what came later. Dates often appear in these summaries, but can be misleading because they are not always relevant. The important thing is to look for *events* and ask yourself if the sport or hobby would have *changed* without the event. If not, then the event itself is not relevant, even if it is connected to a date.

Worked example of a history summary

Stage 1

Read this question based on a past exam paper and underline the keywords.

Read the following newspaper article and then write a summary about the history of greyhound racing. Your summary should be no more than 100 words. You should use your own words as much as you can.

Greyhounds have been bred for thousands of years, but only in the last century have they been used for racing.

The greyhound is an ancient breed of dog whose history can be traced back over 7000 years. Evidence from archaeological excavations shows that it was a popular breed among the ancient Egyptians and Mesopotamians. A marble statue of greyhounds in the Vatican in Rome points to their popularity at the time of the Roman Empire.

The breed's name does not come from the colour grey, but is probably taken from the breed of dog known as Greekhound, which arrived in England from France around 2000 years ago. Because the letter k may have been difficult to pronounce at the time, the name may have become greyhound.

The greyhound, one of the few remaining pure breeds of dog, has a physique which is entirely geared towards speed. But the earliest surviving record of a dog being made to chase an artificial, mechanical hare, or lure, was not until the nineteenth century.

The first attempt to introduce racing took place in a field at Hendon, to the north of London. The event was reviewed enthusiastically in an article in *The Times* on September 11 1876. But the race was over a straight course of 400 yards, and after its novelty had worn off, the sport died out.

The biggest drawback was that the straight course proved no test of a greyhound's skill, and victory almost always went to the fastest runner.

Many attempts were made to invent a lure that could complete an oval circuit. But these met with continued failure and the idea was forgotten for almost a quarter of a century, until it resurfaced in the United States.

A new beginning

Coursing, in which animals chase a live bait, was particularly popular in America at the turn of the [last] century, and a man named Owen Patrick Smith became one of the sport's leading promoters.

But he came up against increasing opposition from anti-blood sports groups, which forced him to consider using a dummy mechanical lure and transferring the events to an enclosed track. One of his first attempts used a stuffed rabbit attached to a motorbike.

By 1919 he had refined his lure to a motorised trolley and, in partnership with coursing enthusiast George Sawyer, opened his first race course at Emeryville in California.

But Smith was anti-gambling, and refused to allow people to bet on the outcome of his races. Public support tailed off, but Sawyer overruled his partner and insisted on bookmakers being allowed to bet on the trackside. Within a couple of years, the sport was booming and in 1925 a deal was struck to allow it to cross the Atlantic back to England.

Greyhound racing made its British debut at the Belle Vue stadium in Manchester on July 24th 1926. But only 1700 spectators arrived, giving the organisers a loss of £50. However, just a week later, 16,000 turned up and the sport was firmly established. A year later, the sport moved to the capital, with a meeting at west London's White City stadium which attracted an estimated 100,000 people. More and more tracks opened up, with 30 in business by the end of the year.

Just before the start of a race, the greyhounds, wearing muzzles and differently coloured jackets with numbers attached, are led into traps. The artificial hare begins its run from behind, and when it is about 11 metres in front of the traps, the doors spring upwards and open automatically to release the dogs.

The greyhounds, which reach speeds up to 61 km/h, use their cunning to gain the position in the field which is most favourable to their particular racing style. This might be the inside position near the rails, or an outside position where the running is less likely to be impeded.

Today, there are 36 tracks, and over 17,000 races run a year. They are watched by over 3.8 million spectators.

It seems that the British public have taken a special liking to seeing man's best friend in the sporting arena.

Stage 2

Skim read the passage paragraph by paragraph, underlining relevant points.

> Greyhounds have been bred for thousands of years, but only in the last century have they been used for racing.

Is there anything relevant to the question? *No.* Continue skim reading.

> The greyhound is an ancient breed of dog whose history can be traced back over 7000 years. Evidence from archaeological excavations shows that it was a popular breed among the ancient Egyptians and Mesopotamians. A marble statue of greyhounds in the Vatican in Rome points to their popularity at the time of the Roman Empire.

Do not be confused by the word *history*. What does the word *history* refer to here? It refers to the history of the *dog itself*, and not to the history of racing (which was asked for in the question). Is there anything relevant to the question? *No.* Continue skim reading.

> The breed's name does not come from the colour grey, but is probably taken from the breed of dog known as Greekhound, which arrived in England from France around 2000 years ago. Because the letter k may have been difficult to pronounce at the time, the name may have become greyhound.

What is the paragraph about? Still the history of the dog, and not dog *racing*. Are there any relevant points? *None.* So move on.

> The greyhound, one of the few remaining pure breeds of dog, has a physique which is entirely geared towards speed. But the earliest surviving record of a dog being made to chase an artificial, mechanical hare, or lure, was not until the nineteenth century.
>
> The first attempt to introduce racing took place in a field at Hendon, to the north of London. The event was reviewed enthusiastically in an article in *The Times* on September 11 1876. But the race was over a straight course of 400 yards, and after its novelty had worn off, the sport died out.

Here we read *the nineteenth century* (did you know that the nineteenth century runs from 1801 till 1900?). What event is this date referring to? *The earliest record of a dog chasing a hare.* Could this be relevant to the question? *Probably.* So underline it.

If you are searching only for dates, then the next one you see is *September 11 1876*. What does this date refer to? *A review article in* **The Times**. What does the article refer to? *The first attempt to introduce racing.* In other words *September 11 1876* is the date of the *article*, not the date of the race. Obviously, the race took place in the same year as the article, so underline the year only.

Remember that you should be looking for ways in which the *first attempt* was different from what came later. Of course, as you read through you do not, as yet, know the answer to that question. So you should look for the significant characteristics at each stage.

So what were the significant characteristics of this *first attempt*? *(It) took place in a field at Hendon, to the north of London.* Is this relevant? *Yes.* Perhaps later in the history of the sport it took place in a different location, and another town. So underline this point.

The race was over a straight course of 400 yards. Is this relevant? *Yes!* Perhaps later in the history of the sport, the shape or length of the course will change. So underline this point.

the sport died out. Why? Read on.

> The biggest drawback was that the straight course proved no test of a greyhound's skill, and victory almost always went to the fastest runner.

The drawback was that the course proved no test of a greyhound's skill. So what needed to be done to change that? Read on.

> Many attempts were made to invent a lure that could complete an oval circuit. But these met with continued failure and the idea was forgotten for almost a quarter of a century, until it resurfaced in the United States.

attempts … to invent a lure … an oval circuit … met with failure … idea forgotten … So was that the end of the sport? If not, why not?

it resurfaced in the United States … a quarter of a century later The next *date* is *1919*. But if you jump to this, you will be missing not one, but *two* important points. So continue skim reading.

> Coursing, in which animals chase a live bait, was particularly popular in America at the turn of the century, and a man named Owen Patrick Smith became one of the sport's leading promoters.
>
> But he came up against increasing opposition from anti-blood sports groups, which forced him to consider using a dummy mechanical lure and transferring the events to an enclosed track. One of his first attempts used a stuffed rabbit attached to a motorbike.

at the turn of the century When does this mean? Rewrite in your own words. This connects to the point mentioned above *a quarter of a century …*

live bait … opposition from anti-blood sport groups Important point? *Yes!* The sport may not remain popular if people are against it. So what effect did this have?

… consider using a dummy mechanical lure … enclosed track.

Note that none of the last few points is connected to a *date*.

… stuffed rabbit attached to a motorbike. This is an *example* of a mechanical lure, so cannot be included. Continue to skim read.

> By 1919 he had refined his lure to a motorised trolley and, in partnership with coursing enthusiast George Sawyer, opened his first race course at Emeryville in California.
>
> But Smith was anti-gambling, and refused to allow people to bet on the outcome of his races. Public support tailed off, but Sawyer overruled his partner and insisted on bookmakers being allowed to bet on the trackside. Within a couple of years, the sport was booming and in 1925 a deal was struck to allow it to cross the Atlantic back to England.

In these paragraphs we come to the date *1919*. What does this refer to? A continuation of the mechanical lure theme, this time *a motorised trolley*. This is just another *example*. Even though it is connected to a date, it is not relevant and need not be included.

The next *date* in the passage is 1925. But again, if you jump to this, you will miss a very important point.

… anti-gambling … public support tailed off. Now the anti-blood sports groups are happy, so why is greyhound racing still not popular? Because of the ban on gambling.

The other partner in the business *insisted … bet on the trackside.* The result? *a couple of years … sport was booming.* As you can see, this is an important point, even though it is not attached to a specific *date*.

Now let's look at the significance of 1925.

a deal was struck … allow back to England. An important point? Perhaps, so underline it. Now carry on skim reading.

> Greyhound racing made its British debut at the Belle Vue stadium in Manchester on July 24th 1926. But only 1700 spectators arrived, giving the organisers a loss of £50. However, just a week later, 16,000 turned up and the sport was firmly established. A year later, the sport moved to the capital, with a meeting at west London's White City stadium which attracted an estimated 100,000 people. More and more tracks opened up, with 30 in business by the end of the year.

Here comes another date! July 24th 1926. Remember, the day and month are not really very important (they are too exact for a summary), only the year.

only 1700 spectators Why? *Only* suggests failure. *the sport moved to the capital … 100,000 people.* The problem had been *location.*

Skim read the next paragraph.

> Just before the start of a race, the greyhounds, wearing muzzles and differently coloured jackets with numbers attached, are led into traps. The artificial hare begins its run from behind, and when it is about 11 metres in front of the traps, the doors spring upwards and open automatically to release the dogs.

What is the paragraph about? *How the races are organised.* Are there any relevant points ? No. Now read on:

> The greyhounds, which reach speeds up to 61 km/h, use their cunning to gain the position in the field which is most favourable to their particular

racing style. This might be the inside position near the rails, or an outside position where the running is less likely to be impeded.

More details about the race. No relevant points. Now read on.

Today, there are 36 tracks, and over 17,000 races run a year. They are watched by over 3.8 million spectators.

Contains statistics about racing today. This is part of the *history*. Underline the points. Now read the last paragraph.

It seems that the British public have taken a special liking to seeing man's best friend in the sporting arena.

Nothing relevant to history.

So, going through this summary shows clearly that if you search for dates alone, you will miss many important points.

Stages 3–6

Exercise 6 Now return to the points you have underlined and rewrite them *in your own words*, before comparing your work with the suggested answer on pages 250–1. Then work through the remaining stages to produce your summary.

■ 'Structure' summaries

The last type of summary can be called the 'function' or 'structure' summary. In this case, the question asks you to write a summary using a certain function or structure of language.

You may be asked to *give advice*, or to explain the *main arguments for and against* something, or to explain the *benefits* of something or the *advantages and disadvantages* of something. Approach the summary in the normal way:

1 Underline key words in the question.
2 Skim read the passage, underlining relevant points.
3 Go back to the points. Write the idea they express in your own words.
4 Group together similar ideas.
5 Check the number of points against the number of words asked for.
6 Write your summary.

In this kind of summary, you should *make a separate list of the structural sentences* asked for, so you do not forget to include them.

In a summary where you are asked to explain the *main arguments for and against*, your list may look something like this:

One of the main arguments in favour of ... is that ...
It can be argued that ...
On the other hand, one of the arguments against ... is that ...

Once this is done, you simply have to fit the points inside the structure phrases.

Worked example of a structure summary

Look at the following question based on a question from a past exam paper.

Stage 1

Read the question carefully and underline the key words.

Read the following article about mountain biking. Then write a paragraph giving advice on ways of making sure that mountain biking is safe and environmentally responsible. Write about 100 words. Use your own words as much as possible.

Out in the wheel world

Mountain biking is the fastest-growing sport in Britain. The saddle of a bike is a far better vantage point from which to explore the countryside than a car, and you see much more than you would walking. On top of this, it's great exercise: a day off-road cycling will have everyone sound asleep at night as soon as their heads hit the pillow. But perhaps the best bit of all is that after every lung-bursting climb comes the thrill of bouncing downhill.

Access is one of the most contentious issues surrounding the sport, with everyone from ramblers and horse riders to farmers and environmentalists wailing about the impact of mountain bikes on the country-side. However, if you are riding on a legal-ly accessible trail, you have just as much right to be there as they do. The main thing, as with all outdoor sports, is to show con-sideration for others: don't tear up behind walkers or riders – warn them of your approach and ride past slowly. As for ero-sion, try not to skid unnecessarily on wet grass and soil, although independent research has shown that mountain bikes cause no more erosion than walkers' boots and a good deal less than horses' hooves.

If you pass through gates, always close or fasten them behind you. Don't disturb livestock, and make sure you always know where you're going, so you don't end up riding through a field of crops after making a wrong turn. Mark your route on a map before you set out (and know how to read it!) so it's easy to follow the trail.

Everyone falls off at some point – a rock, a pot-hole or tree root will catch you out eventually – so the golden rule is to wear a helmet. Always. It's also useful to carry a basic first-aid kit, and, as an expert advises, 'don't stray too far out into the wilds, just in case you do have an accident.' Many of the more experienced riders who go up into the mountains of Scotland and the Lake District take mobile phones in case they come to grief in a remote area. You might agree that this would be a good occasion to have one.

Stage 2

Exercise 7 Skim read the passage and underline the relevant points, marking them at the side of the text with suitable coding. Then check and compare what you have done with the suggested answer on page 251.

Stages 3 and 4

Exercise 8 Make two columns, one for each of the key points. (In the exam, do this on a blank page of the exam question paper, or underneath the reading passage if there is space.) Go through your coding at the side of the text and rewrite each sentence in your own words. Then put your points in order of importance. Check and compare with the answer on page 251.

★ **Remember**
This summary asked for a
paragraph giving advice.

Stage 5

Now check the number of points you have made. Check how many words you have to write (100 words). In other words, you have one line for each point. Don't forget the *advice phrases*, though. When you include the advice phrases, you will have too many words, so you may need to join ideas.

What are the advice phrases? Look back to Section 2, Unit 2 on Friendly letters: advice. There are many phrases to choose from. Try to select ones which are formal ones, and have not been used in the text. For example:

The most important/best/main thing is to …
Remember …
Whatever happens, …/whatever you do, …
Try …
You should/ought to …

Stage 6

Exercise 9 Now write your summary. Then compare your work with the suggested answer on page 252.

LISTENING AND SPEAKING

The first unit in this section sets out the different tasks which you will find in the listening exam. It gives examples of each part in turn, together with hints on how to answer the questions. Unit 2 explains what to expect in the different components of the speaking exam.

UNIT 1

Listening overview

The listening passages in the exam appear in Paper 3 (Core) and Paper 4 (Extended). Both papers consist of three parts and involve listening to six short texts and four long passages.

Paper 3 (Core) lasts approximately 30 minutes.

Paper 4 (Extended) lasts approximately 45 minutes.

- You write your answers in a question paper booklet.
- You must answer in pen.
- You can write down anything you like, at any time during the exam.
- There are blank pages at the back of the question booklet, and you should use these for rough work.
- Any rough notes you make should be crossed through with one diagonal line at the end of the exam.
- Spelling mistakes are not penalised, unless the mistake produces a word with a different meaning which is not appropriate.

■ Part 1

This part of the listening exam is relatively simple and serves as a 'warm up' to Parts 2 and 3. In Part 1 you will hear six short, spoken texts. These could include simple conversations, messages left on an answer machine or a travel announcement. You will hear them all **twice**.

You will need to be able to write down a string of numbers as you hear them – such as a telephone number, and to recognise the difference between similar-sounding numbers, such as *thirteen* and *thirty* when you hear them. You will also need to distinguish between words such as *when* and *where* when you hear them.

These questions test your understanding of very basic vocabulary and involve answering *wh* question words, such as *where? when? why? how? who?* This may involve simple phrases such as telling the time (*what time?, how long?*), amounts of money (*how much does it cost?, how much does he pay?*), days and months (*what is the closing date?, which is the best day?*) or giving directions (*where must you meet?, do you know the way?*).

Part 1 requires very brief answers. Often **one** word is needed, and you should write **as little as possible**. You will see on the question paper that some questions carry two marks. This means that there are two parts to the question and you will need to give **two** answers.

Answering the questions

Before you hear the short, spoken sentences, you will be given time to read the questions.

1 Skim read the questions and underline key words. These will include the main question words such as *how much* or *where*. Other key words also need to be underlined.

Look at the example questions from a Part 1 Core listening paper, where the key words have been underlined.

★ **Exam tip**

The questions often include **names** which may not be familiar to you. Try to say them to yourself so that they do not confuse you and prevent you hearing the answer when you listen to the sentences.

Part 1 (Questions 1–6)

---

1 Carlos needs some petrol for his car. <u>How much</u> will it <u>cost</u> him
  <u>per litre</u>? [1]
2 <u>Which</u> telephone <u>number</u> should Fran ring to contact his <u>father</u>? [1]
3 <u>How long</u> will passengers have to wait for their <u>train</u>? [1]
4 Your class is going on a trip to a local science museum tomorrow.
  <u>Where</u> must you <u>meet</u> and at <u>what time</u> do you expect to be <u>back</u>? [2]
5 Ismail is on a winter snow sports holiday. According to the <u>weather forecast</u>,
  <u>which</u> will be <u>the best day</u> for him to <u>ski</u>? [1]
6 Yasmin and her friend are going shopping. <u>Why</u> does her friend
  suggest buying a <u>bar of chocolate</u>? [1]

In question 1 *per litre* should be underlined. This is because the sentence you hear may say how much it costs Carlos to fill his tank.

In question 2 *father* should be underlined. This is because the sentence you hear may also contain reference to Fran contacting other people.

In question 3 *train* should be underlined. This is because the sentence you hear may refer to other types of transport.

In question 6 *bar of chocolate* should be underlined because Yasmin's friend may refer to other items of shopping.

At the same time, circle questions which need two answers. (Here, question 4.)

2 When you have skim read the questions and underlined key words, read question 1 again.

This time make sure you understand the question. Use the information in the question to guess what the situation you hear may be about, and anticipate (guess) what your answer might be.

3 Listen to the spoken sentence. If you feel confident you know the answer, write it in straight away. If you are not sure of the answer, wait until you hear the spoken sentence a second time.

★ **Note**

Listening passages are not provided in this overview, except for the final exercise on pages 178–9.

4 When you hear the spoken sentence the second time, check your answer or complete any answer you missed the first time. Never leave the answer blank.

Move on immediately to read the next question.

★ **Remember**

There is no need to write complete sentences in your answer. Write as little as possible.

Part 2

In Part 2, you will hear **two** longer spoken texts. Again, these could be a conversation, a monologue (= one person speaking), an interview or a talk. As you listen, you need to use the information to complete gaps on a chart or form. You will hear both texts **twice**.

This part often tests understanding of numbers used for age, measurement, time or cost.

To answer the questions, you often need figures or groups of words. Full sentences are *not* needed.

Answering the questions

You will be given time to look at the form or chart before you listen to the text.

1 Look at the information given in the form or chart. Try to anticipate (guess) the kind of question that needs to be asked in order to provide the answers. Remember that the words you hear used by the speakers are often **different** from those you read on the form.

For example, look at a question from a Part 2 Core listening paper on the next page.

■ Look where the word 'nationality' appears on the career profile form. Do not expect a word from the question to appear in the spoken text. Do not expect the speaker to use the words *What nationality are you?*. Instead you may hear *Where do you come from?* or *Where are you from originally?* or *You're not English, are you?*

■ Look at the career profile form, under 'Problems'. The form says 'two....... on left knee'. What problems can a tennis player have on her knee? Could it be *injuries* or perhaps *operations*? Do not expect the speaker to say, *You had two operations on your left knee, didn't you?* Instead you may hear *Your left knee's been operated on twice, hasn't it?*

Do not expect the words in the spoken text to come in the same order as they do on the form.

2 Listen to the spoken text. If you hear a word and know it is the correct answer, but are not sure how to spell it, write it down anyway. You will not lose marks for incorrect spelling, unless you produce a word with a wrong meaning. For example, in the question in our example about Ruby Chandra's ranking in the world, you know the answer is 'third', but you are not sure how to spell it. If you write 'fird' this will be accepted and if you write 'tird' this will also be accepted. However, if you 'tired' this will *not* be accepted.

3 If you are confident you know the answer, write it in straight away. If you are not sure of the answer, wait until you hear the spoken text a second time.

4 When you hear the spoken text the second time, check your answer or complete any answer you missed the first time. Never leave the answer blank.

Part 2: Exercise One (Question 7)

Listen to an interview with Ruby Chandra, a young international tennis player, and then fill in the details below.

You will hear the interview twice.

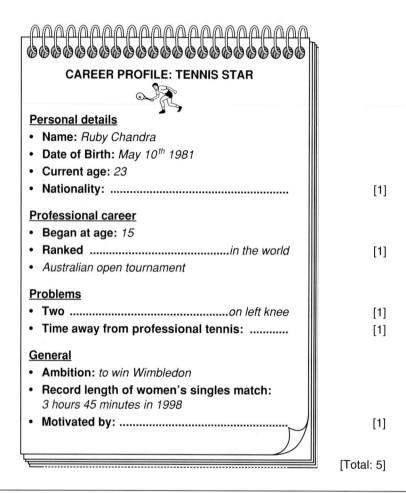

CAREER PROFILE: TENNIS STAR

Personal details
- **Name:** *Ruby Chandra*
- **Date of Birth:** *May 10th 1981*
- **Current age:** *23*
- **Nationality:** .... [1]

Professional career
- **Began at age:** *15*
- **Ranked** ....*in the world* [1]
- *Australian open tournament*

Problems
- **Two** ....*on left knee* [1]
- **Time away from professional tennis:** .... [1]

General
- **Ambition:** *to win Wimbledon*
- **Record length of women's singles match:**
  3 hours 45 minutes in 1998
- **Motivated by:** .... [1]

[Total: 5]

Now look at a question from a Part 2 Extended listening paper on the next page. Using the method outlined in **1** above, anticipate the kind of questions you might hear that will provide the answers.

Part 2: Exercise Two (Question 8)

Listen to an interview with the director of an international airport in India, and then complete the details below.

You will hear the interview twice.

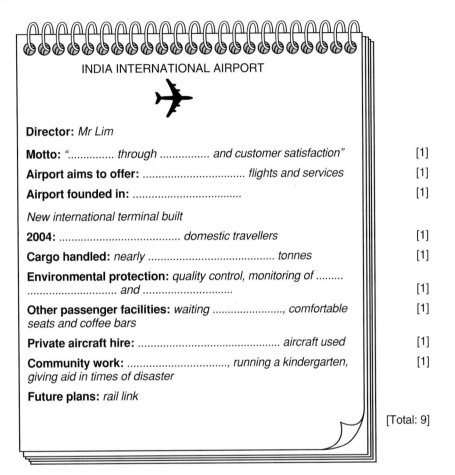

INDIA INTERNATIONAL AIRPORT

Director: *Mr Lim*

Motto: *"............. through .... and customer satisfaction"* [1]

Airport aims to offer: *................................ flights and services* [1]

Airport founded in: *.................................* [1]

New international terminal built

2004: *...................................... domestic travellers* [1]

Cargo handled: *nearly .... tonnes* [1]

Environmental protection: *quality control, monitoring of ....*
.... and .... [1]

Other passenger facilities: *waiting ...., comfortable*
seats and coffee bars [1]

Private aircraft hire: *... aircraft used* [1]

Community work: *..............................., running a kindergarten,*
giving aid in times of disaster [1]

Future plans: *rail link*

[Total: 9]

■ Part 3 (Core)

In Part 3 you will hear **two** spoken texts. Again, these could be a conversation, a monologue, an interview or a talk. You need to decide whether statements about the text are **true or false** and tick the appropriate box.

Answering the question

1 Read the introduction above the statements on the exam paper so you know *what* you are going to hear.

Is it an interview or a conversation, for example? How many people will you hear? Look at the names. Will you hear men or women? What will they be talking about?

2 Read the statements **quickly**, and underline the key words.

3 Then read the first statement again, carefully. Make sure you understand it and keep thinking about it.

4 Listen to the spoken text. Be careful of negatives! Sometimes a negative sentence in the text means the same as the sentence in the question, and sometimes it means the opposite. For example:

a) Harry is popular with all his friends. True or False?

You hear: *I wouldn't say that Harry is universally popular.*

b) Harry is rich. True or False?

You hear: *Harry's not poor these days, is he?*

5 If you feel confident you know the answer, tick the box straight away. If you are not sure, wait until you hear the spoken text for the second time.

6 Check your answers as you hear the spoken text for the second time, and complete any answers you missed the first time. Never leave an answer blank.

Look at the following example question taken from a Part 3 Core listening past exam paper.

Part 3: Exercise One (Question 9)

Listen to an interview about boosting the immune system, and then indicate whether each statement is true or false by putting a tick in the appropriate box.

You will hear the interview twice.

	True	False
(a) Dr Imal has carried out research on an international scale.	☐	☐
(b) Invaders are attacked by our immune system.	☐	☐
(c) Pollution has a big effect on our immune system.	☐	☐
(d) According to the speaker, tiredness does not cause illness.	☐	☐
(e) Sugar helps the effectiveness of the killer cells.	☐	☐
(f) Exercise quickens circulation.	☐	☐
(g) More oxygen in the cells is good for your health.	☐	☐
(h) Good tempered people are likely to be the healthiest.	☐	☐
(i) Stress hormones make us laugh.	☐	☐
(j) The speaker advises us to calm down and enjoy life.	☐	☐

[Total: 5]

■ Part 3 (Extended)

In Part 3 you will hear **two** spoken texts. Again, these could be a conversation, a monologue (= one person speaking), an interview or a talk. You need to write short or sentence-length answers to the questions.

Answering the questions

1 Read the introduction above the questions on the exam paper so you know *what* you are going to hear.

Is it an interview or a conversation, for example? How many people will you hear? Look at the names. Will you hear men or women? What will they be talking about?

2 Read the questions **quickly**, and underline the key words.

3 Then read the first question again, carefully. Make sure you understand it and keep thinking about it.

4 As you listen to the spoken text, establish:

   ■ who is speaking
   ■ their point of view on the subject.

5 Write down anything you think may be relevant to the answer, using the blank pages at the end of the answer booklet, or the space under the questions.

6 Now read the second question again, carefully. Make sure you understand it and keep thinking about it. As before, write down anything you think may be relevant to the answer.

7 Repeat this procedure for each question, remembering that the answers to the questions come chronologically (the answer to question 3 will come before the answer to question 4, for example).

8 When you are sure you have heard the answer to the last question, begin to look through your notes and write in any answers you are confident about. There will be no more relevant information to listen for even though the spoken text may continue. Maximise your use of this time to produce answers from your notes.

9 When writing in your answer, you should not repeat the words in the question. For example:

According to the speaker, which three qualities must a climber have?

Do not answer: *According to the speaker, a climber must have* … Simply list the three qualities in a sentence. For example:

The qualities are …

   ■ Answer the question directly.
   ■ Write a complete sentence.
   ■ Use the same tense as the question.

10 Carry on writing in your answers during the second listening.

11 Stop to listen for any answers you had problems with the first time.

12 Never leave a question unanswered. Marks will not be deducted for a wrong answer, so if you are not sure, just guess!

Hints

1 Listen for phrases such as the following:

What I mean is …

What I'm trying to say is …

In other words …

To put it another way …

In a nutshell …

These phrases are used to indicate that a speaker is going to summarise his thoughts. Very often, the words used in the summary are those needed in your answer.

2 Listen for adjectives. These often indicate a descriptive passage, where there will usually be no answers.

3 Listen for words like these:

however, on the other hand and *whereas* (introducing contrasts)

unfortunately, the down side and *a minus point* (introducing disadvantages).

4 If the question includes the word 'attitude', it means *what does he think about?*

5 Questions often include a phrase like 'How have his feelings changed?' It is important that your answer shows how he felt *before and after* in the situation. This could involve a comparison, such as *happier than*.

6 Presentation is important. Crossings out look messy, and create a bad impression. Only write in your answer when you are happy with it and can put it in a sentence.

7 Cross your notes through with one diagonal line when you have finished.

Part 3: Exercise Two (Question 10)

Listen to this radio interview in which Sally talks about the difficulties of her son, who suffers from autism (a condition where people withdraw from reality), and answer the questions. You will hear the interview twice.

1 Why was Gabriel given a place in his new college?

2 Give *one* example of Gabriel's unusual actions.

3 How have Sally's feelings changed about Gabriel going to this college?

4 What was the effect on Sally of her friends' attempts to help her?

5 How has Gabriel's behaviour changed as he has become older?

6 Why does Sally believe Gabriel is lucky to be going to this college?

Exercise 1 Now ask someone to read the listening text (see page 179) to you, and answer the questions.

Listening text

A In today's 'Family Matters' we begin by hearing the story of Sally and her autistic son Gabriel. Sally, can you begin by explaining what autism is?

B Yes, it's really the name given to people who are severely mentally handicapped and whose behaviour could best be described as 'difficult' or 'challenging'. As you can imagine, autistic children can be very difficult to look after and can completely dominate their families.

A I'm sure that must be true. I understand that Gabriel has a place at a special college. Tell us how this has come about.

B Yes, Gabriel is leaving us soon to go into full-time residential care – he will come back for visits but the college will be his home. I suppose most colleges require good school examination results to get a place, but Gabriel's qualifications were his … I suppose you'd call it 'wild' behaviour. He would eat with his hands or scream constantly or climb out of windows with no regard for his safety. The college deals exclusively with children and young people with disabilities of this sort. But the fact that he's going to college is really wonderful news, although as the actual day approaches I must admit I am a little apprehensive. When we first heard, we all thought it was wonderful news and I could hardly wait for this moment to arrive. Now what I fear most is that he might forget all about us and sometimes I think that it is as if we are abandoning him to strangers. I know perfectly well, of course, that his new carers will give him all the love and encouragement he needs but I still feel rather uneasy about it.

A Hm, I can see that. But I imagine that your friends and family have been very supportive over the years?

B Oh indeed they have. It's hard to see how we could have survived without their support. They are always full of good intentions and often tell us about some new miracle drug that could cure Gabriel, or they 'phone with news about a television programme which offers hope of some new development. Or they might come round with news of some success story about parents who devoted their lives to their difficult children and how, after years of faith and devotion, the child can drive a car or completely look after himself. The trouble with all of that was that while I really appreciated the comfort and support I just became more confused and didn't know whether I should try harder with Gabriel or devote more time to the rest of the family or even to myself.

And over time there have been changes in his behaviour. He still can't speak and prefers to sleep on the floor, but he is much stronger now and more assertive. And instead of merely climbing out of a window he has the agility to get out on the roof and do other horrifying things that as a boy he couldn't have done.

So I suppose I will have very mixed feelings when he goes off to college next week, but I have to remember that he's lucky to have this opportunity, and that not so long ago the future for someone like him would have been in a long-term hospital ward with his behaviour controlled by drugs. I'll be the happiest person in the world when he manages to make a cup of tea or get himself dressed … and his only real hope is this college.

A Thank you, Sally. It looks like changes all round both for you and Gabriel. I am sure all our listeners wish you both the best of luck. Thank you.

Speaking overview

There are two different options for assessing speaking:

- Component 5: examination
- Component 6: coursework.

Your school will probably decide which of these applies to you. Marks for the oral component are not included in the grade you receive for the written papers. For the speaking part of the exam, you will receive a number grade from 1 to 5, with Grade 1 being the highest.

For both components you will be given marks for:

- structure
- vocabulary
- fluency.

■ Component 5

The exam lasts about 10–15 minutes and involves:

- two to three minutes **'warm-up' conversation**, which is *not* assessed. The examiner will ask you a few questions about yourself and things which may interest you, such as your school or your hobbies, to make you feel relaxed and comfortable with the exam situation
- two to three minutes for you to **read an assessment card** and **prepare an answer**. The assessment card will be about a topic such as the role of parents in a family, the advantages and disadvantages of mobile phones, problems faced by teenagers, what makes a good leader, life in the future, health and fitness, and so on. The card will give the topic for discussion and several related points. You do not need to use all of these points or to use any of these points or to use the points in any particular order. These points are given to help you with ideas if you get stuck. You are free to use your own ideas if you prefer. You are not allowed to write anything
- six to nine minutes **assessed conversation**. When the preparation time is over, either you or the examiner will begin the conversation.

■ Component 6

Your school or centre will produce their own oral tasks. You will be assessed on **three** oral tasks such as role play, interviews, telephone conversations, paired or group discussions or debates.

■ Exam hints

1 Listen carefully to what the examiner says.
2 Do not give one-word answers such as *yes* or *no*.
3 Use a variety of different expressions. Instead of repeating *I think*, use other opinion phrases. The same applies to suggestions, advice and so on.
4 Give the examiner a chance to speak!
5 Give sensible answers.

■ How to improve your speaking

Vocabulary

Improve your vocabulary by:

- using the Database of topic-related vocabulary and ideas (see pages 231–44) and adding to it
- reading anything in English, especially newspaper articles where the writer develops an argument
- listening to as much spoken English as possible – TV programmes (especially interviews), radio (World Service), the internet.

Fluency

Improve your fluency by:

- recording just one minute from a TV programme. Listen to one sentence at a time and try to copy it. Record your voice on the tape. Compare the two. Pay attention to pronunciation and intonation
- practising.

Structure

Improve your use of language structures by:

- doing all of the above
- practising.

REFERENCE

Much of this section concerns language you need to know and use in your exam. Unit 1 outlines key ways to change formal sentences into informal ones, while Unit 2 goes on to remind you of some grammar points which should be used correctly in the exam but which often cause problems for students. Unit 3 looks at different uses of prepositions, Unit 4 at word partners and sayings, and Unit 5 at phrases often confused by students, with examples of each, so you know how and where to use them in the exam. Unit 6 helps you improve your spelling by explaining some simple rules, while Unit 7 is a list of words with difficult spelling, which you may need in the exam. Unit 8 examines how to write plans for the writing tasks and gives you some useful final hints on how to approach the writing part of the exam.

UNIT 1 | Register

★ **Remember**
Simplifying a formal word or phrase very often involves expanding your sentence, because a larger number of simple words are needed to explain or replace bigger words.

In the exam, you are expected to show awareness of the differences between formal and informal register and the ability to use the correct register according to the situation in the question. Your relationship with, or 'feel' for, register (different levels of language as discussed in Section 1) comes through experience gained as a result of exposure to the language in a variety of situations. For this reason, it is not easy to 'learn' register from a book. As an IGCSE student, you will probably be more familiar with formal register, so this unit concentrates on helping you to recognise features of formal writing and showing you how to change them in order to produce friendly register.

R1 **Replace an abstract noun with 'person + verb'.**

What is an abstract noun? It is a thing (noun) which you cannot touch or see, for example: *happiness, bravery, arrival, willingness, ability.*

on your <u>arrival</u> → when you arrive
she has the <u>ability</u> → she can
he reached his <u>destination</u> → he reached the place he was going to
in my <u>opinion</u> → I think

Abstract nouns are not always easy to recognise.

R2 **Replace 'verb + ing' (following words such as *after, before, on,* etc) with 'person + verb'.**

The 'verb + *ing*' that you need to replace comes after the following words: *after, before, since, when, while, once, on, until, during, as.*

Knock on the door <u>before entering</u> the room → *... before you go in*
<u>When answering</u> *the phone, give your number* → *When you answer the phone ...*
<u>On seeing</u> *my father, I felt happy* → *When I saw ...*

Sometimes an abstract noun (R1) comes after these words. Replace the abstract noun in the same way, with 'person + verb'.

I met many people <u>during my visit</u> → *... while I was there*

R3 **Replace 'formal' verbs with simple verbs and prepositions or phrases (see pages 201–8).**

to distinguish → *to tell the difference between*
to consider → *to think about*
to postpone → *to put off*

R4 **Replace the passive voice with the active voice.**

Revision should be done → *You should revise*
The music was played by my sister → *My sister played the music*

R5 **Avoid the use of 'which' and 'that'.**

Often the meaning of a sentence does not change when these words are removed.

I was sorry to hear that you feel lonely (formal)
I was sorry to hear you feel lonely (informal)

R6 **Use contracted forms whenever possible in friendly register, as this is the *only* place in the written exam where they are appropriate.**

We will → *We'll*
I have → *I've*

R7 **Avoid listing when writing friendly letters.**

This means when you want to introduce ideas one after another, you should replace words such as *firstly* and *secondly* and so on.
   To introduce the **first point**:

Firstly, → *To start with,*
          ... for a start (at the end of the sentence)

There are lots of ways to revise for an exam. To start with, make a revision timetable.
If you really want to lose weight, you'll have to give up chips, for a start.

To introduce the **next point**:

Secondly, → Another (good) thing is …
What's more
Not only that

What's more, try to have a break from revision every half hour.

Another good thing is to make sure you get a good night's sleep.

To introduce the **final** (and perhaps most important) **point**:

Lastly → And one of the best things
And best of all
Above all
The most important thing

The most important thing is to allow plenty of time to revise.

R8 **Replace joining words, used to develop a point made in formal writing.**

Furthermore,
Besides, } → *What's more/Not only that/That's not all*
Moreover,

However is used in formal register to mean 'but'. *However* is often the first word in a sentence. In friendly written register it is not good style to begin a sentence with *but*. You can **join** two sentences with *but* or you can use …, *though* at the end of the sentence.

However → but

I love most fruit. <u>However</u>, I'm not keen on bananas.
I love most fruit. I'm not keen on bananas, <u>though</u>.
I love most fruit, <u>but</u> I'm not keen on bananas.

The same applies to *on the other hand* which, like *however*, introduces a contrast or opposite point of view:

On the other hand → …, though.

Tourists spend a lot of money in local shops. They can spoil the local environment, <u>though</u>.

Here are a few more words which often appear in formal register and need to be replaced when writing in friendly register:

due to → because of
thus → so
since → because

R9 **Remember and apply the following points.**

a) The word *also* is used in formal register. It does *not* come at the beginning or the end of a sentence. It comes before the main verb.

I love classical music, and I <u>also like</u> jazz.

In friendly register, replace *also* with ..., *too* or ... *as well* at the end of the sentence.

I love classical music, and I like jazz, <u>too</u>.
I love classical music, and I like jazz <u>as well</u>.

b) The word *one* sometimes needs to be replaced with *a*. Look at the following sentences:

I was pleased to hear you're coming to stay for a month.
I have a brother and a sister.
We went skiing for a week.
I lent him a book.

c) *very → really*
d) *be able → can*
e) *many → lots of/loads of*

Exercise 1   Look at the following list of the most common register mistakes made by students and try to produce language suitable for friendly letter writing. Where relevant, indicate which register reference point is being used.

1	I wasn't able	→	
2	during my absence	→	
3	she advised me to	→	
4	I advise you	→	
5	allow	→	
6	in my area	→	
7	your arrival time	→	
8	I hope you will attend the next party	→	
9	before going to bed	→	
10	beneficial	→	
11	will be of great benefit to you	→	
12	I believe	→	
13	celebration	→	
14	concerning	→	
15	contains	→	
16	we entered the shop	→	
17	finally	→	
18	tell me its location	→	
19	many	→	
20	in my opinion	→	
21	prepare	→	
22	after reaching	→	
23	regarding	→	
24	it wasn't successful	→	
25	very	→	
26	during your visit	→	
27	while walking	→	
28	gain weight	→	

Key grammar points

This unit does not cover every aspect of grammar required for the exam. The grammatical points explained here are those which are regularly used incorrectly by students of IGCSE English as a Second Language. Each point is explained through example, where possible, and with minimum reference to grammatical terms.

G1 **Using the past perfect tense.**

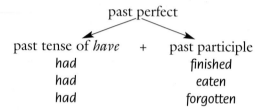

1 Making events sound more interesting

When writing narratives or descriptive narratives, telling stories or giving accounts, you can make events that happened in the past sound more interesting if you join them together using the past perfect.

- When referring to *two* actions and
- when both actions took place in the *past*

the past perfect is used to describe the *first action* which took place – although this may *not* be the *first verb* in the sentence. For example:

I <u>had gone</u> to bed (first action) when I heard a banging noise (second action).

In the example above, the **first** verb in the sentence describes the first action. First I went to bed, then I heard a banging noise.
    Without the past perfect, the sentence would seem much less interesting:

I went to bed. I heard a banging noise.

Here is another example:

I realised (second action) I <u>had lost</u> my keys (first action).

In the example above, the *second* verb in the sentence describes the first action. First I lost my keys. Later I realised this.
    Without the past perfect, the sentence would seem much less interesting:

I lost my keys. Then I realised.

2 Making events clear

The past perfect is useful in narratives, descriptive narratives, stories and accounts because it makes clear to the reader which event happened first. Compare the following two example sentences.

When I got home my brother left.
(using the simple past tense)

    Action 1: I got home. Action 2: My brother left.
    First I got home. *Then* my brother left.
    My brother was there when I got home. He left *after* I got home.

When I got home my brother had left.
(using the past perfect)

> Action 1: My brother left. Action 2: I got home.
> *First* my brother left. *Then* I got home.
> My brother left *before* I got home.

Both sentences are correct, but they have very different meanings, so make sure you know when to use the past perfect.

Here are some other examples relevant to exam topics.

We had been in the city centre looking for a birthday present for Dad.
(used here in a narrative letter, to set the scene)
First we were in the city. *Then* another event took place.

I was disappointed to realise I had missed the opportunity of a lifetime!
(used here in a narrative, perhaps as a conclusion)
First I missed the opportunity. *Later* I realised this.

It turned out that Mum had emptied the pockets before she washed the trousers.
(used here in a narrative letter, perhaps as a conclusion)
First Mum checked the pockets. *Then* she washed the trousers.

It is *not* necessary to use the past perfect when the order of events is clear.

   ✔   I had a shower, got dressed and went for breakfast.
   ✗   When I had had a shower I got dressed. When I had got dressed I went for breakfast.

G2 Sentences with *if*.

Sentences with if are called **conditional sentences**, and consist of two parts.
One part *depends on*, or *results from*, the other part.
   Both parts are usually joined by if.

There are *three* main types of conditional sentences in English, which refer to different times and situations, and use different tense patterns.
   In order to decide which conditional to use, you should ask yourself if you are writing about:

1 a *future* event (the first conditional)
2 an event or situation which is *imaginary* or *unreal* (the second conditional)
3 an event which took place in the *past* (the third conditional).

The first conditional

If you want to talk or write about things that will *very probably* happen in the *future*, use the following tense pattern.

> if + present ... future
> If I see John,   I'll (I will) tell him.

- The verb after *if* must be in a *present* tense, even though it refers to the *future*.
- The two clauses (or parts) can change places, but the verb after *if* must still be in a present tense:

future	... *if* + present
I'll (I will) tell John	if I see him.

- When the sentence begins with the *if* clause, a comma is needed to separate the two parts of the sentence:

If I see John, I'll tell him.

- When the sentence does not begin with the *if* clause, no comma is needed:

I'll tell John if I see him.

This tense pattern can also be used to express:

- **warnings** or **threats** (how a present action may result in a negative action in the future)

You'll put on weight if you eat too much chocolate. (advice letter)

If the government does not improve the standard of living, crime will increase. (formal writing)

- **offers** or **promises** (how a present action may result in a positive action in the future)

If you plan your revision carefully, you'll do well in your exam. (advice letter)

If you come to my school with me, you'll meet my friends. (descriptive letter)

The second conditional

If you want to write or talk about an event or situation which is *imaginary* or *unreal* or *not very probable*, use the following tense pattern.

if + past	... conditional (*would*)
If he had a million pounds,	he'd (he would) buy a yacht.

- The verb after *if* must be in the past tense, even though it refers to the *present* or *future*.
- The two clauses (or parts) can change places, but the verb after *if* must still be in the past tense:

conditional (*would*)	... *if* + past
He'd (he would) buy a yacht	if he had a million pounds.

- When the sentence begins with the *if* clause, a comma is needed to separate the two parts of the sentence:

If Tom had a million pounds, he'd buy a yacht.

- When the sentence does not begin with the *if* clause, no comma is needed:

Tom would buy a yacht if he had a million pounds.

The above situation is *unreal* because Tom has *not* got a million pounds.

It is possible that Tom may have a million pounds in the future, but this is *not very probable*.

Therefore, it is *not very probable* that Tom will buy a yacht.

Tom is wishing for, or dreaming about, something that will probably not happen.

If Sarah married a film star, she'd (she would) be famous.

It is possible that Sarah may marry a film star in the future, but *not very probable*.

Therefore, it is *not very probable* that Sarah will be famous.

Sarah is wishing for, or dreaming about, something that will probably not happen.

If I had a camera, I'd lend it to you.

The situation is *unreal* because I have *not* got a camera.

Therefore, it is impossible for me to lend it to you.

If I had a brother, I'd teach him how to play football.

The situation is *unreal*, or *imaginary*, because I have *not* got a brother.

Here are some other examples relevant to exam topics.

If you met my Aunty, you'd love her sense of humour. (descriptive letter)

Young people would be healthier if they spent less time watching TV and more time playing sport. (formal writing)

This form of the conditional is also used for giving **advice**.

> If I were you,   I'd …
> *If* + past +   *I would* (conditional)

This is particularly useful in friendly advice letters.

If I were you, I'd make a revision plan several weeks before your exam – and stick to it!

The third conditional

If you want to write or talk about an event that took place in the *past*, use the following pattern of tenses.

> *if* + past perfect   …   conditional perfect
> *had finished*   *would have arrived*
> *had eaten*   *would have felt*
> *had gone*   *would have seen*

If I had known you were in hospital, I would have visited you.

■ Nothing can be done to change the situation because the actions in both clauses are completed. The condition is *impossible* because the action is already over and the action in the *if* clause did *not* happen.

■ The two clauses (or parts) can change places, but the verb after *if* must still be in the past perfect tense:

conditional perfect   + *if* + past perfect
I'd (would) have visited you   if I'd (had) known you were in hospital.

■ When the sentence begins with the *if* clause, a comma is needed to separate the two parts of the sentence:

If I'd (had) known you were in hospital, I'd (would) have visited you.

■ When the sentence does *not* begin with the *if* clause, no comma is needed.

I'd (would) have visited you if I'd (had) known you were in hospital.

The example above means I did *not* know you were in hospital, so I did *not* visit you.

Nothing can change the situation, because it all happened in the past.

This construction is often used when looking back at a situation and wishing you could change it. However, as it cannot be changed, this leads to feelings of **regret**.

Consider the following situation: Your exam results have arrived. They are not as good as expected. You look back to your studies and realise that you did not work as hard as you could have. You cannot change the situation, or the results, so you feel sadness or **regret**:

If I had studied harder, I would have got better results.

I did *not* study hard and the results were *not* good.

★ **Remember**
  ❏ *'d* can be the contracted form of *had* or *would*.

  If you'd (= <u>had</u>) been there, you'd (= <u>would</u>) have known what to do.
  ❏ Use the **contracted** form in friendly register.

Here are some other examples relevant to exam questions.

If I hadn't had such a big breakfast before we went to the theme park, I wouldn't have felt so sick on the rides. (narrative)

If the girls had listened to what Miss Matthews told us, they wouldn't have got lost in the museum. (narrative)

These verb patterns can be introduced by *I wish …* and *if only …*.

I wish you'd (had) been there! You'd (would) have known what to do.
If only you'd (had) been there! You'd (would) have known what to do.

You were *not* there, and no one knew what to do.

Sometimes, only one of the two clauses is needed, as the other half can be understood from the story.

I wish I'd (had) taken my mobile (phone) with me!
(But I did *not* take it, so I couldn't call anyone for help.)

If only we'd (had) taken a torch with us!
(But I did *not* take a torch with me. As a result, we had no light in a dark place, so we couldn't see what we were doing/a way out/a signal for help.)

If only he'd (had) told his parents where he was going!
(But he did *not* tell his parents where he was going. As a result, they did not know where to start looking for him/had no idea he was in danger/they couldn't meet him.)

The above three examples are narrative style.
    Look at an example in formal writing.

If the pupils had been given more information, they would not have taken up smoking.

G3   **Using *too* and *very*.**

You cannot use too when you mean 'very' if your sentence has a *positive* meaning.

- ✔   *My mother's cooking is very delicious.*
- ✖   *My mother's cooking is too delicious.*

- ✔   *This book is very interesting.*
- ✖   *This book is too interesting.*

- ✔   *Travelling abroad is very exciting.*
- ✖   *Travelling abroad is too exciting.*

- ✔   *The sky is very blue.*
- ✖   *The sky is too blue.*

In written English, we use too as *part of* the following grammatical construction to express a *negative result*.

    too + adjective + to

Compare the use of too and very in the two following examples:

1   *This table is very heavy.*
    This sentence is a simple statement – it does *not* express *result*.

    This table is <u>too</u> heavy <u>to</u> lift.
    This means I *cannot* lift the table because it is very heavy.
    This is more than a simple statement.
    Being heavy is something *negative*. The *result* of the table being heavy is something *negative*. I *can't* lift it.

2   *I am very tired.*
    This sentence is a simple statement – it does *not* express *result*.

    I am <u>too</u> tired <u>to</u> revise.
    This means I *cannot* work because I am very tired.
    Being tired is something *negative*. The *result* of being tired is something *negative*. I *can't* revise.

This construction (to + adjective + too) does not work if you have a positive sentence. Let's look again at the first set of sentences above and try to apply the complete construction.

My mother's cooking is too delicious to eat.
(This does not make sense. It would mean you cannot eat your mother's cooking because it is very delicious!)

This book is too interesting to read.
(This does not make sense. It would mean you cannot read the book because it is very interesting!)

Travelling abroad is too interesting.
(This does not make sense. It would mean you cannot travel abroad because it is very interesting!)

In the *written* exam remember to use *both* parts of the construction to describe something which has a *negative result*.

My father is too fat to ride a bicycle.
(This means my father cannot ride a bicycle because he is very fat.)

This exercise is too difficult to understand.
(This means I cannot understand this exercise because it is very difficult.)

In *spoken* English it is not always necessary to use both parts of a result clause if the negative result is clear to both speakers in the conversation.

Teacher: *'Why haven't you done this exercise, Peter?'*
Student: *'It's too difficult.'*
(It's too difficult *to do*.)

Friend A: *'Do you want to go to the cinema this evening?'*
Friend B: *'No, thanks. I'm too tired.'*
(I'm too tired *to go*.)

Friend A: *'Shall we join the new sports club?'*
Friend B: *'I don't think so – it's too expensive.'*
(It's too expensive *to join*.)

★ **Remember**
Do not use **too** in a sentence with positive meaning. Replace it with **very**.
In a sentence with a negative result use both parts of the construction:
too + adjective + **to**.

G4 **Joining positive ideas together.**

Sometimes you need to join two *positive* ideas together.

1 *My sister sings.* (positive)   *My sister plays the piano.* (positive)
2 *Windmills are environmentally friendly.* (positive)   *Windmills provide a reliable source of electricity.* (positive)

In *formal* register, the two ideas can be joined using *also*.
also goes *before* the main verb.

1 *My sister sings and she also plays the piano.*
2 *Windmills are environmentally friendly and also provide a reliable source of energy.*

also does not usually go at the beginning of the sentence.

> ✖ *My sister sings. Also she plays the piano.*

In *friendly* register and *spoken* English, *also* is replaced by *...*, *too* or *... as well* at the end of the sentence.

My sister sings and plays the piano, too.
My sister sings and plays the piano as well.

G5 **Joining contrasting ideas together.**

Sometimes you need to join two *contrasting* ideas together.

1 *My brother is naughty.* (negative)   *We love him.* (positive)
2 *Lead-free petrol is expensive.* (negative).   *Lead-free petrol would be less harmful to the environment.* (positive)

Two words you can use to join contrasting ideas are *although* and *but*.

1 <u>Although</u> *he is naughty, we love him.*
   He's naughty, <u>but</u> we love him.
2 <u>Although</u> *lead-free petrol is expensive, it is less harmful to the environment.*
   Lead-free petrol is expensive, <u>but</u> it is less harmful to the environment.

although and *but cannot* be used in the same sentence.

> ✖ *Although he is naughty, but we love him.*

G6 **Words with no plural in English.**

Some of the words you may need to use in the exam do not have a plural form in English, although they may in your own language. So be careful! These words include:

information   homework   advice   luggage   news   furniture   knowledge

I have found <u>some information</u> about England on the internet.
I have got <u>lots of homework</u> to do tonight.
My uncle gave me <u>plenty of advice</u> about studying.
When he came to visit us, he didn't bring <u>any luggage</u>!
I saw something interesting on <u>the news</u>.

G7 **Sequence of tenses.**

If the main verb is in the past tense, the other verbs in the sentence will usually be in one of the past tenses (*not* the present or future).

> ✔ *I felt my friend <u>was</u> unhappy with her results.*
> ✖ *I felt my friend is unhappy with her results.*
> ✔ *I thought of you while I <u>was</u> eating.*
> ✖ *I thought of you while I am eating.*

★ **Remember**
The past tense of *can* is *could*.

★ **Remember**
The past tense of *will* is *would*.

★ **Remember**
Look out for the past perfect.

✔ We went to look for a phone so that we <u>could</u> get help.
✖ We went to look for a phone so that we can get help.

✔ I promised that I <u>would</u> always work hard.
✖ I promised that I will always work hard.

✔ They told him they <u>had been</u> to the police.
✖ They told him they have been to the police.

G8 **Using the present perfect tense.**

As its name suggests, this tense combines elements of the present and the past.

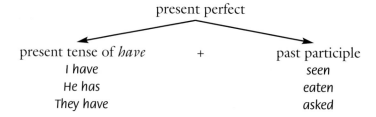

present perfect

present tense of *have*   +   past participle
I have   seen
He has   eaten
They have   asked

1   Talking about the *recent* past

Usually, when talking about an event that happened in the past, we use the past tense and say *when* it happened.

I played tennis on Monday.
I played tennis last week.
I played tennis when I lived near the sports centre.

However, when an event took place in the recent past, *there is no need to say when* because:

■ the event is completed (in the past), but the results can be seen in the present.
■ the event itself is more important than the time it happened.

These concepts are expressed by using the present perfect tense.

I've (I have) cut my finger!

The action of cutting is completed. We know it happened recently because we can see the bleeding finger, so there is no need to say *when* it happened.
    The fact that the finger is cut is more important than information about when it happened.

I've passed all my exams!

The action of passing the exams is completed. We know it happened recently because you are holding the results in your hand, so there is no need to say when.
    The fact that you passed the exams is more important than information about when you passed them.

You can emphasise the action by adding *just*.

You'll never guess who I've just seen!

However, if you use the present perfect (+ *just*) in your sentence you cannot say *when*.

He started jogging round the park at eight o'clock.
He started: past tense; *eight o'clock* tells us when.

He started jogging round the park in July.
He started: past tense; *in July* tells us when.

He's (just) started jogging round the park.
He's (just) started: present perfect; nothing in the sentence to say when.

2   Using *since* or *for*

If you want to talk about a situation that began in the past and has not changed up until the present moment in time, you must use the present perfect + *since/for*.

Since	For
is used for a specific moment in time	is used for lengths of time
Monday, Sunday March, September 3 o'clock lunchtime this morning last week my birthday Delia's party the wedding the war 1920, 1986, 2000	ages days (two) weeks (six) months (ten) years a long time a while some time

I have lived here since 1993. (and I still live here now)
We have lived here for three years. (and we still live here now)
I have had this pen since my birthday. (and I still have it now)

I've had short hair since Christmas.

★ **Remember**
Use the contracted, or short form, in friendly register.

3   Using *ever, never, yet, already*

Other words used with the present perfect to connect the past to the present include: *ever, never, yet, already*.

Have you ever been to China?
This means at any time in your life, since you were born until now.

He's (he has) never visited India.
This means at anytime in his life, since he was born until now.

Have you started your revision yet?
This means at any time in the past until now, this moment.

She's (she has) already finished her homework!
This means at some unspecified time in the past before now.

G9 **Sentences with questions inside them.**

There are many ways of asking questions in English. Look at four different types of question:

Type 1 *Where is he?*
Type 2 *Where does he live?*
Type 3 *Where has he lived?*
Type 4 *Is he happy?*

If you want to ask a question, but also use an introductory phrase (such as those given below) *before* the question, it is important to realise that the whole structure of the question changes, and it does not behave like a question any more.

Introductory (or prefix) phrases A

I'd like to know …
I don't know … / I didn't know …
I want to know … / I wanted to know …
I wonder … / I wondered …
I'm not really sure … / I wasn't really sure …
I have no idea … / I had no idea …
I can't remember …
I couldn't remember …

Type 1 questions

These begin with a *wh* question word:

who, what, where, when, why, how + *am / is / are / was / were*

If you use an introductory phrase in front of a Type 1 question, you must do the following.

1 Make the question into a *statement* by changing the word order:

Where	is am are was were	+ subject	→	subject +	is am are was were
(Where)	is	he?	→	he	is
(How)	was	she?	→	she	was

2 Then select an introductory phrase + *wh* question word.

I don't know + *where* + *he is.*

Look at the examples on the next page.

Original question	Prefix phrase	*wh* word	Statement
Why *was he* late?	I wonder/*I wondered	why	*he was* late.
What *are you* doing?	I don't know *I didn't know	what	*you are* doing. *you were* doing.
Who *is he*?	I'd like to know	who	*he is*.
Where *am I*?	I can't remember *I couldn't remember	where	*I am*. *I was*.

★ **Remember**
If the main verb is in the
*past tense, the other verbs
will probably be in one of the
past tenses.

Type 2 questions

These begin with a *wh* question word:

who, what, where, when, why, how + *do/does/did* + main verb

If you use an introductory phrase in front of a Type 2 question, you must do the following.

1 Make the question into a *statement* and change verb forms and agreement as necessary.

(What) *does he like?* → *he likes* …
(Where) *did she go?* → *she went* …

2 Then select an introductory phrase + *wh* question word.

I don't know + what + he likes.

Look at the following examples.

Original question	Prefix phrase	*wh* word	Statement
Who does she meet?	I don't know	who	she meets.
Why doesn't he phone?	I wonder	why	he doesn't phone.
Where do they live?	I'd like to know	where	they live.
Where did we go?	I can't remember	where	we went.
What did she study?	I want to know	what	she studied.
How did you revise ?	I have no idea	how	you revised.

Type 3 questions

These begin with a *wh* question word:

who, what, where, when, why, how + *has/have/had* + main verb

If you use an introductory phrase in front of a Type 3 question, you must do the following.

1 Make the question into a *statement* by changing the word order:

$$\text{(Where)} \begin{cases} \text{have} \\ \text{has} \\ \text{had} \end{cases} + \text{subject} + \text{main verb} \rightarrow \text{subject} + \begin{cases} \text{have} \\ \text{has} \\ \text{had} \end{cases} + \text{main verb}$$

(Where)   has   he   gone?   he   has   gone

2 Then select an introductory phrase + *wh* question word.

I don't know + where + he has gone.

Look at the following examples.

Original question	Prefix phrase	wh word	Statement
Who *have they* visited?	I don't know	who	*they have* visited.
Why *hasn't he* phoned?	I wonder	why	*he hasn't* phoned.
Where *have they* gone?	I'd like to know	where	*they have* gone.
Where *had they* been?	I couldn't remember	where	*they had* been.
What *have you* done?	I want to know	what	*you have* done.
How *has she* managed?	I have no idea	how	*she has* managed.

Type 4 questions

These do not have a *wh* question word.
If you use an introductory phrase in front of a Type 4 question, you must do the following.

1 Make the question into a statement.
2 Select an introductory phrase.
3 Use *if/whether*.

I have no idea + if + she drives.
I wonder + whether + he is hungry.

Look at the following examples.

Original question	Prefix phrase	wh word	Statement
Is Tom lonely?	I don't know	if/whether	Tom is lonely.
Do they play tennis?	I'd like to know	if/whether	they play tennis.
Did they tell him?	I have no idea	if/whether	they told him.

In all the examples of Type 1, 2, 3 and 4 questions, the sentence is no longer a question and does not need a question mark.

Introductory (or prefix) phrases B

Some introductory phrases are questions *themselves*, for example:

Do you know?
Can you tell me?
Have you any idea?

When these are used, you still need the *statement* form of the verb, but with a *question mark* at the end of the sentence.

Look at the following examples.

Type 1 questions

Original question	Prefix phrase	*wh* word	Statement + ?
Where *is Tom*?	Do you know	where	*Tom is*?
What *is her name*?	Can you tell me	what	*her name is*?
When *is Tom* arriving?	Have you any idea	when	*Tom is* arriving?

Type 2 questions

Original question	Prefix phrase	*wh* word	Statement + ?
Who does she like?	Do you know	who	she likes?
Why doesn't he phone?	Can you tell me	why	he doesn't phone?
Where do they live?	Have you any idea	where	they live?

Type 3 questions

Original question	Prefix phrase	*wh* word	Statement + ?
Who *has she* invited?	Do you know	who	*she has* invited?
Why *hasn't he* answered?	Can you tell me	why	*he hasn't* answered?
What *have they* bought?	Have you any idea	what	*they have* bought?

Type 4 questions

Original question	Prefix phrase	*wh* word	Statement + ?
Is Tom lonely?	Do you know	if/whether	Tom is lonely?
Do they play tennis?	Can you tell me	if/whether	they play tennis?
Did they tell him?	Have you any idea	if/whether	they told him?

Essential prepositions

Wherever prepositions occur, they can cause problems for students of English. Unfortunately, they do need to be learnt accurately: wrongly used prepositions make a very bad impression on examiners.

Common prepositions									
about	before	down	for	in	of	past	through	under	with
after	below		from	into	off		to	up	without
along	beside				on				
above	between				over				
around	by								
at									

This unit does not concentrate on the grammatical names of the various phrases containing prepositions, or the rules concerning their formation: this information is not essential for the exam. However, the phrases themselves are extremely important.

The following four groups list key phrases containing prepositions, carefully selected as being suitable for use in the exam. Make sure you allow plenty of time before the exams to learn them and try to practise using them until you feel completely comfortable with them. Try to produce sentences using the prepositions in as many different situations as possible. Ask your teacher to check them for you.

Whenever you read anything in English (books, articles, magazines), try to recognise these phrases and other similar ones: mark them and note *how* and *when* they are used. If you have a chance, record a conversation from the radio, play it back and examine the phrases with prepositions.

■ Group 1

The phrases in this group are produced when a common, simple verb combines with various prepositions or adverbs to produce a variety of meanings. In some cases, each word in the phrase keeps its own meaning and so there is no problem with understanding: for example, *sit down*.

On the other hand, it is often not possible to see a logical relationship between the original verb and the phrase produced when that verb is combined with a preposition. Or, to put it another way, you cannot guess the meaning of the phrase, even if you understand the meaning of each word in the phrase: for example, (*to*) *turn up* = (*to*) *arrive, appear unexpectedly*.

The situation is complicated by the fact that each combination may have two or three different meanings.

As explained in Section 1, Unit 2 on friendly register, to simplify language usually involves using a larger number of simple words to replace bigger words. That is why the phrases in Group 1 often appear in informal, or friendly, register.

How are you getting on with your homework? = progressing

The example shows how the two or three simple words in the prepositional phrase can replace a single, 'formal' word: (*to*) *get on with* = (*to*) *progress*.

Used in the appropriate places, these phrases will help to convince the examiner that you are familiar and comfortable with the different registers in English, and this is required in the exam. The list that follows has been carefully selected from the thousands of phrases found in English, and each one comes with example sentences relevant to the exam. You should learn them by heart and try to put them into sentences of your own. Aim to learn five a day. This may seem very difficult at first, but it will become easier. Ask someone to test you on them every day. *Listen* for these combinations when watching TV or talking to English people.

Break – broke – broken

- **Break down:** Stop working/functioning because of a fault. Usually relates to a car, bus or train. Also used with 'talks', 'discussions', 'negotiations', etc.
  Narrative: I'll never forget the night our car broke down and we had to walk home.
  Formal: Communication often breaks down between parents and teenagers.

- **Break in:** Enter somewhere (locked) by force. Usually relates to a thief, a burglar.
  Narrative: I was alone in the house, when I heard banging and realised that someone was trying to break in.

- **Break out (1):** Begin suddenly. Used to describe war, fire, disease, argument, panic.
  Narrative: We were in the supermarket, when a fire broke out.

- **Break out (2):** Escape.
  Narrative: We were locked in the museum, and thought we would have to break out.

- **Break up:** Finish, end. Usually relates to school term, meetings.
  Descriptive: School breaks up on 6 July for the summer holidays.

Bring – brought – brought

- **Bring in:** Introduce a new rule or law.
  Formal: The government has brought in a new law making it compulsory for passengers in the back seats of cars to wear seatbelts.

- **Bring on/about:** Cause to happen, result in.
  Advice: Sitting in wet clothes will certainly bring on a cold.
  Formal:
  .... will bring about
  }
  a change in attitude
  an awareness/understanding of
  an improvement in

- **Bring out:** Produce, cause something to be seen.
  Formal: Giving teenagers responsibility brings out the best in them.

- **Bring round (1):** Bring someone who has fainted back to consciousness.
  Narrative: ... fainted when she heard she'd won the competition and we had to throw water on her face to bring her round.

- **Bring round (2):** Bring something to my/your/his house.
  Descriptive: At weekends my friends bring their favourite CDs round and we listen to them on my brother's system.

- **Bring up (1):** Raise. Usually relates to a child.
  Formal: If children are brought up in a violent environment, they may grow into violent adults.

- **Bring up (2):** Highlight or refer to, remind others of a question/subject/topic.
  Descriptive: You'll recognise my Dad straight away – he's always bringing up the subject of exams!

Call – called – called

- **Call for:** Collect.
  Descriptive: My friend calls for me at eight and we walk to school together.

- **Call off:** Cancel.
  Descriptive narrative: When I heard the weather forecast, I had the feeling sports day would be called off.

Carry – carried – carried

- **Carry on:** Continue.
  Narrative: We carried on banging on the door, hoping someone would hear us.

Catch – caught – caught

- **Catch up with:** Reach the same level (when you were behind).
  Descriptive narrative: I was only ill for three days, but it's taken ages to catch up with the rest of the class.

Clean – cleaned – cleaned

- **Clean out:** Thoroughly clean and tidy.
  Descriptive: I've cleaned out the spare room and got it all ready for you.

Come – came – came

- **Come across:** Find (something) unexpectedly.
  Narrative: I was looking through the drawer for a pen, when I came across an old photograph.

- **Come up with:** Think of an idea.
  Descriptive: I've come up with a brilliant idea for the end-of-term party!
  Narrative: My sister always comes up with a good excuse for not doing her homework!

Cut – cut – cut

- **Cut down on:** Reduce.
  Descriptive: I've been cutting down on the time I spend playing computer games.

- **Cut out:** Stop (using/taking).
  Advice: If I were you, I'd try to cut out junk food.

■ **Cut out for:** (Often in negative sentences) Suited, good at, enjoy.
  Descriptive: I'm not really cut out for gardening/sport.

Do – did – done

■ **Do away with:** Abolish.
  School magazine: How many of you feel we should do away with school uniform?

■ **Do up:** Fasten.
  Narrative: I rushed out into the rain without doing up my jacket.

Drop – dropped – dropped

■ **Drop in:** Visit someone without official invitation or arrangement.
  Descriptive: At weekends my friends often drop in for a chat or to borrow a DVD.

Fall – fell – fallen

■ **Fall out:** Quarrel, have a disagreement.
  School magazine: Have you ever fallen out with one of your friends?

■ **Fall through:** To not be completed, not happen.
  Descriptive narrative: ... to let you know that my plans to go camping have fallen through because the weather has been far too wet recently.

Find – found – found

■ **Find out:** Discover (through effort).
  Descriptive: When they find out how fast you run, they'll put you in the athletics team.

Fix – fixed – fixed

■ **Fix up:** Arrange.
  Descriptive: You'll be glad to know I've fixed up for us to join the tennis club.

Get – got – got

■ **Get away from:** Have a chance to leave.
  Descriptive: ... old Uncle Sam started telling me about how life was when he was a boy, and I just couldn't get away (from him).
  School magazine: Now the holidays are on the horizon, I'm sure everyone is looking forward to getting away from school, at least for a while.

■ **Get away with:** Commit an offence or do something wrong and not be caught or punished.
  School magazine: We must not allow students to get away with bullying.

■ **Get on with (1):** Progress, ask about how well somebody is doing something.
  Descriptive: How are you getting on at school?
  How are you getting on with the driving lessons?

- **Get on with (2):** Have a positive, friendly, personal relationship with someone.
  Descriptive: I've never got on well with my sister – she's so extrovert!
  I'm sure you'll get on well with my Dad – he's mad about cars, just like you!

- **Get over:** Recover from. Usually relates to illness, shock, problem.
  Descriptive: I hope you've got over the flu.
  He's just getting over the disappointment of losing the match.

Give – gave – given

- **Give out:** Distribute.
  Descriptive narrative: There was a clown giving out brightly-coloured balloons to all the youngsters.

- **Give up (1):** Stop. Usually relates to a habit, or a school subject.
  School magazine: How many of us would like to give up maths!
  Formal: The government has a responsibility to encourage smokers to give up smoking.

- **Give up (2):** Stop trying to achieve something.
  Advice: I know how hard it is for you to lose weight, but you mustn't give up!

Go – went – gone

- **Go ahead:** Proceed.
  School magazine: The committee has gone ahead with plans for a new library.

- **Go back:** Return.
  Narrative: When I got the shoes home, I didn't like them, so I went back to the shop and changed them.

- **Go out (1):** Spend time away from your house for entertainment.
  Descriptive: At weekends I go out with my friends.

- **Go out (2):** Extinguish.
  Descriptive narrative: The party was in full swing, when suddenly the lights went out.

- **Go over:** Repeat (often verbally).
  Narrative: As we waited our turn to jump out of the plane, the instructor went over all the safety steps.

- **Go through:** Examine in detail.
  Advice: If I were you, I'd start going through your notes a few weeks before the exam.

- **Go up:** Increase.
  School magazine: Have you heard that the price of petrol is going up again?

Hold – held – held

- **Hold up:** Delay.
  Narrative/school magazine: ... the bus was held up in the traffic and we missed half of the play.

Keep – kept – kept

- **Keep on:** Continue.
  School magazine: Do your parents keep on telling you how important it is to study?

- **Keep up:** Maintain an effort.
  Advice: You've lost a lot of weight since you started eating sensibly. Keep it up and you'll soon be able to wear your favourite jeans.

Let – let – let

- **Let in:** Allow to enter.
  Narrative: When we eventually got to the club, they wouldn't let us in because we weren't wearing ties!

Look – looked – looked

- **Look after:** Take care of.
  Narrative: … we were looking after their dog while they were on holiday.

- **Look forward to:** Expect or anticipate something with pleasure, happiness.
  Descriptive: I'm really looking forward to seeing you.

- **Look out on:** Overlook. Usually relates to windows, buildings.
  Descriptive: … my bedroom looks out on the snow-covered mountains.

- **Look up:** Search for something in a reference book, such as a phone book, dictionary, address book.
  Narrative: I couldn't remember where she lived, so we had to look her address up in the phone book.

- **Look up to:** Respect.
  School magazine: Most of us have someone we look up to in our lives; a parent or relative, a sports star or even a pop star!

- **Look down on:** Not have respect for something.
  Advice: … whatever happens, don't think other teenagers look down on you because you are a bit overweight.

Make – made – made

- **Make for:** Go towards.
  School magazine: … in the summer holidays many of us make for the beach.

- **Make up:** Invent.
  Descriptive: … my younger brother is always making up stories about ghosts.

- **Make up for:** Compensate.
  School magazine: During the weeks of revision you may have missed quite a few workouts in the gym: but now the holidays have (finally!) arrived, you can make up for the lost exercise.

Move – moved – moved

- **Move in:** Take your belongings and put them into a different house, room etc., where you intend to stay.
  Descriptive: … I've been busy moving in to our new house.

Pick – picked – picked

■ **Pick up (1):** Collect and take someone (or something) with you, often in a vehicle.
Descriptive: … *the school bus stops to pick us up at the end of my street.*

■ **Pick up (2):** Learn, gain something without effort or expense.
Descriptive: *If you come and stay in France for three weeks, you'll soon pick up French.*

Pull – pulled – pulled

■ **Pull down:** Demolish. Usually a building.
School magazine: *Have you heard that the old library is going to be pulled down?*

■ **Pull up:** Stop driving, somewhere at the side of the road where you can stop without obstructing the traffic.
School magazine: *If you're feeling tired, why don't you pull up for a rest?*

Put – put – put

■ **Put across:** Explain.
School magazine: *We have to put across our ideas about school uniform if we want a change.*

■ **Put away:** Put something out of sight in an organised manner.
Descriptive: *My younger sister never puts away her toys.*

■ **Put forward:** Suggest.
School magazine: *This is a chance for you to come and put forward your ideas about how to save the environment.*
Formal: *Suggestions have been put forward concerning control of air pollution.*

■ **Put off:** Postpone.
School magazine: *If you're hoping for good exam results, do not be tempted to put off revision till the last minute.*

■ **Put on (1):** Wear, dress in clothes, accessories, cosmetics, perfume.
Advice: *What about putting on your new jacket and the cologne you got for your birthday?*

■ **Put on (2):** Perform. Usually of a play, concert, show.
School magazine: *We're looking for volunteers to put on this year's school show.*

■ **Put up:** Offer accommodation.
Descriptive: *We can camp if you want, or I have a friend who can put us up for a couple of nights.*

■ **Put up with:** Tolerate, stand, bear patiently.
Descriptive: *I'm afraid you'll have to put up with my younger brother playing tricks on you.*

Run – ran – run

■ **Run away with:** Assess quickly without careful thought or consideration. Usually + negative.
Descriptive: We live in the middle of the countryside – but don't run away with the idea that there's nothing to do!

■ **Run into (1):** Collide. Usually of vehicles.
Narrative: Dad slammed on the brakes suddenly, and the car behind ran into us.

■ **Run into (2):** Meet by chance.
Narrative: You won't believe who I ran into in town yesterday! Mr Brown, our old physics teacher.

■ **Run out of:** Reach the end of a supply.
Narrative: The car stopped. We thought it had broken down – but we had actually run out of petrol!

■ **Run over:** Drive on top of.
Narrative: The cyclist wobbled and fell off her bike. We braked hard and swerved, missing the girl, but running over her bike and squashing it.

See – saw – seen

■ **See off:** Say goodbye to someone as he catches his train, plane or gets into a car to leave.
School magazine: All the parents came to see us off at the airport, but we were so excited about catching the plane that we hardly noticed them.

Set – set – set

■ **Set off/out:** Begin a journey.
School magazine: On a cold, winter morning, 36 excited girls and four members of staff set off on the adventure holiday.

Show – showed – shown

■ **Show off:** Display some ability, only with the intention to impress.
Descriptive: My younger brother tries to annoy me by showing off his computer skills!

Stand – stood – stood

■ **Stand out:** Be noticeable, easily seen.
Narrative: The outline of the house stood out against the clear night sky.

■ **Stand up for:** Defend. Usually in words.
School magazine: We must stand up for victims of bullying.

Take – took – taken

■ **Take after:** Be like a parent or older relative in looks or ability.
Descriptive: I'm afraid I don't take after my mother when it comes to cooking!

■ **Take up:** Begin. Usually a sport or hobby.
  Advice: What about taking up tennis? It'd keep you fit and …

Talk – talked – talked

■ **Talk over:** Discuss.
  School magazine: If you're being bullied, you must talk it over with your parents or someone in authority at school.

Try – tried – tried

■ **Try out:** Test.
  Advice: The good thing is that you can try out the new equipment in the gym.

Turn – turned – turned

■ **Turn away:** Not allow to enter.
  Narrative: They turned us away from the club because we were under 18.

■ **Turn down (1):** Reject.
  School magazine: Our request for a swimming pool has been turned down, so why not raise the funds for it ourselves?

■ **Turn down (2):** Lower the volume, pressure, etc.
  Advice: If the noise of your friend's radio is disturbing your concentration, why not ask him to turn it down?

■ **Turn on/off:** Switch on or off the lights, radio, TV, AC, etc.
  Advice: … don't turn on your radio while you're studying.

■ **Turn out:** The end result (unexpected); it was revealed.
  Narrative: It all turned out well in the end.
  He didn't want to tell his parents about his exam results, but it turned out they knew already.

■ **Turn up:** Arrive, appear.
  Descriptive narrative: Everything was ready for the dinner party, but none of the guests turned up – we had put the wrong date on the invitation!

Wash – washed – washed

■ **Wash up:** Wash plates, dishes after a meal.
  Descriptive: I usually help my mother wash up/do the washing up after dinner.

■ Group 2

This is a list of words followed by prepositions, suitable for use mainly in formal writing. It is important to learn the relevant preposition and construction that follows each of the words.

Word	Preposition	Construction	Example
accustomed	to	+ noun + verb + *ing*	hard work working hard
afraid	of	+ noun + verb + *ing*	cats, spiders, hard work flying
angry	with	+ noun	someone *for* doing something
annoyed	with	+ noun	someone *for* doing something
annoyed	about	+ noun + verb + *ing*	the decision, the arrangements forgetting your birthday
apologise	for	+ noun + verb + *ing*	his behaviour being rude
approve	of	+ noun + verb + *ing*	marriage, single sex schools giving money to charity
ashamed	of	+ noun	myself, the truth, the way (something is done) …
aware	of	+ noun	the difficulties, the situation, the seriousness of the problem
bad	at	+ noun + verb + *ing*	tennis, maths, English, sport cooking, driving
blame someone	for	+ noun + verb + *ing*	the condition of hospitals, the standard of education neglecting the environment
capable	of	+ noun + verb + *ing*	change improving, solving, overcoming
concentrate	on	+ noun + verb + *ing*	revision providing, improving, studying
(have) difficulty	with	+ noun	homework, tennis, music
(have) difficulty	in	+ verb + *ing*	losing weight, concentrating
disagree	with	+ noun	my parents, my sister, the idea of …
disappointed	with	+ noun	someone
disappointed	with/about	+ noun	my results, the decision
disapprove	of	+ noun + verb + *ing*	cheats, bullies smoking, endangering
enthusiastic	about	+ noun + verb + *ing*	sport, the trip playing tennis, organising
excited	about	+ noun + verb + *ing*	the trip, the party visiting, taking part in, seeing
fond	of	+ noun + verb + *ing*	fast food playing tricks, exaggerating

Word	Preposition	Construction	Example
frightened	of	+ noun + verb + *ing*	the dark, thunderstorms drowning, forgetting
furious	with	+ noun	someone (*for* doing something)
furious	about	+ noun + verb + *ing*	the exam results, the decision breaking, losing, missing
good	at	+ noun + verb + *ing*	tennis, English, sport swimming, cooking, writing
the idea	of	+ noun + verb + *ing*	marriage, single sex schools walking, studying with friends
impressed	with	+ noun	the results, his behaviour, his cooking
influence	on	+ noun	someone, someone's behaviour
insist	on	+ verb + *ing*	paying, helping
interested	in	+ noun + verb + *ing*	sport, music saving the environment
(no) intention	of	+ verb + *ing*	improving, changing, rectifying
kind	to	+ noun	you, others, animals
laugh	at	+ noun	someone, something
listen	to	+ noun	someone, the radio
object	to	+ noun + verb + *ing*	the idea, the suggestion, the noise being treated like a child
pleased	with	+ noun	someone, the news
pleased	about	+ verb + *ing*	passing, winning
proud	of	+ noun + verb + *ing*	you, the school, the achievement winning, being successful
pessimistic	about	+ noun + verb + *ing*	the chances of, the outcome, the future saving, reaching
responsible	for	+ noun + verb + *ing*	(their) behaviour, (her) actions protecting, providing
succeed	in	+ noun + verb + *ing*	life passing the exam
save	from	+ noun + verb + *ing*	starvation losing
scared	of	+ noun + verb + *ing*	heights, failure losing my way, getting lost
smile	at	+ noun	him, you, the teacher
speak	to	+ noun	someone
the thought	of	+ noun + verb + *ing*	the winter, the exams, the holidays getting the results, going to university

■ Group 3

The prepositions in this group are part of a series of expressions used very regularly in daily situations. Most of these expressions are taught at an early stage of language learning. If you make a mistake when using them, this indicates to the examiner that your basic knowledge of English is poor.

The following list is of time-related phrases introduced by simple prepositions. Many of these are often confused. Make sure you *know* which prepositions to use. Cover them up and test yourself.

Preposition	Usage	Examples
at	an *exact* or *specific* time for festivals	At six o'clock At the crack of dawn At the moment At midnight At Christmas At Easter At weekends At the weekend
on	a *particular* day a date	On Thursday On Monday morning On Christmas Day On Friday night On 3 September
in	months, years and long periods of time	In April In 1993 In the past In the future
since	a *specific* time	Since January Since Monday Since my birthday Since 1920 Since the results came
for	a *length* of time	For ages For years For a while For ever For six months

Make sure you are totally confident about using these simple expressions. A small preposition may not seem important to you but it is *essential* to be accurate.

Now check through the following list of commonly misused simple prepositions.

at	by	for	on
at home	by car	go for a walk	on the radio
at school	by bus	go for a drive	on foot
at work	by plane	go for a swim	on the phone
at university	by train	go for a jog	on (the) television
at the cinema	by bike		
at the office	by air		

The phrases below can be particularly confusing.

■ **On time**
At the exact time: not early, not late.
The flight from New York arrived on time.

■ **In time**
Not late, early enough.
We had to run to the station, but we were in time for the last train.

■ **At the beginning/at the end**
These phrases refer to something that lasts for a *known* length of time or has a *known* length, such as a show, a TV programme, a journey, a school term, a book etc.
At the beginning (of the detective book/programme) you are made to think that the murderer is Alan, but his true identity is only revealed at the end (of the book/programme).
At the beginning of a formal letter, you write Dear Sir, and at the end you write Yours faithfully.

■ **In the beginning/at first/to begin with**
These phrases indicate a *change* of situation.
In the beginning, the snow was easy to walk on, but as we moved north it got deeper and difficult to cross.
At first, I found the food tasty, but after a while, it made me feel sick.
To begin with, we found the heat unbearable, but we soon got used to it.

■ **In the end/at last**
After some time, eventually.
Every time I tried Sarah's number it was engaged – but I got through in the end.
After what seemed like ages, the lift doors opened at last.

◼ Group 4

This is a list of idiomatic expressions containing prepositions, which native speakers use regularly, and which will make your writing much more natural. However, if they are used inappropriately the examiner will suspect you have learnt them without fully understanding them. Go through them one by one. If there are some you do not feel happy about, do not worry about them, but do not try to use them in the exam. Concentrate on the ones you are confident about.

■ **Out of the blue:** (Informal) Suddenly, unexpectedly, without warning.
Narrative: *We were having dinner when, out of the blue, the phone rang and we heard we had won a holiday!*

■ **In the same boat:** (Informal) In the same situation, having the same experience.
Advice: *I know what it's like to be lonely – I was in the same boat last year when my friend moved away to another town.*

- **On the brain:** (Informal) Think continuously about (something).
  School magazine: At this time of year, for one reason or another, many of us have exams on the brain!

- **Without a break:** (Formal/informal) Without stopping, continuously.
  School magazine/advice: If you spend hours doing revision without a break, it'll do more harm than good.

- **For a change:** (Formal/informal) (Do) something different.
  Advice: If you're bored with drinking water, why not squeeze some fresh orange juice for a change?

- **Off colour:** (Informal) Unwell.
  Narrative: I decided to stay at home because I was feeling a bit off colour.

- **In the dark:** (Formal/informal) Uninformed, ignorant.
  Descriptive narrative: We kept her in the dark about the party because we wanted it to be a surprise.

- **Out of date:** (Formal/informal) Old fashioned.
  Descriptive: I'm sure you'll find our science labs out of date – we haven't had any new equipment for years.

- **Up to date:** (Formal/informal) Informed, fashionable, modern.
  School magazine: Today's technology helps keep us up to date, but …

- **On a diet:** (Formal/informal) Trying to lose weight.
  Descriptive narrative: … and Jo, who's supposed to be on a diet, ate most of the chocolate cake!

- **On edge:** (Formal/informal) Tense, anxious, excited.
  School magazine/advice: … gentle exercise and plenty of sleep should stop you feeling on edge before the exams.

- **At a loose end:** (Informal) Having nothing to do, bored.
  School magazine: Do you think you're going to be at a loose end during the long school holidays?

- **On fire:** (Formal/informal) Burning, alight.
  Narrative: It wasn't until I saw flames coming out of the roof that I realised the supermarket was on fire.

- **On holiday:** (Formal/informal) Time spent relaxing away from school or work.
  Descriptive: I'm sorry I haven't written for so long, but I was on holiday and forgot to take my address book!

- **In a hurry:** (Formal/informal) Quickly.
  School magazine/descriptive: … often do their homework in a hurry so they can play computer games.

- **On the increase:** (Formal) Becoming greater in size, amount, etc.
  School magazine: The number of cars on the road is on the increase.

■ **At the latest:** (Formal/informal) Not later than.
  School magazine: Put your suggestions in the box outside room 12 by Friday
  lunch time at the latest.

■ **Between the lines:** (Formal/informal) Understand the true meaning from
  what is implied.
  Advice: Reading between the lines, it seems you are still feeling lonely.

■ **On my mind:** (Formal/informal) Thinking about.
  Advice: I've had your problem on my mind all day.

■ **In two minds:** (Formal/informal) Undecided.
  Narrative: I was in two minds whether to stay with my friend or go for
  help.

■ **In the mood:** (Informal) Mentally prepared for something.
  Advice: Don't try to revise if you are in the mood for socialising – you'll be
  wasting your time.

■ **Out of order:** (Formal/informal) Not working/functioning. Usually
  relates to machines.
  Narrative: We had to use the stairs because the lift was out of order.

■ **For your own sake:** (Formal/informal) In your own interests, for your
  benefit.
  School magazine: If you are a victim of bullying, you must report it to the
  authorities for your own sake, or the situation may get
  worse.

■ **In pain:** (Formal/informal) The feeling you have in your body when you
  have hurt yourself.
  Advice: Remember to do warm-up exercises, or you'll be in pain later!

■ **Out of place:** (Formal/informal) Different, not appropriate for a situation.
  Descriptive narrative: I was the only one wearing jeans, so I felt very out of
  place.

■ **Out of practice:** (Formal/informal) (To be) less good at doing something
  than you were because you have not spent time doing it recently.
  Descriptive: I used to play tennis at school in the past, but I'm out of
  practice now.

■ **At random:** (Formal/informal) In any order.
  Descriptive narrative: The winners were picked at random from a hat.

■ **As a rule:** (Formal/informal) Usually.
  Descriptive: As a rule, I spend about three hours every evening on
  schoolwork.

■ **In the long run:** (Formal/informal) Eventually, in the end.
  School magazine/advice: It may be fashionable to smoke when you are
  young, but remember that in the long run you are
  damaging your health.

■ **From scratch:** (Informal) From the beginning.
  School magazine/advice: Make sure you revise all your notes from scratch.

- **Behind the times:** (Formal/informal) Out of date, unfashionable.
  Descriptive narrative: Aunty May was there in a hat and gloves! You know how behind the times she always is!

- **Out of tune:** (Formal/informal) Not in harmony.
  Descriptive: You should have heard everyone singing 'Happy Birthday' – it was awful – all out of tune!

- **In touch:** (Formal/informal) Not lose contact with someone (for example, a friend if one of you moves away).
  Descriptive: I'm sending my new phone number and e-mail address – so please keep in touch!

- **Under the weather:** (Informal) Unwell (but nothing serious).
  Descriptive narrative: I was sorry to hear you've been under the weather.

- **Without warning:** (Formal/informal) Suddenly.
  Narrative: We were on the way to the theatre when the driver stopped the bus without warning.

Word partners and sayings

■ Word partners

'Word partners' refers to two words regularly used in combination with each other. There are many more than those listed here, which have been selected as relevant to IGCSE topics. If you want to improve your knowledge of these, try to listen to interviews in English on the radio and television (try the BBC World Service) or on the internet, or read good quality newspapers.

Look at the second word in the partnership. It could be a word you want to use in your formal writing. Then look carefully at its partner – the word in front of it. Try to use both words together, as this will make your English sound much more natural and fluent.

Word partners		Definition/Expansion	Examples
tremendous	achievement	= something you have done which you are very proud of	Taking part in the school play was a tremendous achievement for my shy sister. Raising funds for our school swimming pool was a tremendous achievement.
helpful	advice	give … to someone get … from someone go to someone for … about revision/… on how to revise	My teacher gave me some very helpful advice about revision.
acutely	aware	= very aware be … that be … of the (problem(s)/ difficulties/dangers	Many people are acutely aware of the problems caused by bad eating habits.
total	commitment	something depends on/ requires/demands/can only be achieved as a result of …	To be a professional footballer demands total commitment.
disastrous/ serious	consequences	something will lead to/ result in …	Continual emission of greenhouse gases will lead to disastrous consequences. Refusing to wear a seat belt can have serious consequences.
senseless	cruelty		Keeping wild animals locked up in cages is senseless cruelty.
incurable	disease		A hospice is a special nursing home for people suffering from incurable diseases.

Word partners		Definition/Expansion	Examples
reckless	driver	= someone who drives without respect for traffic rules	Safety awareness campaigns should result in a reduction in the number of reckless drivers on our roads.
incredibly/ remarkably	fit	= very fit	To become an Olympic athlete you need to be incredibly fit.
foreseeable	future	in the .../for the ...	Man will colonise space in the foreseeable future.
virtually	impossible	= almost impossible	It is virtually impossible to lose weight without doing exercise.
noticeable	improvement	+ in There has been a ... in	Regular exercise will result in a noticeable improvement in your health. If you plan your revision carefully, there will be a noticeable improvement in your results.
substantial	increase	+ in a ... in the volume of traffic on the roads	In recent years, there has been a substantial increase in smoking-related illnesses.
fundamental/ underlying	problem	there is a ... with (something) the ... is	The fundamental problem of pollution needs to be resolved.
capital	punishment	= death for serious crimes ... should be abolished/ introduced	Many countries have abolished capital punishment.
considerable/ substantial	reduction	... can/will cause, result in	Building a ring road would result in a considerable reduction in the number of road accidents.
disappointing/ impressive/ pleasing	results		Bad planning can lead to disappointing results.
harmful/ unknown	side effects	something can produce/ have/cause/result in ...	Violence on TV, smoking, eating junk food, and car exhausts can all produce harmful side effects.
practical	solution		We must find a practical solution to the problem of pollution.
irresistible	temptation	= something which is extremely difficult to resist	When you are on a diet, chocolate cake can be an irresistible temptation.
sorely	tempted	= something you want to do very much (but know you shouldn't)	Students are sometimes sorely tempted to stay in bed and miss lectures.

■ Sayings

There are many sayings in English. You may know some already. The following list is a very short selection of sayings which you may be able to include in your writing. Never use a saying unless you are completely sure of its meaning and that you are using it appropriately.

■ *All work and no play makes Jack a dull boy.*

If you spend all your time working, without having a break and being with other people, you will have no interest in life and will become a boring person.

■ *Turn over a new leaf.*

To decide to change the way you think about or do something to produce an improvement. (Decide to give up fast food in order to feel fitter. Decide to plan your revision carefully so your results are better than last time.)

■ *Bury your head in the sand.*

Try to escape from a problem by pretending you are unaware of it.

■ *Jump on the bandwagon.*

To become involved in an activity that is likely to be successful.

■ *If you can't beat them, join them.*

If everyone around you is doing something which you do not approve of, you can try to stop them. If they continue in spite of your efforts, then you will be 'the odd one out' – in other words, left alone. If this happens, you are in the minority, which suggests what they are doing may not be as bad as you thought. So – why not join them? (Sport/fitness/relaxation classes/self-defence classes.)

■ *Every cloud has a silver lining.*

No matter how bad a situation may seem, something good will usually result from it. (The misery of revision/the joy of passing the exam. The misery of being on a diet/the pleasure of fitting into fashionable clothes.)

Now note the ways in which sayings can be introduced into your writing.

■ To a friend who needs advice on exam revision:

You know what they say, 'All work and no play makes Jack a dull boy.'

■ To a friend who needs to start a fitness programme:

'If you can't beat them, join them' *– or so they say.*

■ To a friend who has moved away and is feeling lonely.

As my grandmother used to say, 'Every cloud has a silver lining.'

Confused phrases

The following list contains phrases which regularly cause confusion for students.

Student's mistake ✘	Correct sentence ✔
A room of myself	A room of my own A room to myself
To your surprise	Believe it or not Funnily enough You may be surprised to hear
I hope you would	I hope you will I wish you would
To sit in home	To stay at home
Sleep early	Have an early night Go to bed early
For my luck	Luckily for me I'm lucky because
Lucky for not coming	It's a good thing/job you + negative
You were lucky you weren't there	Thank goodness + negative What if you + had + negative
My small sister	My younger sister
She's a brilliant cooker	She's a brilliant cook
Invite my friends to my home	Invite my friends round
To enjoy my time	To enjoy myself To have a good time
You know how it is like	You know what it is like You know how it is
As you know that	As you know, (I am terrified of heights) You know that (I am terrified of heights)
To sit with someone	To spend time with someone
In my point of view	In my view From my point of view
I feel sorry that you didn't come	It's a shame that you couldn't come
I feel regret for you not coming	I'm sorry that you couldn't come
All people	Everyone
Almost at my age	The same age as me
All what you hear is …	The only thing you hear is
I don't have except	I only have
Today morning	This morning
To make/do an accident	To have an accident
It will do you a lot of help	It will help you a lot It will do you a lot of good
Something wrong will happen	Something will go wrong

Spelling tips

Spelling is very important in the exam. Learning a few rules will improve your spelling. Some of the spelling rules and exceptions to the spelling rules are complicated and not relevant to the exam, and so have not been included in this unit.

Vowels are: a, e, i, o, u.
Consonants are all the other letters which are not vowels.

1 When do you double a consonant?

Consonants can only be doubled if they are at the end of a word.

Words of *one* syllable which end in one vowel + one consonant double the final consonant when you add 'er' or 'ing'.

thin → thinner
get → getting
cut → cutting
swim → swimming, swimmer
run → running, runner

Words of *two or more* syllables which end in one vowel + one consonant double the final consonant *when the stress falls on the last syllable.*

be'<u>gin</u> → beginning, beginner
up'<u>set</u> → upsetting

Compare with the following verbs where the stress falls on an earlier syllable:

de'<u>velop</u> → developed
'<u>benefit</u> → benefited

2 When you add 'full' to the end of a word, the second 'l' is dropped.

wonder + full = wonderful
beauty + full = beautiful
Note also,
till → until

3 Adverbs are formed by adding 'ly' to the adjective, so adjectives ending in 'l' make adverbs with double 'l'.

Adjective   Adverb
beautiful + ly = beautifully
awful   + ly = awfully

4 Learn the simple rule: 'i' before 'e' except after 'c'. This will help you if you always confuse words which contain the same sound, but have different spelling, such as:

bel**ie**ve   and   rec**ei**ve

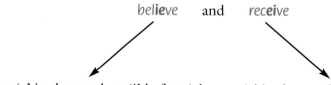

no 'c' in the word, so 'i' before 'e'   'c' in the word, so 'e' before 'i'

The exceptions to this spelling rule are fairly common and simple words which you use regularly:

eight	either	foreign	height	leisure
neighbour	neither	their	weight	weird

You will notice that none of these words has the same pronunciation as *believe, receive*, in other words /i:/.

5 Words ending in a consonant +'y' usually change the 'y' to 'i' when something is added.

easy → easier
carry → carried
happy → happily

This change does *not* happen if the letters added begin with 'i'.

study → studying
carry → carrying
baby → babyish

Words ending in a vowel + 'y' do *not* change.

buy → buying
play → played
enjoy → enjoyment

6 Words which end in a consonant + 'e' drop the 'e' if the letters added begin with another vowel.

make → making
hope → hoping

Words which end in a consonant + 'e' keep the 'e' if the letters added begin with a consonant.

hope → hopeful
manage → management

7 Words ending in 'ise' or 'ize'

■ In American English, only 'ize' is used.
■ In British English, words with two syllables end in 'ise': *advise, surprise*.
■ Longer words in British English can be spelt either way: *computerise/computerize*.

★ **Note**
If you have learnt American English, there will be other differences in spelling. American spellings will be accepted in the exam, if they are used throughout.

Problem spellings

Make sure you can spell these words which are regularly spelt wrongly by students.

A
absolutely
accommodation
actually
address
answer
apologise
appearance
appropriate
assure

B
beautiful
beginner
beginning
believe
benefit
boring
breath
breathe
business
busy

C
centre
chocolate
chosen
college
colourful
coming
competitive
completely

D
decision
delicious
develop
different
disappointment
documentary

E
embarrassed
enthusiastic

equipment
especially
except
excited
exercise
extremely

F
fabulous
fascinating
favourite
finally
fitness
fortunately
forward
friend

G
gorgeous
guitar
gym

H
habit
handsome
hear
here
hoping
horrified

I
immediately
impression
intelligent
interesting

L
laugh
listened
loose (adj)
lose (v)

M
marvellous

museum
mysterious

N
neighbour
nervous

O
occasion

P
panicked
planning
politely
practically
practice (n)
practise (v)
prefer
preferable
private
professional
programme

Q
quiet
quite
quiz

R
raining
really
receive
recipe
relieved
riding

S
safely
settled
shopping
sincerely
souvenir
spacious
specially

stereo
stopped
studying
succeed
surprise
swimming

T
terrifying
their
there
they're

thoroughly
throughout
truly

U
understanding
until
usual

V
video

W
weight
wear
weather
where
whether
without
writing

Exam hints for the writing exam

Managing your time is essential in the exam. Put your watch on the table and keep aware of the time. Do *not* be tempted to turn to the compositions and write them first.

The exam starts with reading comprehensions requiring short answers, and these are intended to 'warm you up': as you read you are reminded of vocabulary, structures and ideas and this, in turn, builds up your confidence. In other words, the reading comprehension section *prepares* you for the writing section.

■ Planning

Why write a plan?

- A plan gives you time to **think**. If you think for a few moments, it will stop you rushing into the question and probably making mistakes or writing an irrelevant answer.
- A plan will also allow you to remember ideas, structures, phrases and vocabulary that you may otherwise forget.
- A plan also means fewer crossings out; a messy presentation is annoying for the examiner. A neat presentation indicates confidence.
- A plan gives you a chance to produce the best possible composition, including all the important elements of logic, register, development, vocabulary and presentation.
- A plan indicates a methodical, serious approach which will impress the examiner.

Time is precious, so make sure your plan is worthwhile and *useful* to you. Whatever happens, a plan should not be simply another version of the composition and should never be written *after* answering the question. In fact, if you run out of time, your plan should give the examiner a clear outline of what you intended to include.

How long should a plan take?

Allow three to five minutes. This means you should have studied, practised and become familiar with the relevant vocabulary, prepositions, word partners, grammar and register, together with the features of style and writing techniques outlined in this book *before* you sit the exam. Plan to write four paragraphs, each containing 25–40 words (Core) or 40–50 words (Extended).

How to write a plan

You will need a slightly different plan for each type of writing task. You should aim to write a basic plan and then write into it any vocabulary and language structures you may want to include in your answer. Write your plan in pencil.

Draw a line through any plan you write when you have finished with it. Do *not* rub it out – you want the examiner to see your effort!

★ **Remember**
Your plan is to *help* you.

Plan 1: Descriptive/advice letter

First analyse the question, using the methods outlined in the relevant units of this book. Then, on a blank sheet of the exam question paper, in pencil, write 'Plan'. Next, write a sub-heading 'Intro' or 'Intro and transition'.

Select the appropriate introduction and if necessary adapt it to reflect the question or to personalise. **Write it down** in note form. For example:

... Lovely to get letter, but sorry to hear about ...

Do the same for the transition sentence. For example:

I thought I'd drop you a line ... been in the same boat

Write a heading 'Body'. Decide on two ideas you want to include. Then decide on the support for each. **Write them down**.

Write down a selection of phrases relevant to the type of letter, for example, advice phrases. Take a moment to select the most appropriate ones. Write down any word partnerships/sayings/preposition phrases you want to include.

Look at the following friendly advice writing task:

A good friend of yours has moved to a new area and is feeling lonely. Write a letter to make him feel happier and help him like his new life better.

How should you approach this task? What might your plan look like?
First, analyse the question. Elements to notice:

- a good friend
- moved away (so *you* miss him, too!)
- sad, lonely (so are you)
- writes to you hoping you will make him feel happier. You may need to give him advice or encouragement.

What kind of introduction is appropriate? Does it need to be adapted?

Your plan might look something like this:

Plan

Intro and transition:

... lovely to get letter ... *but* ... sad to hear lonely ... miss you, too

Body:

The best thing you can do is ...

Why don't you ...?

Whatever happens, ...

Ideas	Support
1 Get involved in after-school activities; drama, music, choir	Get to know school friends on a social basis.
2 Join a sports club	Keep you busy. Do you good. Meet people with the same interests.

Down in the dumps/under the weather/in the same boat/at a loose end/from scratch/drop in/find out/fix up/take up/in touch.

Ending

Why don't you come over in the holidays? Keep writing.

Plan 2: Narrative/descriptive narrative letter

Look at the following narrative writing task:

You were taking a pleasant walk by yourself when you fell down some steps and twisted your knee. You were unable to get help and had to wait several hours for help to arrive. Write a letter to a friend explaining what happened.

How would you approach and plan this question?
An example is shown below.

<u>Plan</u>

<u>Intro and transition</u>:

You'll never believe what happened …

I was out on my usual walk/favourite path through the woods.

Feelings – daydreaming/head in the clouds/walking happily along.

<u>Body</u>:

Paragraph 1: (events/feelings/time sequence + vocabulary)

1 *Out of the blue I slipped on the steps/covered with leaves/must have been wet*

2 *I was just about to get up. Felt as if my leg was cut in two.*

3 *The moment I realised my knee was twisted, it made my blood run cold.*

Paragraph 2:

1 *Nothing for it but to wait.*

2 *Sang songs/recited geometry theorems/had pretend conversations.*

3 *After what seemed like ages. Mr … found me – taking Rex for 4pm walk.*

4 *Never felt so relieved to see that dog!*

<u>Ending</u>

It all turned out well in the end. Nothing broken.

Must dash to tell … about it.

Plan 3: Opinions/suggestions composition

Write the following basic plan and include points relevant to the subject.

1 Intro: *Nowadays/the majority of … /in my opinion …*
2 Support: *Firstly,/because of … /due to … /which …*
3 Support: *Another reason …*
4 *To sum up,/I believe … /it would be a good idea if* (+ past).

Plan 4: Views and arguments composition

Write the following basic plan and include points relevant to the subject.

1 Intro: *These days/a large number of …* 'explaining the importance of the subject'.
2 Points in favour: *One of the main arguments in favour of …/ Furthermore … /which means that …*
3 Points against: *On the other hand, …/moreover… /consequently …*
4 *To sum up, … /in my opinion … /it would be a good idea if …*

◼ Check your answer

You *must* allow a few minutes to check through each composition. Try not to check a piece of writing as soon as you finish it; your mistakes will not be obvious if you have just written them. Write both compositions, then go back and start to re-read them, starting with the first.

The following checklist is for *basic* mistakes, such as grammar and spelling.

1 Each student has his own 'favourite' or repeat mistake. Be aware of yours and check for it.
2 Check that each sentence is *complete* (has a subject, verb and object) and is correctly *linked* to the next. In a long sentence, you may have changed constructions without realising.
3 Check that the sequence of tenses is maintained: if the main verb is in the *past*, all other verbs are usually in one of the *past* tenses.
4 Check that singular subjects have single verbs (+ 's' for *he/she/it* in the present tense) and plural subjects have plural verbs.
5 Check that verbs are followed by the correct preposition and relevant construction.
6 *Then*, remembering that corrections should be minor and neat, look for:

- words with no plural form, such as *homework, information*
- muddled constructions: *hope + will* (avoid *wish*)
- words that can be removed in friendly register: *that, which*
- position of *also* (correct it with arrows)
- *so* + adjective + *that* / *too* + adjective + *to*
- repetition.

★ **Remember**
There is not enough time to make major changes. These should not be necessary anyway, if you wrote a plan first. You want to maintain neat presentation.

■ A last few helpful hints and reminders

Write your answers in *pen* not pencil (but your plan should be in pencil). If you need more space for your answers, use the blank pages at the end of the answer booklet. Write at the bottom of the lined answer page 'continued on blank page number …'.

Friendly register

Support any information you give, such as advice or personal details, with simple, relevant explanations. Personalise to indicate your relationship with the reader, and to reveal personal details.

Sometimes, in narratives, a 'plan' is given, for example:

- Explain how you got lost.
- What did you do when you realised you were lost?
- How did you resolve the problem?
- Describe how you felt.

All points in this plan should be covered by your answer, but it is only a base; in other words, you can develop it as much as you want. Remember to include **feelings**, **incidents** and **atmosphere**.

★ **Remember**
Do not use words from the question when writing in friendly register, because the words of the question are written in formal register.

Formal register

Sometimes, in views and arguments compositions, prompts are given; for example, a list of comments from other people on the subject. Do *not* include them all. Select one or two to explore with support and examples. Use the relevant language structures. Give relevant support for maximum marks.

Check if the question specifies 'school magazine' or 'newspaper'. Then use the correct **register** and link your views to the interests of the reader.

If the question asks you to present your formal writing composition as 'a letter to a newspaper', then the only modification in layout you need to make is to write:

Dear Sir,

before beginning your introduction, and then at the end add:

Yours faithfully,
A. Student

When writing your signature, use your normal handwriting and write either:

- the initial of your first name, followed by your family name (if you have more than one family name, use only the last one)

  or

- your first name followed by your family name (again, only one).

Finally, underneath your signature write the same name in capital letters.

If the question asks you to present the formal writing as a 'letter to your *local* newspaper', in addition to following the same style shown above, remember that a *local* paper is very different from a *national* paper. All the readers are familiar with the local area and what is happening there – if an airport is being planned, everyone will know about it and will be putting forward their own views about it.

In many ways, what you write may sound like a school magazine article, with the use of 'we' to emphasise solidarity. You should mention local places, even local people by name to try to create the friendly atmosphere of a small community. As an example, let's look again at the 'windmills' composition from Section 4, Unit 1, and imagine it being written for a local newspaper. What differences would there be?

■ The use of 'we':

We have all heard about the plans to build windmills on <u>our</u> beautiful hills/behind <u>our</u> beautiful woods/along <u>our</u> lovely riverbank.

■ When outlining the arguments against windmills, try to think *who* in the local community would be against them:

– People owning small hotels; give them names to make them sound real: *Mrs Moore of the Lakeside Guest House*
– Local wildlife group; give the name of the leader, how many years the group has been meeting or how many members it has.

■ *Why* are they against the windmills?

– Fewer guests are staying because the ugly windmills have spoiled the natural beauty of the area.
– A rare species of owl/fox/badger – only found locally – may be frightened away by the noise of the blades.

■ Do the same thing when considering points in favour of windmills.

Summary writing

Remember to:

■ write a list of points
■ put the points into logical order
■ write the points using your own words
■ write headings for notes
■ check to see if you need to include functions, such as advice
■ use formal register
■ *not* exceed the number of words asked for
■ *not* write an introduction.

Throughout the exam, pay careful attention to your **spelling**, **punctuation**, **grammar** and general **presentation**.

This section contains key words and phrases relevant to a number of topics which are regularly covered in the IGCSE exam, and which you would be expected to know at this level. Some of the vocabulary has appeared in appropriate units of this book, but has been included again here to provide a complete list. The table below lists the topics that are covered, together with the different registers you need to show knowledge of in each case.

Words or phrases suitable for a particular register are marked as follows:

Fr	=	Friendly
F	=	Formal
SM	=	School magazine

Sometimes it can be difficult to think of basic ideas. To help you, where a topic can be developed for discussion, ideas have been included under separate headings in the form of opinions, suggestions, and views and arguments sentences.

The separate headings are usually based on past exam questions, although they obviously apply to the topic in general. Some words or phrases may appear under different headings. You may have different ideas and opinions of your own, in which case you should use the sentences given as a structural basis for your sentence.

	Friendly	Formal	Article/School magazine
School and education	✓	✓	✓
Hobbies, sport and health	✓	✓	✓
Holidays	✓	✓	✓
Crime and social issues	✓	✓	✓
Smoking		✓	✓
Television	✓	✓	✓
Importance of appearance	✓	✓	✓
Environment		✓	✓
Tourism		✓	✓
Safety and driving		✓	✓
Animals		✓	✓
Past, present and future		✓	✓
Home and family	✓		

■ SCHOOL and EDUCATION

comprehensive school – a government school which is free and available to everyone.

private/independent school – parents must pay fees to send their children to these schools.

traditional school – uniforms, discipline, academic, competitive sport (play to win), compulsory sport (you must do it whether you want to or not. There is no choice. It is not optional.).

progressive school – no uniform, prefer continuous assessment and coursework to exams, may abolish compulsory sport (would be optional), may abolish competitive sport (would be for fun, exercise, social reasons).

boarding school – you sleep, eat, relax, do your homework in accommodation owned and run by the school. Pupils/students can be *weekly boarders* (they go home or to relatives at weekends), or they can board for the term. This is a convenient option for parents who work abroad. However, it is not possible to board at a comprehensive, and boarding is *very* expensive – usually double the fees of a private day school.

day school – not a boarding school. You go home each day when school ends.

to win a scholarship – to obtain a place at a school on merit, based on the result of a written entrance exam. Parents do not need to pay school fees.

Head/Headteacher
Headmaster
Headmistress

lots of/loads of/not much homework (SM/Fr)

a heavy/light workload (SM/F)

classroom: open plan, rows of desks
science laboratory (or lab. for short) equipment
sports hall
gym
games pitch (for cricket, football, hockey)

well-equipped (of laboratory, library, gym, etc.)
out of the ark = very old
up-to-date (used adjectively)

tuck shop – sells crisps, sweets, snacks, for mid-morning break
(to have) school lunch

after-school activities (clubs, societies, sports teams)
extra-curriculum/curricular activities (F)

to take + a subject (Fr/SM)
What subjects are you taking? (Fr/SM)
Are you taking English? (Fr/SM)
a popular subject (SM/F) = many students study the subject

optional (SM/F) = you have a choice
compulsory (SM/F) = no choice, you must do it

to work hard – more common than 'study'
to get good marks
If we want to go to a good university, we have to get good marks.
to be under pressure
parental pressure (SM/F) = parents encouraging/forcing you to work
peer pressure (SM/F) = students the same age as you, influencing you or persuading/forcing you to dress or behave a certain way

to settle into = get used to, accustomed to, begin to feel comfortable with somewhere new
My sister did not like her new school at first, but now she's settled in (= settled into the new school), *she really enjoys it.*
to settle down to = to start something seriously, with serious intent
Before dinner, I organise my books and check my revision timetable, so that I can settle down to work straight after eating.

Exams and revision

(to do) revision
to revise
cramming
to cram

allow time to revise (SM/F)
give yourself time to revise (Fr)
plan ahead

work out/make a revision timetable/study plan
stick to/keep to a timetable
don't put it off (Fr) = do not delay

distract (your attention)
distraction (F)
disturb (your concentration) (F)
stop you concentrating (Fr)

willpower
self-discipline

learn facts by saying them over and over again
pick out important facts
highlight key facts
write key facts on revision cards
record notes onto tape
draw labelled diagrams
make your subject more visual
draw cartoons so you can 'see' the information

to be under a lot of stress (Fr)
to ease stress (F)
to relieve tension (F)
stress

headaches
feeling permanently tired
aching limbs   } all signs of stress
tense muscles
to ache all over

to crack up (under the stress) = to become mentally
    unable to cope with exams and revision

don't overdo it
don't work for long stretches without a break
don't be tempted to …
don't think you can …
don't burn the midnight oil = don't study late into
    the night
don't drink too much coffee: it'll mess up your
    sleep pattern

listen to music
unwind/relax before you go to bed
have regular breaks (every half hour or so)
do regular exercise
eat/have fruit and vegetables as snacks
make sure you still see friends
go out at the weekends

to improve your concentration (F)
to help you to concentrate better (Fr)
to help to keep you alert
to make you feel more confident
to build up your confidence (F)
to help you to relax
to feel under less pressure
to achieve more
to have time to relax as well

the night before the exam …
… have a warm, relaxing bath
… have an early night

on the day of the exam …
… get up early so you don't feel rushed
… have some breakfast

to take an exam (also, to sit an exam) = to go to
    the examination centre, sit and write your
    answers to the exam questions
He's taking the English exam on Monday.
He'll have taken the exam by lunchtime.
He's not here at the moment, he's taking an exam.

to pass an exam = to get/obtain the number of
    marks necessary to succeed
to fail an exam = to not pass, to not reach the
    necessary standard to pass
If you don't pass/If you fail this exam, you'll have to
    resit.

to do well = to get good results
to do badly = to get bad results
to make more effort = to try harder

There's no time to lose = start (revision) immediately
to get down to work = concentrate on study
Look on the bright side = think positively about a
    depressing situation
Put your nose to the grindstone = start to make
    real effort
Pull your socks up = try harder
Keep up the good work = keep working to the
    same standard

All work and no play makes Jack a dull boy = if you
    work all the time and never relax or do anything
    you enjoy, then you become dull and boring

Strike a reasonable balance between schoolwork
    and other activities.
Short bursts of study with frequent breaks are
    better ((F) = more effective) than long stretches
    without breaks.
When you finish, reward yourself with a rest or a
    fun activity.

How to improve school

build better sports facilities/a swimming pool
provide language laboratories
enlarge the library to include
    modern/contemporary fiction

more/less discipline

treat students as responsible members of society

committee (of staff and students?) to deal with bullying

smaller classes and friendly teachers (but remember friendly teachers should be good teachers, too)

a wider range of subjects, including practical subjects

educational trips

Teachers should motivate students to learn for interest, not just to pass exams.

Introduce your ideas with phrases using the second conditional (see Section 7, Unit 2, Key grammar points):

I'd like to see/have …
There should be …

The school should } *provide …*
offer …

I think it'd
It would } *be nice if …*

The school would be better if …
We would enjoy school more if …

The problem of bullying

What is bullying?

Wanting to frighten or hurt someone by:

- name-calling
- damaging their property
- making threats.

What are the effects of bullying?

The victim becomes distressed, miserable and insecure, and … his performance at school may be affected.

If the bullying lasts a long time, his personality may be affected.

In other words, the effects are very serious and damaging.

What can be done?

The school should have a zero-tolerance approach to bullying.

The school should take bullying seriously.

Every student in the school should be able to recognise bullying and not be afraid to report it.

The victim should socialise more. Loners (= people without friends, or who prefer to be alone) are more vulnerable (= at risk). Safety in numbers.

The victim has a responsibility to report bullies to the authorities, or talk about it to his parents.

There should be a support group for victims.

A committee formed from staff and other students could decide on appropriate punishment for the bully.

Bullies should be encouraged to make friends with the victim to understand how the victim feels.

Bullies should be made to take responsibility for their actions.

The objective is to break the cycle of bullying in a way that changes the behaviour of the bully, with the best result for the victim.

School uniform

Arguments in favour of school uniform

no distinction between backgrounds, wealthy or poor

no time wasted each morning deciding what to wear

no need to impress

students feel they 'belong', like a family – leads to pride, self-esteem

main reason for going to school is to learn, not to show off your clothes

you can change out of uniform after school and at weekends

it is more appropriate to express your personality outside the school environment

everyone wears a 'uniform': you would wear different things when cleaning/cooking or entertaining friends and different again when going to work (shirt/blouse, tie, suit, smart shoes)

Arguments against school uniform

school uniform is boring, does not suit everyone

feel like a prisoner

students like to feel mature, responsible enough to select their own clothes

no chance to be an individual

Are these arguments relevant to different age groups throughout the school?

Single sex or mixed school?

depends on the individual school

depends on the family background
a child from a reserved family
a child from a sheltered background

depends on the individual child
self-conscious, inhibited (describes a shy child)
a sensitive child
an only child = a child with no brothers or sisters
feel awkward, embarrassed
feel comfortable, relaxed

adolescent/teenager = describes the age group
    from 13 to 19
mature = behave(s) like an adult
to reach maturity
well-adjusted

balance
to interrelate/relate with each other
segregation = the separating of boys from girls

there are many factors to consider
(have to) look at it from the point of view of the
    individual child
(have to) look at it from the education point of view

a child from a sheltered background may feel more
    comfortable in a single sex school
parents may feel a single sex school is more suitable
    for a sensitive child
but society is mixed. The child will have to come
    to terms with this sooner or later
Will the child feel awkward/embarrassed/not
    know how to deal with the opposite sex when he
    leaves school?
Will the single sex school have boosted her
    confidence so that by school-leaving age she will
    feel less awkward in the presence of the opposite
    sex?

Adolescence is a notoriously difficult stage for
    many teenagers. Is there any evidence that
    segregation from the opposite sex reduces
    bullying or emotional conflicts?
Is the problem worse *in either case* for teenagers
    who are overweight, have spots or are weak
    academically?
Having members of the opposite sex present may
    distract a teenager. He may pay more attention
to his appearance, hair, clothing, trying to be
    noticed or to make an impression, than on
    studies.

Research shows that boys and girls learn in a
    different way/react to information differently.
Good teachers should be aware of this. In single
    sex schools teachers can suit the lesson to either
    boys or girls.
Statistics show that single sex schools consistently
    obtain better results in public examinations than
    mixed schools.

In mixed schools, teachers must make sure there
    is a balance between the interests of both
    sexes.
Mixed schools may 'teach' children of both sexes
    how to have respect for each other, what makes
    the other sex tick and what compromises need
    to be made for both sexes to exist together
    harmoniously.
This is a slow and difficult process, learnt through
    experience.
For many people, this process continues through
    life/only becomes possible once they have
    matured.
Should this lesson be learnt at the expense of
    academic success/basic education?

University offers the opportunity for more mature
    interaction.

Interview advice

no need to be worried
just relax
be confident
be yourself

nothing too trendy (Fr)
remember to polish your shoes for a change (Fr)

sit still, don't fidget/twiddle your hair/tap your
    feet (Fr)
be your usual, polite self (Fr)
so much depends on … the overall impression you
    make (F)
neat, smart appearance (SM/F)
look the interviewer straight in the eye (Fr/SM)

be polite – just as you always are

■ HOBBIES, SPORT and HEALTH

to have a good appetite (usually applies to
    someone who eats a lot)
junk food
fast food
convenience food (F)
a balanced diet
to eat the wrong things
healthy eating

to be fit/unfit/out of condition
out of shape = unfit
to be off colour/under the weather
to feel rotten
to feel sick = to be about to vomit
to suffer ill-health (F)

as fit as a fiddle = very fit
incredibly/unbelievably/remarkably fit

to feel on top of the world
to feel great
to feel full of energy/go/beans

boost your energy (level)
to get rid of (Fr)/break down (F) (fat)
to build up (muscle)
to tone up flabby muscles

improve body shape (F)
improve appetite/circulation/posture
make your heart stronger
help you sleep better
do you good

to lose weight
to be on a diet
cut down = reduce
cut out = stop completely
to reduce the calorie intake (F)

to take up + noun
… thinking of taking up tennis/rowing
to join a gym/health club/fitness centre

out in the open/fresh air
a sense of freedom
to meet people with similar interests
a fitness fanatic = someone who is very keen on
    being fit

good ⎫
brilliant ⎪
quite good ⎪
not bad ⎬ at
hopeless ⎪
no good at all ⎭

keen on + verb + *ing*

all you need is …
it doesn't cost much
it doesn't need complicated equipment

tennis racket
tennis court = where you play tennis
football match
football pitch = where you play football

to play (tennis) for fun
to warm up
do some warm-up exercises

hobby
pastime (F)
recreation (F)
to spend time + verb + *ing*

change your lifestyle
change your eating habits

■ HOLIDAYS

tourist
holiday-maker
coach tour
full-board = all meals included
bed and breakfast

it'll make a nice change to …
it'll be fun to …

there were clear blue skies
there was not a cloud in the sky

the weather couldn't have been better
it couldn't have been a better day
there was not a breath of wind

the sky was overcast and threatening rain
the weather couldn't have been worse
it couldn't have been a worse day

it started to pour with rain
it started to throw it down = to rain heavily
it was raining cats and dogs = raining heavily

the heavens opened = it suddenly began to rain
   heavily
to run for shelter
to make a dash for it = to try to reach shelter
   without getting too wet
soaked to the skin

waterlogged = flooded
The whole sports field was waterlogged in no time.

dressed up to the nines = beautifully dressed ready
   for a night out

in a relaxed mood
in a festive mood
strolling around
to enjoy yourself
to have a good time

to go sightseeing
to see the sights
to visit local places of interest
local entertainment
colourful folk dances
traditional costumes

to buy souvenirs to take home
to charge tip-top prices
to take photos
to have a photo session
to buy postcards

Carnival/festival

people/visitors flocked in their hundreds
refreshment stall/tent
to do a good business
dying of thirst = very thirsty
to quench their thirst = to stop them feeling thirsty

in a relaxed mood
in a festive mood
strolling around
wandering around
licking ice-creams
joining in the fun

twinkling fairy lights
(decorated with) brightly coloured bunting = flags
   used as decoration
dancing display
colourful folk dances
traditional costumes
sideshow/stalls
tug-of-war

float (main event) = lorry decorated in the theme
   of the carnival, which drives slowly through the
   streets
procession
tombola/raffle

smell of onions frying
candy floss/toffee apple
makes you feel hungry

noise of the music
deafening
couldn't hear yourself think/speak
traditional instruments
marching band

■ CRIME and SOCIAL ISSUES

juvenile = youth, under 18 years old, not legally an
   adult
juvenile delinquent = young trouble maker

vandal = someone who spoils other people's
   property by smashing it, breaking it, just for fun
to vandalise
hooligan = trouble maker
football hooligan = someone who starts fights or
   damages property at football matches
hooliganism

thug = someone who is physically aggressive to
   other people
young offender
mugger = someone who knocks over a victim in
   order to steal a handbag, wallet etc.
mugging

burglar = someone who breaks into houses,
   buildings to steal the contents

graffiti = writing of slogans, rude words on public
   walls and surfaces, usually with spray paint

to be given a prison sentence
to be sent to prison

capital punishment/the death penalty = killing a
   criminal (by electric chair, lethal injection,
   hanging, etc.) who has committed a serious
   offence, such as murder
capital punishment is supposed to act as a deterrent
   = the thought that their actions may result in
   their death should make criminals think twice

shoplifter = someone who steals from shops
pickpocket
joyriding = breaking into a car, stealing it to drive dangerously at high speed without a licence
joyrider
unrepentant (F) = not feeling sorry, not asking for forgiveness

poverty can drive people to crime; people without basics, such as food, have no choice but to steal

prosperity nurtures crime (F) – in a materialistic society, people steal to obtain things (mobile phones, for example) because they see other people with phones and feel they should have one, too

drug-related crime – drug addicts have to steal in order to have something to sell to get the money they need for drugs
theft becomes a way of life to support a drugs habit (F)

influence of violent films on TV and DVDs

break-up of the traditional family (high rate of divorce, children from broken homes)

to take a tough stand
to enforce legislation (F)
to introduce new laws (F)
to bring in new laws (Fr)

■ SMOKING

passive smoking – this applies to people who do not smoke, but breathe in smoke from others who do. This is especially important for children with parents who smoke.

the rights of the non-smoker
no-smoking areas
smoke-free zones

lung cancer
brain tumour
nicotine-stained fingers
yellow teeth
unfashionable

Are you one of the set who thinks it is 'cool' to smoke? (SM)
Do you think you know everything there is to know about smoking? (SM)

many of us know someone who has died as a result of smoking

if the idea of cancer does not seem real to you, maybe the thought of yellow fingertips and foul smelling breath will make you think twice (SM)

if you smoke already, it is never too late to give up (SM)

nowadays, due to scientific research and the mass media, we are all aware of the dangers of smoking (F)
it would be a good idea if we …

smokers are becoming social outcasts, forced to smoke outside office buildings, as more and more places become smoke-free zones
smokers are now made to feel outsiders

smokers 50 years ago were unaware of the dangers and were simply smoking to be fashionable. With today's information, it makes sense never to smoke

■ TELEVISION

influence of TV/the internet
educational
entertaining
controversial topic
satellite channels – 24 hours a day, multi-cultural programmes of poor quality, often not suitable for younger viewers

a TV addict = someone who wants to watch TV all the time
a couch potato = someone who sits in a chair in front of the screen, without moving, for the whole evening

Are you fed up with parents controlling what you watch on TV? (SM)
Do you find yourself rushing to finish your homework so you can collapse in front of the TV screen every night? (SM)

Remember: everyone *knows* TV is supposed to be bad for your eyes and that it is addictive, that time flies when you watch it. People also become anti-social, because they prefer to watch TV rather than go out and socialise.

If you want to include these points, start by saying 'we all know that…'

However, as everyone has heard these arguments many times before, do not attempt to use them to persuade students not to watch TV. You have to think of a *new approach*, a different angle.

Bearing this in mind, always try to appeal to your fellow students' maturity and sense of responsibility.

Do we really want to be reminded of all these things and go through all this fuss every time we want to watch TV? If not, we have to ask ourselves 'is TV really worth it?' (SM)

Stand back for a moment and see how boring the programmes really are, how you are wasting your life watching TV, when you could be doing something interesting and useful – like playing tennis with friends. (SM)

Break the TV habit. (SM)

it is argued that by the age of 10, children are discerning viewers, which means they can recognise what is real and what is not

… controlling what children watch makes them more interested in the 'censored' programmes

it would be a good idea if a censor board were set up to classify programmes

it is time media classes were introduced into the school curriculum to help children interpret what they see on TV

… youth clubs and schools could organise activities for youngsters to curb the influence of TV

TV threatens our relationships with each other and our own identity

it can become an obsession, with people organising their lives round TV programmes

some local activity centres, such as the ice rink, have had to close down, as young people choose to slump in front of the TV instead of taking part in physical activity

it can be used to mislead and misinform
it can brainwash us into buying things we may not really need
it has the potential for education, language teaching
it could be used to promote national culture
the cost of producing a good quality programme is high

advertisers (who help finance programmes) like to be associated with feelings of happiness and contentment, not documentaries about AIDS, depression and debt

■ IMPORTANCE OF APPEARANCE

Do you worry about how you look? (SM)
Are you one of the many teenagers who lose sleep over their appearance? (SM)
we should not judge people by their appearance
the way you look says a lot about your personality

TV and magazines always show slim, attractive people, and this has made us insecure
glamorous stars on TV and in glossy magazines have made us over-concerned about our looks

there is no need to follow the trends. Do not be afraid to be yourself
some people may argue that people who look good get better treatment
not everyone can afford or has the time to look glamorous
personal qualities are more important – looks can mislead
dress within acceptable limits

eat a balanced diet and do regular exercise. Not only will you feel fitter, your skin will look healthy and you will stay slim

I think it is important to be clean, wear respectable clothes and let your personality shine through

■ ENVIRONMENT

Note: This topic should be considered from different points of view.

natural or scientific considerations, such as climate change, global warming, natural disasters (floods, drought, earthquake)
damage caused by man/humans (pollution, damage to ozone layer, deforestation)
effect on life (human health, animals, vegetation)

environmentally friendly
environmental issues (F)
natural resources = oil, gas, gold, etc.
conserve natural resources = be careful not to use them up completely

natural resources are being depleted = used up, squandered = wasted
a threat to the environment

recycling (helps to conserve natural resources)
compare the costs of recycling with cost of manufacturing
landfill site = an area where compacted rubbish is dumped

an eyesore
to upset the balance of nature

catalytic converter = fitted to car exhaust systems to reduce pollutants
pollution
to poison the air/atmosphere/the seas/the land
layer of smog = a mix of smoke and fog which sometimes hangs over industrialised areas, cities etc.
number of cars/volume of traffic has grown at an alarming rate

danger to public health
health hazard = danger to health
the situation is getting out of hand
things are getting steadily worse

to damage/spoil
consider the future
deforestation = cutting down of forests
natural habitats are being destroyed
endangered species

global warming/climate change
urban growth
skyscrapers/high-rise blocks

to tackle/address an issue

Arguments in favour of wind farms

environmentally friendly, no dangerous fumes, no air pollution
more attractive than a conventional power station
provide a reliable source of electricity
make small industries possible, which …
… create employment in the area

Arguments against wind farms

ugly, eyesore, spoil the natural beauty of a place
may put tourists off, reduce tourism – bad for the economy

noise pollution, may disturb local wildlife
distracting, especially for motorists
may cause pollution by blowing dust and dirt around
will need large area of land – which may be used for farming

■ TOURISM

package tour = a holiday where all the accommodation and travel are arranged by a travel agent for you, and is not very expensive
popularity of package tours has produced an increase in tourism
more tourists than ever before
a marked increase in tourism
cut-price and discount airlines provide more opportunities for more people to travel

tourist
tourist guide

comfort
convenience
coach tour

souvenir sellers
to charge tip-top prices

brings money into the country
tourists spend a lot of money in local shops, etc.
provides work for many local people, often in isolated areas where there would be no other way of earning a living

to spoil the natural beauty
areas of natural beauty are at risk
to pollute the environment
to respect the environment
to drop litter

the way you behave reflects the country and society you are from

■ SAFETY and DRIVING

to commute = to travel a long distance to and from work each day
the rush hour = 7.30–9.30 am and 4.30–6.30 pm: the time when commuters are travelling to and from work
traffic jam

traffic comes to a standstill
congestion

bumper to bumper = heavy traffic in a queue, moving slowly
to crawl along = move slowly due to heavy volume of traffic

ring road = a road which takes traffic around the outside of a city or town to reduce congestion and speed up the traffic flow
by-pass = a road which avoids going through the centre of a town or city
city driving

to slow down
to brake hard
to slam on the brakes = to apply the brakes suddenly and sharply
to skid … and crash into (for describing an accident)
to run into the car in front = to hit the car from behind
to swerve = change the direction of the car to avoid an accident
to have an accident
to crash
to run over
a head-on collision
a write-off = a vehicle which is so badly damaged in an accident that it cannot be driven again

to overtake = if the car in front of you is going slowly, you move in front of it by overtaking

a learner = someone who is learning to drive
to take/fail/pass your driving test

emergency services = fire, police and ambulance
on the spot
at the scene
soaring cost of petrol

pavement = path
zebra crossing = markings on the road where pedestrians have the right to cross
a roundabout
a junction
traffic lights
pedestrian = someone on foot

a bus/cycle lane
to have the right of way

Ways to make driving safer

wear a seatbelt
observe the speed limit
use of speed cameras
(on the spot) fines

Reducing pollution caused by cars

Are you counting the days until you can drive? (SM)
Are you looking forward to following in the footsteps of your parents/siblings (brothers and sisters)? (SM)
Are you looking forward to getting behind the wheel? (SM)
Are you reaching the driving age? (SM)

Driving is associated with freedom, independence, maturity (SM/F)

Have you stopped to consider the down-side? (SM)
Stop for a moment to consider the down-side.

We are all aware, from our topic work and the environment awareness campaign carried out by Year 10, of the dangers to the environment caused by car exhaust. (SM/F)

What we can do

use lead-free petrol (SM/F)
do not use the car for short journeys (SM/F)
keep the car serviced/maintained/tuned up for maximum efficiency/minimum exhaust fumes (SM/F)
take passengers where possible (SM/F)

No need to sacrifice freedom and independence,

… just be considerate and environmentally friendly (SM)
… just be considerate and think of the damage you could be doing to the environment (SM)

What the government can do

An improved network of ring roads should be built to prevent traffic jams which result in a build-up of pollutants/exhaust fumes in the air. (F)
Cars should be serviced to ensure minimum exhaust levels. (F)

The government should encourage drivers to leave their cars at home in favour of public transport. (F)

The government has a responsibility to provide reliable and affordable public transport. (F)

There should be a public awareness campaign to highlight the dangers to public health and the environment from car exhaust. (F)

The price of petrol should be raised and the profit put into improving public transport. (F)

Advantages of cars

convenient

comfortable

door-to-door: keep you dry in wet weather

sense of freedom

no need to rely on others: feeling of independence

greater degree of mobility

can choose fellow travellers

not restricted to timetables

can take unlimited luggage with you

Disadvantages of cars

expensive to run, insure, maintain, park

we become conditioned to our car and always use it even when we could walk

make us lazy

modern day driving is very stressful – can lead to road rage (= bad language, rude gestures, verbal arguments or even physical fights between drivers)

tired and stressed drivers may fall asleep at the wheel

cars are regularly broken into or stolen by thieves

Advantages of public transport

reduces number of cars on the road, which means less air pollution

kinder to the environment

Disadvantages of public transport

inconvenient – and probably not much cheaper

uncomfortable

■ ANIMALS

cruelty to animals

endangered species

in danger of extinction

becoming extinct

natural habitat disappearing

urban growth = spreading of towns, cities into countryside

animal rights groups = people who campaign on behalf of animals

in captivity

behind bars

in cages

senseless cruelty

intolerable conditions

safe breeding environment

conservationist

inhumane treatment

educational value of zoos

entertainment value of zoos

zoos provide many jobs

safari parks

wild animals suffer away from natural environment

cruel to keep wild animals in cages

to save animals from extinction

safe breeding environment

day trips

educational experience

to provide employment for local people

needs less space than a safari park

pets

■ PAST, PRESENT and FUTURE

In the past

life was less complicated, carefree, slower, more relaxed, there was less stress

there was harder physical work to do

there were stronger personal relationships/social ties/closer knit communities

there was no electricity/technology

there was more leisure time

people were more aware of nature and the natural cycles

there were incurable diseases, poor living conditions, lack of education

People look back with nostalgia to the 'good old days'.

In the present

Today, we have

- technology
- medical advances
- travel
- education
- stress and stress-related illnesses
- the rat-race
- competition
- increased crime due to breakdown of social values
- everything impersonal, materialistic
- no concern for the environment

In the future

Advances in technology, such as computers, mobile phones and the internet will result in more free time. This is not necessarily a good thing. It could result in boredom and increased crime rates, as can be seen in areas affected by high unemployment.

Effect of computers

could eventually replace teachers at school
could replace schools as we know them. Every student could study at home on a computer linked to a teacher on a computer in her home.
lose human aspect/contact/interaction
books in a school library will be accessed by computer. Books themselves may have been replaced by CD-ROMs
workers, too, will be home-based. Fewer commuters will mean less air pollution, less stress
people will become isolated at home and have no contact with others. In time, we may forget how to communicate with people and socialise – both essential elements of our nature
computers of today will seem hopelessly out of date, huge and slow

Family

Will not be like the family unit of today. 'Test-tube babies'. Cloning. No need for couples.
Everyone will live alone with a computer to work at, which will also serve him (or her).

Travel

Travelling to other planets will be common. Spaceships will be larger and fuelled by a new resource – possibly discovered on a trip to another planet.

■ HOME and FAMILY

Home

a detached house
a flat
a semi
a terraced house

a block of flats
a skyscraper

on the ground floor
on the third floor

upstairs
downstairs

in the suburbs of
on the outskirts of
not far from
about 10 minutes' walk/drive/bus ride from
(quite) near the city centre
(right) in the centre/heart/middle of the city

overlooking
with a lovely/great/fantastic view of

the spare room
the guest room
to share my room
to get the spare room ready

Family

a kind-hearted sort of person
an easy-going kind of person
easy to talk to
easy to get on with
young at heart
… ready to lend an ear

… looks like …
… takes after …

… is very different from …
… are very similar in some ways …

a practical joker
to tell jokes
to play tricks on …
to pull someone's leg
cheeky

a computer/TV/junk food addict/enthusiast/fan
mad about …
keen on …
… fancies himself as a …

a bookworm

fashion conscious
dressed up to the nines
at a loose end
up to date
out of date

to get on well (with)
to see eye to eye (with)
his bark is worse than his bite
… sings at the top of her voice
… plays his music at full volume

to have a sweet tooth
to have a second helping
to be on a diet

brilliant at
hopeless at
excited about
afraid of

Family celebration

to have a party
to throw a party
to hold a party
I thought you might like to know how the party
    went

to get smart
a frilly white blouse
a gaudy dress = very brightly coloured
glittery material
shocking pink
to spend ages trying to decide what to wear
to make up your mind = to decide

dressed up to the nines = dressed beautifully

a cheerful character
a piercing voice
laughing eyes
to be the centre of attention
to tell a joke
to crack a joke
to be bored to tears
to have a good time
to burst out laughing
to burst into tears

to be in full swing = at its most lively
it was a bit dull at first, but quite good once it got
    going
the small hours = after midnight/early the
    following morning
it went on well into the small hours

to have a sweet tooth = to enjoy eating sweet
    things
to tuck into (the cake) = to eat something with
    great pleasure, almost greedily
to have a second helping = to have another serving
    of food

a delicious smell
a sizzling sound (of something frying)

the music was much too loud for my liking = I did
    not like the music because it was loud
in tune
all/completely out of tune
to put up with/someone's behaviour/
    remarks/jokes
I got stuck with Uncle George and had to put up
    with his usual, boring advice for what seemed
    like ages until May came and rescued me.

to run out of cake/coffee
to go round
I had to eat my cake/chicken off a paper serviette,
    as there weren't enough plates to go round.
to go without
Nora's spicy chicken was such a hit/so popular that
    it soon ran out and a few of us had to go
    without.

ANSWERS TO EXERCISES

■ SECTION 1 UNIT 2

Exercise 1, page 4

Suggested answers:

1 If you work in a holiday camp for kids, you'll get to do lots of exciting things.
2 Every two years people use twice as much water.
3 We must do something to stop car drivers speeding.
4 It is good for you to exercise regularly, and it can help you lose weight, too.
5 When there are tourists, it's good for the country because it means a lot of money is coming in.

■ SECTION 2 UNIT 2

Exercise 1, page 36

1 'Apology' introduction not appropriate. Friends asking for advice need a quick reply. Sounds disinterested. More interested in your study than your friend's problem.
2 *meaning to write for ages* – not appropriate. Friends asking for advice need a quick reply.
3 Good introduction, showing concern for your friend. *I have been in the same boat before* – misuse of register and phrase. → *I've been in the same boat* or *I was in the same boat before* (see G8, page 194 and R6, page 183).
4 Good content for an introduction. Quick reply **this morning**, and reassuring. *I've been in the same boat before* – see number 3.

Exercise 3, page 40

1 **You … hours** – use of *also* is formal (see R9, page 184). No support.
   Another helpful … them – listing. No support or personalising. Use of *advice* is formal (see R1, page 182).
2 **I think … people** – listing, or repeating the same idea? Use of *also* is formal (see R9, page 184).
   as you know – a good attempt to personalise.
   because … own – a good attempt to support.
   I think you should – repetition of advice phrase – select an alternative.
   as this would – a good attempt to support.
   the same interests as you – good attempt to personalise.
3 **You can** – select a better advice phrase.
   your great parties – personalising.
   I'm sure … love it – support.
   they will → they'll.
   The best thing – should be first piece of advice.

■ **SECTION 2 UNIT 3**

Exercise 2, page 57
Suggested answer:

> I was enjoying myself looking at the funny cards, trying to choose one for **Susan's birthday (don't forget, it's next Tuesday)❶**.
>
> **I was just about to❷** make up my mind, **when❷** there was a deafening noise behind me. I looked over the counters **and❸** was **terrified to see❹** a man with a dirty scarf over his face holding a knife at the cashier.
>
> **I panicked❺**, and couldn't think what to do **at first❻**. **It took a few moments before❻** I remembered I had my mobile phone in my hand, **although❼, as you know❽**, I'm not very good at using it!
>
> Anyway, **by the time❾** I started calling the police, **Pedro❿** and two of his friends **from the judo club❿** had come into the shop.
>
> **I have never felt so relieved to see⓫** Pedro! **Before⓬** they even realised what was happening, **though⓭**, the would-be robber dropped his knife and had run away **in no time⓮**.
>
> So now you know all about the excitement at the shop. I must go now – I want to tell Alex about it.

❶ Personalising
❷ Time sequence × 2
❸ Connector
❹ Feelings
❺ Feelings
❻ Time sequence × 2
❼ Connector
❽ Personalising
❾ Time sequence
❿ Personalising × 2
⓫ Feelings
⓬ Time sequence
⓭ Connector
⓮ Time sequence

Exercise 3, page 57
Suggested answer:

> I'm dying to tell you what happened to me on the way home from school just now.
>
> Mai had her usual tennis practice, so I was on my own, and everywhere was quiet as it always is at dinnertime.
>
> **As❶** I stepped in the lift, I was wondering what Mum was making for dinner. **The minute❶** the lift doors closed, **I knew something was wrong❷, because❸** the lights dipped **and❸** there was a strange noise – **it set my teeth on edge❹**.
>
> **I was just about to❺** press the button for a lower floor, **when suddenly❺** the lights went out **and❻** I **was horrified to realise❼** the lift had stopped moving and I was stuck. **I felt my blood run cold❼. You know❽** how terrified I am of the dark.
>
> I don't know how, **but❾ for the first time in my life❿**, I managed to **keep a cool head⓫ and⓬** groped around **till⓬** I found the alarm button.
>
> I suppose it must have been **about ten minutes later⓭** –though, **as you can imagine⓮, it seemed like ages⓯, I was relieved to hear⓰** voices and banging so I calmed down a bit. **Soon⓱** the doors opened and **at last⓱** I climbed out to safety.
>
> I think it was the scariest moment in my life. I wonder what you'd have done? I must go now for tea.

❶ Time sequence × 2
❷ Feelings
❸ Connector × 2
❹ Feelings
❺ Time sequence × 2
❻ Connector
❼ Feelings × 2
❽ Personalising
❾ Connector
❿ Time sequence
⓫ Feelings
⓬ Connector × 2
⓭ Time sequence
⓮ Personalising
⓯ Time sequence
⓰ Feelings
⓱ Time sequence × 2

Exercise 4, page 58
Suggested answer:

> **As soon as❶** I got to the airfield I was given clear instructions on how to use the parachute. **About two hours later❶**, after lots of practice, **it was time to❶** get in the plane. **Up until then❶** I hadn't felt **nervous❷**, but **by the time❸** it was my turn to jump, **I was terrified❹**. **If only you'd been there❺** then – **you know❺** how **scared I am❻** of heights.
>
> **Just as❼** I was about to change my mind, the instructor gave me a friendly push, **and❽ before❾** I knew it, **I was amazed to find❿** myself falling through the air!
>
> **It only took a few minutes⓫** to reach the ground, **and⓬ although⓬** it was a fantastic experience, **I can't tell you how relieved I was to⓭** touch down safely.
>
> So now you know I can parachute jump – and I can thoroughly recommend it! Must go now and find something else to do tomorrow!

❶ Time sequence × 4
❷ Feelings
❸ Time sequence
❹ Feelings
❺ Personalising × 2
❻ Feelings
❼ Time sequence
❽ Connector
❾ Time sequence
❿ Feelings
⓫ Time sequence
⓬ Connector × 2
⓭ Feelings

■ SECTION 3 UNIT 2
Exercise 1, page 87
1 (Surely) schools could help promote awareness of the dangers of smoking.
2 I (would) suggest introducing laws to deal with the problem of pollution.
3 I (would) suggest that drivers should take a more difficult driving test.
4 It would be a good idea if children were made aware of the importance of good eating habits.
5 Tourists have a responsibility to respect the places they visit.
6 It is (high) time doctors gave more advice on health.

■ SECTION 3 UNIT 3
Exercise 1, pages 88–9
1 As far as I am concerned, we should judge a person by his actions and not by his appearance.
2 As I see it, it is high time schools educated children about the dangers of taking drugs.
3 Personally, I feel that countries could take steps to reduce the negative aspects of tourism.
4 In my opinion, schools have a responsibility to preserve the environment for future generations.

5 As far as I am concerned, sport should be part of every school timetable.
Suggested answers:
6 In my view, seatbelts could prevent serious injuries in car accidents.
7 I believe that it would be sensible if ring roads were built around major cities.
8 Many people believe that schools have a responsibility to make students aware of the problems caused by pollution.

Exercise 2, page 89
Suggested answers:
1 The vast majority of parents feel that it would be a good idea if schools motivated children.
2 Almost all teenagers think that it is high time parents listened to their point of view.
3 A large number of people believe that we have a responsibility to begin to respect the environment.
4 On the whole, people think it is high time the government reduced the price of petrol.
5 Most students feel they should be treated as responsible members of society.

Exercise 6, page 91

Suggested answers:

1 I object to the way people are cruel to animals.
One thing I dislike about people is the way they are cruel to animals.
One thing that annoys me is the way people are cruel to animals.

2 Computers that never do what you want infuriate me.
One thing I dislike about computers is the way they never do what you want.
One thing that infuriates me is the way computers never do what you want.

3 I like the way teachers always try to make lessons interesting.
One thing I like about teachers is the way they always try to make lessons interesting.
One thing that infuriates me about teachers is the way they never make lessons interesting.

4 I object to the way cars pollute the environment.
One thing I dislike about cars is the way they pollute the environment.
One thing that worries me about cars is the way they pollute the environment.

Exercise 7, page 91

1 It is hard to imagine that some people cannot read.
2 It is upsetting to hear that crime is on the increase.
3 It is easy to understand why/how/that travelling broadens the mind.
4 It is frightening to realise how/that pollution is destroying the environment.
5 It is easy to see why/that revision is important.

■ SECTION 3 UNIT 4

Exercise 1, page 92

Suggested answers:

1 One of the main arguments against modern technology is that it is damaging our planet.
Some people would argue that modern technology is damaging our planet.
Many people think that modern technology is damaging our planet.

2 The main argument in favour of windmills is that they are environmentally friendly.
It can be argued that windmills are environmentally friendly.
Many people think that windmills are environmentally friendly.

3 One of the main arguments against team sports is that they can cause aggression.

Some people would argue that team sports can cause aggression.
It can be argued that team sports can cause aggression.

4 One of the main arguments in favour of competitive sports is that they encourage a spirit of co-operation.
Some people would argue that competitive sports encourage a spirit of co-operation.
It can be argued that competitive sports encourage a spirit of co-operation.

Exercise 2, page 93

Suggested answers:

1 It seems to me that television programmes often mislead and misinform viewers.
2 I firmly believe that appearance reflects personality.
3 I am very much in favour of rear seat passengers wearing seatbelts.
4 Personally, I would argue that the breakdown of social values has resulted in increased crime.

Exercise 3, page 93

Suggested answers:

1 Many psychologists would argue that competitive team sports can lead to violence.
2 The majority of teachers believe that mixed schools are appropriate for life in a mixed society.
3 Doctors argue that regular exercise is good for your health.
4 The government argue that tourism benefits the national economy.
5 A large number of sociologists would argue that poverty and crime are linked.

■ SECTION 4 UNIT 1

Exercise 5, page 110

Introduction

For many years, football has been a popular international sport, attracting large numbers of spectators.

Recently, however, there has been a marked/noticeable increase in

(incidents) of violence ⎫
violent/ugly incidents ⎭

at football matches worldwide ⎫ *which*
associated with football ⎭

are giving the sport a bad ⎫ *name.*
⎭ *reputation.*

Paragraphs 2 and 3

It seems to me that there are several ways of

dealing with }
overcoming } *this problem.*

In the first place, I feel that it is high time the government

enforced
brought in — *new laws to* — curb } — *violence.*
introduced — — prevent }

They should impose heavy fines and prison sentences on offenders to act as a deterrent to others.
Furthermore, in my opinion, football clubs

have a responsibility to }
should }

ban alcohol from football grounds, as, in the vast majority of cases, violence tends to be linked to drinking. The use of metal detectors at the entrance gates to check for knives or other potential weapons should also be introduced.
Moreover, a spectators' club could be formed to collect the names of offenders and prevent them from entering football grounds.

Conclusion

I feel confident that, if these measures were taken, the problem of football violence would soon be a thing of the past and the game would be restored to its former glory.

■ SECTION 5 UNIT 2

Exercise 1, page 157

Suggested answer: grouping the ideas in the following order: (2,3,1) (8) (4,5,6,7)

The majority of boys often choose to spend their free time on computers because they are confident about using computing technology and tend to be more interested in something if it involves computers. For this reason, it has been suggested that giving boys interesting work to do on the computer at home may improve their concentration. Computers also give boys confidence because they do not need to worry about their handwriting. This means they are happy to write more and makes them keen to use a variety of styles to improve the appearance of their work.

(96 words)

Exercise 2, page 163

- Inside her cardboard box, Rocky went everywhere with me
- now a seasoned traveller
- perched on her own log on the back seat of my car

Michael takes Rocky everywhere with him. To begin with, she travelled in a cardboard box, but now she has her own perch in the back of his car.

- The helpless baby owl – abandoned by her mother
- I had to hand-rear the chick
- I persuaded the chick to eat during the day and sleep at night. Every two hours I had to cut up food and feed the owlet thin layers of meat small enough to swallow whole.
- For the first two weeks she dozed endlessly on a bed of towels.

The owlet was all alone in the world and Michael had no alternative but to feed it himself. It was a time-consuming process that meant changing the owl's natural eating and sleeping pattern. The selfless way Michael prepared the owl's food shows his dedication and concern for her well-being. The task became even more demanding when Rocky learnt to call for him every time she wanted food. At first the owl was sleepy most of the time, but as she began to grow she became more of a responsibility for Michael.

- I would have preferred Rocky to have grown up naturally in the wild where she could have soared freely
- The companionship … has enriched my life
- Hopefully, she will be with me for many years to come

Michael enjoys having Rocky as a companion, and appreciates the way she has changed his life. He is looking forward to the future with Rocky, although he regrets that she will never be able to fly free.

- Within six days I had been completely accepted as 'mother'
- As time goes on our relationship grows and intensifies
- Every morning before anyone else is up we call to each other.

It took less than a week for Rocky to bond with Michael and now they communicate privately with each other.

■ Despite our mutual affection – mutual trust – she is unique

Their relationship is special/unusual, based on mutual trust and affection.

Exercise 3, page 163

4 Michael takes Rocky everywhere with him. To begin with she travelled in a cardboard box, but now she has her own perch in the back of his car.

2 The owlet was all alone in the world and Michael had no alternative but to feed it himself. It was a time-consuming process that meant changing the owl's natural eating and sleeping pattern. The selfless way Michael prepared the owl's food shows his dedication and concern for her well-being. The task became even more demanding when Rocky learnt to call for him every time she wanted food. At first the owl was sleepy most of the time, but as she began to grow she became more of a responsibility for Michael.

5 Michael enjoys having Rocky as a companion, and appreciates the way she has changed his life. He is looking forward to the future with Rocky, although he regrets that she will never be able to fly free.

3 It took less than a week for Rocky to bond with Michael and now they communicate privately with each other.

1 Their relationship is special/unusual, based on mutual trust and affection.

Exercise 4, page 163

Note how the words underlined have been removed and/or replaced using fewer words.

1 Their relationship is special, based on mutual trust and affection.

2 The owlet was all alone in the world and Michael dedicated himself to preparing her food and feeding her. Soon Rocky learnt to call him every time she wanted food. At first the owl was sleepy most of the time, but as she began to grow she became more demanding and more of a responsibility for Michael.

57 words

2 As the owlet was *orphaned*, Michael dedicated himself to *feeding her*. Soon Rocky learnt to call him *when* she wanted food, At first *Rocky slept* most of the time, but as she *grew* she became more demanding and more of a responsibility.

42 words

3 It took less than a week for Rocky to bond with Michael and now they communicate privately with each other.

20 words

3 Rocky quickly bonded with Michael and…

6 words

4 Michael takes Rocky everywhere with him. To begin with she travelled in a cardboard box, but now she has her own perch in the back of his car.

28 words

4 …goes everywhere with him. She used to travel in a cardboard box, but now has a perch in his car.

20 words

5 Michael enjoys having Rocky as a companion, and appreciates the way she has changed his life. He is looking forward to their future together, although he regrets that she will never be able to fly free.

36 words

5 Michael appreciates the way Rocky has changed his life and looks forward to their future together, although he regrets she will never fly free.

24 words

After this editing work, the number of words has been reduced from 151 to 102. (Notice that 100 words is smaller than you may think.)

Exercise 5, page 163

The relationship between Michael and Rocky is unusual, based on a special understanding and trust. As the owlet was orphaned, Michael dedicated himself to feeding her. Soon Rocky learnt to call him when she wanted food. At first, Rocky slept most of the time, but as she grew she became more demanding and more of a responsibility. Rocky quickly bonded with Michael and goes everywhere with him. She used to travel in a cardboard box, but now has a perch in his car. Michael appreciates the way Rocky has changed his life and looks forward to their future together, although he regrets she will never fly free.

107 words

Exercise 6, page 168

■ *1876 greyhound racing began* (this indicates the beginning of the history) *in a field* (the location is going to change later) *near London* (do *not* write *Hendon*; this is too exact an example) *with dogs chasing a mechanical lure along a straight course* (this is important because the shape of the course is going to change later).

- **Early 1900s sport** (note form – no need to include 'the') *became popular in USA with dogs chasing live bait* (this will change later).
- **Animal rights groups** (anti-blood sports) *protested and a dummy hare* (this is a new development) *was used in an enclosed track* (this is new, too).
- *1919 first racecourse opened in the United States.*
- *Gambling was introduced and this increased popularity of sport* (note – no need for 'the').
- *1926 sport returned to Manchester,* (important to mention this here, to contrast with London later) *England. Not very popular* (do not give exact figures) *at first* (note – no need for full sentence).
- *Before long, moved to capital. Huge crowds* (do not give exact numbers) *attended meetings.*
- *Today, tens of thousands* (do not give exact numbers) *of races run, watched by nearly four million fans* (no exact numbers).

Exercise 7, page 169

Suggested answer:
e = environmentally responsible
s = safe

Mountain biking is the fastest-growing sport in Britain. The saddle of a bike is a far better vantage point from which to explore the countryside than a car, and you see much more than you would walking. On top of this, it's great exercise: a day off-road cycling will have everyone sound asleep at night as soon as their heads hit the pillow. But perhaps the best bit of all is that after every lung-bursting climb comes the thrill of bouncing downhill.

Access is one of the most contentious issues surrounding the sport, with everyone from ramblers and horse riders to farmers and environmentalists wailing about the impact of mountain bikes on the countryside. However, if you are <u>riding on a legally</u>
e <u>accessible trail</u>, you have just as much right to be there as they do. The main thing, as with all outdoor
s sports, is to <u>show consideration for others: don't tear up behind walkers or riders – warn them of your</u>
e <u>approach and ride past slowly. As for erosion, try not to skid unnecessarily on wet grass and soil</u>, although independent research has shown that mountain bikes cause no more erosion than walkers' boots and a good deal less than horses' hooves.

e If you pass through <u>gates, always close or fasten them</u>
e <u>behind you. Don't disturb livestock, and make sure</u>
e <u>you always know where you're going, so you don't end up riding through a field of crops</u> after making a
s wrong turn. <u>Mark your route on a map before you set out</u> (and know how to read it!) so it's easy to follow the trail.

Everyone falls off at some point – a rock, a pot-hole or tree root will catch you out eventually – so the golden
s rule is to <u>wear a helmet</u>. Always. It's also useful to
s carry <u>a basic first-aid kit</u>, and, as an expert advises,
s '<u>don't stray too far out into the wilds</u>, just in case you do have an accident.' Many of the more experienced riders who go up into the mountains of Scotland and
s the Lake District take <u>mobile phones</u> in case they come to grief in a remote area. You might agree that this would be a good occasion to have one.

Exercise 8, page 169

Environmentally responsible	Safe
Only bike where you are allowed	Slow down behind others
Don't skid on wet grass	Wear a helmet
Close gates behind you – especially farmers' fields	Carry first-aid kit
Plan trip from beginning to end	Don't go off the beaten track
Don't ride through fields of crops	Take a mobile phone

Note that the original sentences in this summary were simple, and so it is more difficult to change them when you rewrite them in your own words.

Environmentally responsible	Safe
2 Only bike where you are allowed	5 Slow down behind others
5 Don't skid on wet grass	1 Wear a helmet
4 Close gates behind you – especially farmers' fields	2 Carry first-aid kit
1 Plan trip from beginning to end	3 Don't go off the beaten track
3 Don't ride through fields of crops	4 Take a mobile phone

Exercise 9, page 170

Suggested answer:

The most important thing when you go mountain-biking is to plan your route from beginning to end, so you can be sure that you are biking where you are allowed, and do not find yourself riding through fields of crops. Whatever happens, be considerate to others and the environment by riding responsibly and remembering to close gates behind you, especially in farmers' fields.

Whatever you do, wear a helmet at all times and carry a first-aid kit with you. Try to keep to recognised paths, but take a mobile phone with you in case of emergency.

96 words

■ SECTION 6 UNIT 1

Exercise 1, page 178

1 He was given a place because of his wild behaviour.
2 He eats with his hands/screams constantly/climbs out of windows/sleeps on the floor.
3 Sally was very pleased when she first heard, but now she is worried.
4 They made her become confused.
5 He is now much stronger/more assertive/more agile.
6 She knows it is his only hope of getting better. Without the college, his future would be in hospital on drugs.

■ SECTION 7 UNIT 1

Exercise 1, page 185

Note that the letter R in the second column refers to points in the Register unit on pages 182–5.

1	I wasn't able	→ R9	I couldn't
2	during my absence	→ R2	while I was away
3	he advised me to	→	he suggested/he said I should/he told me to
4	I advise you	→ R3	why don't you/what about/how about/have you thought of
5	allow	→ R3	let
6	in my area	→ R1	where I live/here/there
7	your arrival time	→ R1	what time you arrive/when you arrive
8	I hope you will attend the next party	→ R3	I hope you'll come to/go to the next party
9	before going to bed	→ R2	before I go to bed
10	beneficial	→	good (for)
11	will be of great benefit to you	→ R1	will really do you good
12	I believe	→	I think
13	celebration	→	party/get together
14	concerning	→	about
15	contains	→	is full of
16	we entered the shop	→ R3	we went into the shop
17	finally	→ R7	in the end
18	tell me its location	→ R1	tell me where it is
19	many	→ R9	a lot of/loads of
20	in my opinion	→ R1	I think
21	prepare	→ R3	get ready
22	after reaching	→ R2	when (she) reached/got to
23	regarding	→	about
24	it wasn't successful	→	it didn't succeed/it didn't work
25	very	→ R9	really
26	during your visit	→ R2	while you are here
27	while walking	→ R2	while (you) walk
28	gain weight	→ R3	put on weight

INDEX